A COUNTRY TO BE

RECKONED WITH

The true story of Australia's pioneer stock agent

Patsy Trench

Copyright 2018 Patsy Trench
All rights reserved

ISBN-13: 978-0-9934537-2-4

Prefab Publications, London

Cover design by **Michael Burge**

This project has been assisted by funds allocated to the
Royal Australian Historical Society through the Heritage
Branch of the NSW Office of Environment and Heritage

REVIEWS

"... a most entertaining and well-written publication. Author Patsy Trench has made it clear what her factual sources are, and where her imagination has filled the gaps, with comprehensive references and chapter notes."

History magazine, RAHS

"This is an accessible approach to history and aims for a wide readership of those who want more than dry history and facts. It ... contains the stories of people to be reckoned with, along with the country itself. Good Australian stories."

Descent magazine, SAG

Contents

Prologue: Richmond, New South Wales	1
Introduction: Wagga Wagga, New South Wales	3
PART ONE: New South Wales	
Chapter 1: Head of the family	9
Chapter 2: Staying on	17
Chapter 3: Scandal	22
Chapter 4: The Hawkesbury	32
Chapter 5: The Aboriginal connection	41
Chapter 6: At home	47
Chapter 7: Distraction	52
PART TWO: London 2015	
Chapter 8: The convict stain	59
Chapter 9: Crime and punishment	68
PART THREE: Bound for Botany bay	
Chapter 10: Mary and John	79
PART FOUR: Sydney	
Chapter 11: The little brown jug	89
Chapter 12: The smile	95
Chapter 13: Robert Aull	101
Chapter 14: Upper Richmond	107
Chapter 15: Interpreting our ancestors	112
PART FIVE: New South Wales	
Chapter 16: Death & marriages	119
Chapter 17: William Scott	124
Chapter 18: The land of golden soil	128
Chapter 19: The big journey	133
Chapter 20: The drover	137

Chapter 21: Three expeditions	142
Chapter 22: The squatter	151
Chapter 23: Moree	156
Chapter 24: The puzzle explained	160
Chapter 25: Dispossession	164
Chapter 26: The price of capitalism	173
Chapter 27: The women	177
Chapter 28: The law and the Aborigines	183
Chapter 29: Self government	189
Chapter 30: Local matters	192
Chapter 31: Australia and how to find it	197
Chapter 32: The romance of the bush	202
Chapter 33: The law and the Europeans	207
Chapter 34: Birth of a salesman	210
Chapter 35: Politics	217
Chapter 36: Railroads and rivalry	223
Chapter 37: Weddings & inundations	228
Chapter 38: Manly Beach	233
Chapter 39: The Mauritian connection	241
Chapter 40: Anna Sparrow	245
Chapter 41: Kirribilli	251
Chapter 42: The North Shore Lazarus	256
Chapter 43: Captain Cook, then and now	260
Chapter 44: Julia	265
Chapter 45: Pitt, Son & Badgery	268
Chapter 46: The world without a sun	276
Chapter 47: Battling on	280
Chapter 48: Conclusion	284
Epilogue	290
Afterword	295
Acknowledgments	296
Author biography	298
References and chapter notes	299
Bibliography	326
Index	334

George Matcham Pitt (Elders Ltd)

Prologue

1896: Richmond, New South Wales

On the afternoon of Tuesday 13 October 1896 the town of Richmond came to a halt. Shops and businesses closed their doors and pulled down their shutters. A hot wind blew through the empty streets and a church bell began to toll as a funeral cortege proceeded slowly down the road from the railway station along Windsor Street to St Peter's Church.

The horse-drawn hearse was accompanied by a long line of carriages containing the relatives, friends and business associates of the dead man – around 150 of them in all. From behind their windows residents of the town looked on. It was the best part of 30 years since the grand old man had lived in Richmond but if they had not met George Matcham Pitt – known colloquially as GM – they knew him by reputation. They'd have known he was born some 82 years earlier in Richmond and brought up on a farm near the Hawkesbury River, grandson of the early pioneer Mary Pitt, the first woman to be granted land in her own right at the beginning of the century. They may have known that as a young man he travelled on foot to the outer reaches of New South Wales to take up land in the Gwydir district, and later near Wellington, before he gave up farming to form one of the colony's earliest stock and station agents called Pitt, Son & Badgery. They may or may not have been aware that in his later life he moved from Richmond to the North Shore and served for several years as mayor of East St Leonards.

They would also, some of them, have heard stories of the great man's generosity of spirit, and of size; of how when GM took a ferry across to the city the ferryman brought along counterweights in order to balance his boat and save it from sinking beneath the mass of his worthy passenger. Of how he regaled fellow passengers with jokes and anecdotes, peppered with quotes from Shakespeare and Robbie Burns; of his readiness to dig into his pockets for those he considered less lucky than himself; his fondness for firing off sharply-worded letters to the press bemoaning the behaviour of the government; his patriotism, his enthusiasm and his limitless energy, whether it was to do with affairs of state or the local community.

However much they knew or didn't know of the man who had now brought the entire town of Richmond to a halt, there was no questioning the fact that GM Pitt had been a notable pioneer in the still young colony of New South Wales; and that his lifetime, that spanned the best part of the 19th century, had seen the most remarkable changes in the rapidly-evolving country called Australia.

Introduction

2017: Wagga Wagga, New South Wales

I am standing inside an auction house at a cattle saleyards in the country town of Wagga Wagga, New South Wales. With me is my brother Tony, who lives here, and a friend called Chris McCarthy, who has spent his life farming sheep and cattle. I am here to get a taste of the life of my great great grandfather GM Pitt, farmer, auctioneer, entrepreneur and stock and station agent in 19th century Australia.

To say this is far from my comfort zone is an understatement. I am a townie, a Pom. I've lived in London virtually my whole life. I barely know a ram from a goat, yet I've undertaken to write the story of my great great grandfather. That is why I am here: to try to experience something of the world of country people in Australia who make their living from the land.

The auctioneer stands on a podium, surrounded by a team of 'spotters', gabbling incomprehensibly into his mike and now and again banging his gavel to conclude a sale. The buyers, all men and all wearing identical hats, sit motionless and expressionless behind desks, from time to time lifting part of a forefinger to indicate a bid. The objects of the bidding are shoved into the pen and out again before they've had a moment to look around and figure out what the hell is going on. Whips are cracked but don't, I am told, connect.

Outside the auctioneer walks along a gantry above the cattle pens, again with his team, all of them in uniform indicating the company they represent, only this time he has no mike and his assistant makes notes on a pad of paper. My fear that by taking photos on my phone I might find myself leaving with a herd of Herefords is unfounded. There is no one here among the buyers who is not known to someone apparently.

Beyond the auction house pens stretch as far as the eye can see, some containing small huddles of cows or calves – many of them disturbingly young and still looking for their mothers – and here and there a single cow, or a mother and calf. The bewildered-looking animals are fed from one pen to another through clanging gates, mostly by girls, as the selling proceeds. Young men and women ride on horseback up and down between the pens, leaning back in their saddles eating apples and herding the cattle from hither to hence. Everyone wears a hat. It's like something out of a Western, both exotic and industrial, a countryside Las Vegas, a vast, complicated and well-oiled machine that is spanking new and as old as the hills.

The smell of cowshit is overwhelming and still lingers, weeks afterwards, on the soles of my shoes. It is a reminder of this extraordinary world, so utterly different to everything I have ever known: the world of my great great grandfather.

~

It has taken a leap of faith, and a good deal of nerve, to think I can understand enough of the world of 19th century rural Australia to be able to write about one of its self-made – and well-known – legends.

I am not a total stranger to Australia. I was born and bred in London to an Australian mother and British father. I even emigrated there as a ten pound Pom in my youth, and while I eventually returned to live in England I have been visiting Australia regularly over the past twenty years or so, researching and writing about my family history. I know about the country's beginnings as a penal colony and its fight for survival in the early years; how it was initially regarded by the colonists – or invaders, as some view them in the 21st century – as the worst country in the world; a phrase that became the title of the first book in my family story about my four times great grandmother Mary Pitt. Exactly why Mary, a widow with five children, decided to migrate to New South Wales at that time is a matter for speculation. Suffice to say on her arrival in 1801 she was one of fewer than 40 free settlers who'd dared to chance their arm in what was still a penal colony, and an experiment like no other in history.

What a story that was! And now here we are again, with Mary's grandson, born and bred in New South Wales, at a time when the newly-named Australia was just beginning to be thought of as a land of promise for new migrants from the old country. In they came, these interlopers, mostly young men who'd heard of fortunes to be made on the land which – since the country had been officially declared *terra nullius*, or 'no-man's land' by the powers that be in Britain – they had been led to believe was up for grabs. For the most part they were, like me, totally ignorant of farming. (One of them, Edward Bell, arriving in the colony in 1839, admitted his researches were confined to reading books on the journey out. Otherwise, he cheerfully acknowledged, 'my general information regarding live stock was limited to a confused knowledge of sheep by their distinctive titles of rams, wethers, and ewes, and a vague idea of cattle as heifers, cows, bulls, and oxen, and as beasts that had horns, and made a great bellowing'.) But they had money, most of them, and what skills they lacked they assumed they could pick up on the way. They became known as 'new chums', and the locals, born in the colony, took great pleasure in taking the mickey out of them. (They still do.)

When I first heard about the new chums I was both surprised and reassured. Surprised at the *chutzpah:* to imagine they could travel across the globe, these young hopefuls, to make their fortunes in a strange country doing something they knew nothing about – not to mention the kind of welcome, or lack of, they could expect at the hands of the indigenous population whose land they were intending to take possession of; reassured because I recognised myself in many ways as one of them.

If the new chums could make a go of it, I thought (and many of them did), so can I. Once again, as I delved into the life and times of my great great grandfather I uncovered a story of such diversity and fascination I could not bear not to write about it. I could not sit back and let someone else tell the tale not just of a man, but of a country that during that man's lifetime transformed itself from a makeshift penal colony to a thriving entity with its own parliament, legal system, sophisticated infrastructure and, above all, its own distinct personality.

So here it is: the story of an entrepreneur who made his living from the land; of convicts and Aborigines, squatters, drovers and bushrangers; of appropriation and dispossession; fortunes, litigation and bankruptcies; births, marriages, illegitimacy and abscondence; of governors, parliamentarians and legislators racing to keep up with the rapidly-changing reality of people's lives. Most of it is gleaned from newspapers of the day, and there's plenty of information to be had about GM – in particular concerning his larger than life personality, his astonishing powers of rhetoric and his fondness for quoting from poets; none of which his biographer would have thought to invent.

But as with any history there are gaps, which once again I have filled with my imagination, as I did with my first book: dramatising scenes and inventing the odd fictional character in order to bring GM to life, setting him within the context of the developing nation of Australia, and including my own observations on the country I have been visiting regularly over the years. Again the chapter notes make it clear what is true and what I have invented. As with Mary, so I have tried to take the reader with me as I embark on yet another extraordinary adventure into my family history.

PART ONE

Richmond, New South Wales

Chapter 1

1821: Head of the family

George Matcham Pitt became head of the family at the age of not quite seven years old.

His father had been on his way home from a business trip to Sydney on a hot January day when, as so often happens in the land of extreme weather, the wind changed and out of what had been a clear blue sky came a torrent of rain as if someone had pulled the plug out of a bath. Thomas arrived at the farm in Richmond drenched to the skin and feverish, and on orders from his young wife he took immediately to his bed.

He never left it.

Soon after, neighbours were summoned to the house to witness his will, and eight days later, on Saturday 28 January 1821, Thomas Pitt, aged 39, died.

His obituary read:

> 'On Sunday morning last, in his 40th year, at Richmond, Mr. Thomas Matcham Pitt, Gent. a distant relation of the late Lord Nelson, leaving a widow and five orphans to deplore the loss of a tender and affectionate husband and parent. His death was occasioned by a severe cold contracted in going home from Sydney; which terminated in a fever that brought his existence to a period in the short space of a few days... The probity of

his heart could only be equalled by the complacency of his manner; and as he was universally esteemed, so will he now be as universally lamented.'

He left a 24-year-old widow and five children under seven.

In my version of events Thomas's widow, Elizabeth, retreated into her room and did not emerge for several days. The children – George and his five-year-old sister Mary, Robert, William and Eliza, aged three, two and a few months respectively – were looked after by a succession of aunts, uncles, neighbours and anyone else who happened to call round. There were hugs and kisses for the littler ones and a handshake and a pat on the head for George, and a 'Head of the house now, young man,' from uncle William.

Head of the house? What could that mean?

Lacking any other kind of instruction George went about the usual daily tasks his father had set him on the farm: making sure the pigs were fed and their huts cleaned, clearing out the chicken coop, checking for eggs and placing them on the specially-grooved shelf in the kitchen and turning them every day. It had also been his duty, along with William Scott, the adopted farm worker, to move the cattle and pigs onto high ground whenever it rained heavily. Other tasks, such as making sure the horses were 'looking happy' as his father put it, came along as and when. But now there was a 200-acre farm to look after, to make decisions about. Was this what 'head of the house' meant?

There was only one person George could ask. Uncle William Faithfull, whose wife Susanna had died only a few months before, was too busy locked in discussion with his mother about her future, along with George's other uncle Sam Laycock, his mother's brother. Uncle James and aunt Hester Wilshire paid a fleeting visit from their house in Sydney and aunt Lucy, a widow herself, gave him hugs and wept over him for quite a long time. Last to arrive was George's grandmother Hannah, his mother's mother. She buried her grandson in her bosom for some time before holding him at arm's length and saying, 'Hold up, young man. Your mother and I will soon sort things out'.

But what George needed right now was man-to-man advice, and the only man available was William Scott.

Scott was the only male worker living on the farm at that time who was not a government servant. He'd arrived at Pitt Farm two and a half years ago with his sister Margaret and younger brother James, who'd been sent to live in an orphanage not long after. Quite why his father had taken the family under his wing, and then had young James committed to an orphanage, George never thought to ask.

As a free man twenty-year-old William was entitled to work for whoever he chose, and the sudden demise of his employer left not just the farm but his own future in limbo. Moreover the mistress of the house had taken to her room and looked as if she might never come out. There was no one to oversee the convict workers and no one to make decisions. It could mean opportunity or it could spell disaster. He reckoned he'd give it a week to see what happened and then think about moving on.

He was locked into this thought one morning when he looked up to see the eldest child standing not two feet away from him with his hands on his hips and a question mark on his face.

'Hello,' he said to George.

'What should I do?'

William squinted down at the boy and smiled. 'Why are you asking me, I'm not the boss.'

'Yes you are.' George stood his ground, bare-footed, trousers rolled up to the knee, four square on his little legs, just like his father. It was all William could do not to chuckle.

'Says who?'

'I am head of the house now, they told me.'

'If you're head of the house it's up to you what you do, isn't it?'

The little boy didn't reply immediately, and William saw he was trying not to cry.

'Look, I'm sorry about your father,' he said, laying a hand on the boy's shoulder, which George immediately shook off. 'But I'm damned if I know who's in charge here now.'

'Well I'm the head of the house and I say you are.'

William did laugh then, quite heartily. 'In that case,' he pushed his hat back from his face and wiped his arm across his forehead. 'You could give me a hand with this, for a start.'

'This' referred to the plough, which he was at that moment harnessing to one of the horses. 'Want to give it a try?' he suggested. 'Go on then.' And he stood back and watched as the young lad, with more determination than skill, looped the collar over the horse's head, wrapped the strap around the horse's girth and the tug around its belly, then stood back and waited for signs of approval.

William nodded. 'Not bad.' He tightened the girth slightly and adjusted the harness at the horse's neck. 'Now what?'

'I dunno.' George resumed his position with arms akimbo, waiting.

'Grab holds of the straps, hook 'em onto this, here.' Now it was William who stood with his arms folded as George fiddled and twisted until one way or another he had the plough attached to the horse. 'Right, now grab hold of the handles, that's the way, and crack the whip.'

There was a moment while George looked around. 'I can't see a whip.'

'In that case,' said William with a smile, 'we'll have to think of another way to get him moving. Keep hold of the handles, like that, keep him steady.' Then he gave a brief whistle and stood back and watched as the great horse, with a toss of its head, set off on its slow journey across the paddock, the small child behind him pushing the plough with all the strength in his stocky little body. The older man called out now and then to keep the horse going and looked on as horse, machine and boy wove an uneven path across the paddock.

It was the start of a tough week. From sunup to sundown George was out there in the paddocks, working away at whatever his mentor told him to do. He learned how to de-burr the horses' tails and check the cattle for signs of bloat (the extreme cure for which was a knife in the cow's gut to let the air out). He even learned how to use a stock whip, after a fashion, without garrotting himself. His mentor was tougher than his father ever was, and a lot less protective. When George complained he was tired and his feet hurt William told him it was his own fault for not wearing shoes. When William spotted two convicts having a prolonged smoko round the back of the cattle shed he told the boy to go and tell them off for idling.

'You do it,' George remonstrated.

'I can't tell them what to do. They won't listen to me. You're the head of the house, it's your job. You've seen your father do it plenty of times.'

The boy scowled.

'And remember not to shout,' said William as the young lad strode off in the direction of the shed. 'Your father never shouted. Keep your voice down, it shows authority.'

'What's authority?'

'You'll soon find out. If they do as you say you have it. If they don't, you don't.'

George scowled again and kept on walking.

It took a while, twenty minutes or so, before the government men were back at work. 'Not bad, for your first time.' William ruffled George's hair and the boy flinched. 'It's not easy for grown men to take orders from a kid but they'll soon get used to it. As will you,' he added as an afterthought.

George learned more in that week than most six-year-olds before him; and perhaps most important of all, the work kept his mind off the terrible loss of his father.

'You will stay, won't you?' He asked William at the end of it.

William shook his head, and then nodded. 'Maybe I will, maybe I won't.'

~

A week after Thomas's funeral Elizabeth finally emerged from her room, the baby Eliza in her arms and her brother Sam alongside, to make an announcement.

'I am letting the farm,' she said.

There was silence.

'Just for a few years. I've placed an advertisement in the newspaper.'

She had called the family together in the front room. The afternoon light blazed through the window casting deep shadows on the wooden floor. Her four elder children stood in a straight line facing their mother and their uncle, like soldiers awaiting inspection.

It was Mary who spoke first. 'Where are we going to live?'

Elizabeth glanced at her brother. 'We're going to live with my mother,' she said.

'In Sydney?' Little Mary's eyebrows shot up.

Elizabeth nodded.

'Why?' George's question snapped out like a ball from a musket, louder than he intended.

Elizabeth smiled wanly at her son. 'There is no one to take care of the farm, darling, it's too much for me.'

'I can.'

'Can you?' Elizabeth laughed gently. 'You and who else?'

'William. Me and William. Me and William have been looking after it already. We know what to do.'

Elizabeth hesitated a moment. 'I'm sorry George but the decision is made.'

'What'll happen to William then?' George thrust out his chin.

'William is free to do as he likes. He could stay here, with Margaret. It's up to them.'

'What if he doesn't want to?' The boy had gone quite red in the face now. 'William says he doesn't want to work for anyone else so if you leave the farm so will he.' He bit his lip, thrust his hands behind his back and crossed his fingers and glared at his mother like the small boy who's been into the biscuit tin.

'Anyway I'm not going,' he declared finally.

'It's only for a couple of years darling – three, five at the most. We'll be back, maybe, when you're older.' And then as George stood there shaking his head, 'You'll like it in Sydney, it'll be fun, and you'll have people to play with, cousins, lots of them, aunt Hester's and . . .'

'I'm not leaving. You can't make me. It's my birthday tomorrow, I'll be seven.' He added, inconsequentially.

'So you will.' Elizabeth nodded thoughtfully. She sighed again. 'You know I don't really want to leave either, George.' She crouched down in front of her son and gently pushed his hair back from his face with her finger. 'This is the house where I met your father all those years ago. I love it too, and the farm.' She glanced back at her brother fleetingly. 'But I don't see how we can cope, not without your father.'

'He doesn't know.' George pouted.

'Who doesn't know?'

'Him.' George jerked his head over his mother's shoulder at his uncle Sam. 'Was it his idea? Me and William have been working it out. He doesn't know, he didn't see us.'

'This is true,' said Sam, with a chuckle. He stood at the far side of the room leaning against the wall, legs crossed and arms folded.

'I'm not leaving,' George ploughed on regardless. 'I wasn't told, and I'm the eldest.' He shook his head. 'I don't want to live in Sydney, we don't want to go anywhere.' He glanced at his elder sister and his two younger brothers. 'Do we?' he demanded.

They stared back at him uncomprehendingly. Then five-year-old Mary started to cry and, seeing her, the faces of the two younger boys began to pucker. 'See?' George demanded, pointing rudely.

Elizabeth straightened up. 'I've already placed the advertisement,' she said. And then, almost as an afterthought she added, 'I'll have a word with William.' She looked into the face of her eldest son and brushed a hand across his cheek. 'All right?'

George glowered, and then nodded, and then stifled a tear, and then stood stiff as a rod while his mother, still holding the baby, once more bent down to envelope him in her arms.

Chapter 2

1821: Staying on

What George's father Thomas would have made of strangers taking over the properties he had spent nineteen years nurturing and coaxing into submission is anyone's guess.

The two 100-acre plots were the original grants given to his mother Mary and himself in 1802, soon after the family's arrival in the colony the previous year. They had named them Pitt and Nelson's Farms in acknowledgement of their patron Admiral Nelson, whose brother in law George Matcham, Mary's first cousin, was responsible for the Pitts' migration in the first place.

In those nineteen years Thomas, with help from his four sisters and three government servants, had transformed their 200 acres from dense woodland into, as described by Elizabeth in her advertisement in the *Sydney Gazette*:

'. . . a valuable farm, at Richmond, containing two hundred acres, 150 of which are cleared, with capital House and convenient outhouses thereon erected, has four acres of well cultivated garden, containing some choice fruit trees, forming a complete country residence for a Respectable Family. For particulars apply to Mr [sic] E Pitt on the premises, or, to Mr S Laycock, Toll-gate,

Sydney.'

It was here that Thomas had met and married the sixteen year old Elizabeth Laycock back in 1813, when he was 31 years old. It was here that their five children were born and raised. To uproot the children from the only home they had ever known was no small matter.

~

Among the many visitors to Pitt and Nelson's Farms at around that time was a middle-aged woman I have named Mrs Pursip. This gentlewoman, whom I have invented for the purpose of this story, was what was known in the colony as an Exclusive, or Pure Merino (after the sheep); being – like Mary Pitt – a member of that rare species that had arrived in the colony free and uncoerced.

Mrs Pursip, who was otherwise known in the Pitt household (behind her back) as Mrs Parsnip by George's father and Mrs Purselip by his mother, was also known in the adult world as a 'd***** busybody and therefore not necessarily welcome at Pitt and Nelson's Farms. Needless to say this was not enough to deter a woman like Mrs Pursip, and of course once the boss had passed away and his widow was left vulnerable and helpless, and she only a slip of a thing, the door to the Pitt family home was in her view open to all-comers. Moreover it became perfectly clear from her first visit that the poor children, the eldest ones in particular, were being completely ignored by their distraught mother and had no one to take proper care of them.

So Mrs P made herself busy, welcome or not, in the Pitt kitchen, getting in the way of the housekeeper and bossing everyone in sight. She had little Mary fetching and carrying and peeling potatoes and preparing vegetables, and had she had a chance she would have turned her attention to George. Only George was far too busy helping to run the farm.

It was Mrs Pursip who first asked George about William Scott. As in why it was that a young man who was really no more than a farm labourer was not only allowed inside the farmhouse but seemed to spend an immoderate amount of time there, chatting away with the lady of the house as if he were her equal. Everyone knew that while an overseer might just be permitted onto the veranda, and then only by invitation, welcoming a mere labourer into the house itself was quite beyond the pale. The poor bereaved widow obviously did not know what she was doing. When George responded that William was already part of the family *and* he'd saved the farm and if it hadn't been for him they'd have all had to move to *Sydney* of all places, she merely harrumphed.

~

William had arrived on the veranda just as the sun was setting behind him, his outline black against the yellow sky. 'You wanted to talk to me?' he asked.

'Yes.' It was later on the day Elizabeth had dropped what turned out to be a bombshell on her family.

'I should have spoken to you before,' she said, looking out at the horizon, or somewhere. 'I haven't been thinking very clearly this past week.'

William propped his back against the veranda post and waited.

'I'm leasing out the farms, just for a few years,' she said.

'I know.'

Elizabeth nodded. 'George told you. Of course.'

'May I ask why?'

'We can't stay here, it's out of the question.'

'Who says?'

'No matter who says,' she shook her head with irritation. 'The question is, what happens to you and Margaret. I feel a responsibility.'

'No need. We're free people.'

Elizabeth squinted briefly up at him, shielding her eyes from the sinking sun with her hand. 'I was hoping you might stay on for the new tenants, you and your sister. Would you do that?'

William removed his hat and twirled it in his hand.

'Depends on who they are.'

'Well there's no way of knowing that of course. But if you'd be prepared to give it a try.'

'Where are you planning on going?'

She wanted to tell him it was none of his business but instead she said, 'We're going to Sydney. My mother has a house.' She turned away from him. She didn't like him staring at her.

'So it was your mother's idea.' William nodded, and smiled briefly. 'She doesn't think we can handle the property on our own.'

'It isn't that. She doesn't think . . .'

William waited.

'She doesn't think a woman out here is safe on her own, is that it?' he offered eventually. Then when Elizabeth did not reply he went on, 'And what's your view on the matter?'

Elizabeth heaved a great sigh that was almost a sob. 'I don't know.' She touched a hand on the veranda railing. 'George's reaction took me by surprise.'

'It's the only home he's known.'

She gazed out across the paddocks, gleaming gold in the dying sun. 'And now,' she smiled weakly, 'he refuses to speak to me.'

William nodded.

'He told me you'd been working together on the farm, all week, keeping it going.'

'All part of the job,' said William.

She turned to look at him. There was a flash of humour in his eyes that she thought, at times, may have been mocking her.

'The point is, William, I am not my husband. I know virtually nothing about the land – except for the garden of course – there is no way I could manage all this without him.'

'According to whom?'

'Besides, yes, it isn't safe for a widow on her own, with children.' She paused for a moment. 'Unless of course . . .' she stopped.

He wasn't going to make it easy for her, even if he had a strong idea what she was going to say next.

She took a breath and spoke right at him. 'Look, tell me, if you would agree to stay on here for let's say a year, could you guarantee me that?'

'Depends on who I'm working for.'

'Me of course. And George. All of us.'

'Is that what you want?'

Elizabeth thought for a moment. 'Yes,' she said eventually. 'As a matter of fact it is.' She cocked her head and smiled slightly. 'So?'

William shrugged. 'If you like.'

'I need more than that William.'

'I will stay here for a year, Mrs Pitt, on my honour. And beyond, if needs be.' He put a hand on his heart and gave a little bow. 'How's that?'

Elizabeth laughed, and gave a little bow in return. 'Thank you William,' she said.

Thus it was, according to this writer's speculation, that the Pitt family decided to stay put at Pitt and Nelson's Farms.

Chapter 3

1824 Scandal

'I do think,' pronounced Mrs Pursip, 'if we are to make a go of this country we should above all maintain standards, don't you agree?'

Elizabeth glanced sleepily at her neighbour. She felt very tired.

'Are you trying to tell me something, Mrs Pursip?'

'Agnes, please. Not at all my dear, but I couldn't help noticing your – overseer, is he now your overseer? – taking what you might call liberties.'

Elizabeth smiled. 'What kind of liberties?'

'He seems, if you don't mind me saying, to be assuming an over-familiarity with you Mrs Pitt – Elizabeth. Taking advantage of a vulnerable woman on her own.'

She stopped, and waited.

Oh Lord, thought Elizabeth, am I really expected to respond?

Agnes Pursip was one of the earlier arrivals in the colony, along with her husband and children. Like the Pitts the (imaginary) Pursips were free settlers and had been granted land on the Hawkesbury, which Mr Pursip farmed quietly and efficiently while his wife took on the task of guardian of the colony's morals.

'Elizabeth? Do you hear what I'm saying?'

'I'm afraid it's a bit late for that, Agnes.'

She was three months gone in her pregnancy and for some reason this one was making her feel excessively tired. It might have been the company or it might be a sign that at the age of 27 Elizabeth was past it.

'What do you mean?'

'Nothing. Just that – it's the way it is. William's become rather indispensable you see,' – in more ways than one, she said to herself – 'and I can't see it's doing any harm. Is it?'

Mrs Pursip pursed her lip. 'I'm not sure you're hearing what I'm saying Elizabeth. It's a question of standards and traditions and it's so important here, far more important don't you agree than back in England?'

'To know our place, yes Agnes, I am hearing you. I am simply trying to say that just because I allow my overseer to cross my threshold doesn't mean he takes advantage, or treats me with less respect. It's just the way it is, we are working together you could say. As a team. It doesn't make sense to confine him to the paddock, or even the veranda.'

Mrs Pursip shrugged her stiff shoulders with disapproval and stared down her nose at the floor. 'And I have to add, forgive me Elizabeth, what kind of example is it setting your children?'

'Oh Lord, Agnes, what possible harm is it doing to them?'

'And you're not looking particularly well. Are you sure you are looking after yourself?'

Underneath all the snobbery there was a heart, thought Elizabeth. She didn't like to offend people and besides, it was her own acute loneliness following Thomas's death that had led her to tolerate the presence of her nosy if good-hearted neighbour in her house in the first place. She'd needed someone to talk to, a fellow settler, a wife and mother, like her someone who was brought up in England. But frankly now the woman was becoming a bit of a trial.

It was partly because of this same loneliness that she had

first allowed William Scott to also cross her threshold.

Having made the decision to stay on at the farm Elizabeth needed constant reassurance, from both her eldest son and the man who was to become her overseer. After all William was still a young man – three years younger than herself – and there was no reason why he should take a particular interest in the farm beyond the general day-to-day maintenance. Lacking both experience and confidence herself she relied on him more than she would have liked, and now and again she would turn to her eldest son for reassurance that she'd done the right thing.

'Don't worry mama,' George told her, with a paternal pat on the arm, 'everything's under control.'

'Elizabeth?'

'Oh, yes. What? Yes. I'm perfectly all right, thank you Agnes. Just tired.' She rubbed her stomach involuntarily.

'Are you eating properly?'

'Yes. You're very kind to be concerned. But there's really no need to be. I am doing very well. Very well indeed.' Very well indeed, indeed.

Agnes frowned. She wasn't stupid. This girl is playing with me, she thought. Well so be it. There is only so much that a woman can do. She'd made her point.

'And now if you'll excuse me,' Elizabeth rose rather stiffly to her feet. 'I have to get on. It's been very good of you to call, Agnes.'

'I'll drop by again in a day or two,' said the good woman, with a stern nod. 'Keep an eye on you. Someone needs to.'

Someone already has, thank God, thought Elizabeth as she ushered her guest to her door.

~

She had asked William to give her regular updates, which he duly delivered, from time to time, in the comfort of her living room over a cup of tea. These mini conferences, which she'd requested in order to keep abreast of affairs on the farm in a way she had never properly done when her husband was alive, became more frequent, and longer, as they extended into conversations beyond the day-to-day goings on concerning the care of stock. She told William something of her own background: born in Sydney, yet brought up and educated in England and brought back to her native country, somewhat against her will, when she was fourteen years old. Then finding herself at the age of sixteen marrying a man twice her age, and the challenges of adjusting to that marriage, and to country life and children. They shared their memories of the old country they had left all those many years ago, when they were both still youngsters. It all helped to stem the awful loneliness that hung over Elizabeth, especially throughout the long dark nights of winter.

So it was that in time William became a part of the family. After a few months – even Elizabeth was aware of etiquette, and she didn't like to rush things – she began inviting him for dinner, where he amused the children with tall tales of his childhood spent back home in Scotland, riding wild horses bareback through the glens and dancing with Selkies by the light of the Easter moon.

Then there was a night when, unable to sleep, she rose from her bed and walked out onto the veranda, where she stood for some time, leaning against the balustrade and gazing out over the blackness. It was a still night, just the faintest breeze shuffling through the casuarinas. There was no moon, but there was a spill of light. It came from the little hut down the paddock beyond the orchard where William lived. Curious without knowing why, she stepped out in her slippers onto the grass, skirting the apple trees, feeling her way in the dark through the garden she knew so well until she was at his door, on which she tapped.

He opened it immediately, staring out into the darkness in some alarm.

'What's up?' he rapped.

The suddenness caused her to take a step backwards.

'Oh, nothing, I'm so sorry Will.' She clutched her shawl

around her, feeling ridiculous. 'I couldn't sleep,' she said, then, 'and I saw your light and wondered what you were, well . . .'

'You wondered what I was up to?' He smiled, or she thought he did as with the light behind him she couldn't see his face properly. 'You wondered if I wasn't entertaining a strange woman. Mm?' He added the query as an afterthought.

'Of course not!'

He chuckled.

'I thought no such thing. You have every right.'

She wasn't sure that was true. She wasn't really sure what his rights were, or if he had any in the first place, seeing as he was working for her and living on a property that belonged to her. Having given her his guarantee for a year, the future was not something they'd ever discussed; and she wondered now if they should have drawn up some kind of contract, after all there was nothing to keep him there now, and nothing to stop her getting rid of him either.

'Come in,' he said, and stood aside as she stepped gingerly over his threshold.

She saw a simple room with an open fire at one end of it. A table, a chair, a stool and a few shelves, not many home comforts. There were kangaroo skins on the rough wooden floor, and strips of hessian at the glassless windows passed for curtains; the whole lit by a single tallow candle enclosed within a bottle that stood on the table, casting its flickering light over sheets of paper and what looked like a ledger.

There was, needless to say, no one else there. Just the table and the flickering light, and the ledger.

'What are you doing?'

'What it looks like. The books.'

'The books?' She spoke as if she didn't know what the words meant. But she wandered to the table and trailed her fingers over its rough cover, as if to assure herself it was real.

'Somebody has to.' He eased himself round to the other side of the table. 'Did you not know?'

'Of course.'

'No fancy woman. Sorry to disappoint you.'

'Disappoint? What do you mean?'

'Not as exciting perhaps, but easier to control. And cheaper.' He tapped the cover of the ledger, as if it were a pet.

'Then I'm sorry to disturb you.'

'You do not disturb me Elizabeth. Not in the way you mean. I am delighted to be disturbed.'

The use of her first name was a surprise, she wasn't sure he'd done that before. She felt the faintest shiver of an intimacy, almost as if she had caught him with a woman.

'Now you're here I could offer you a drink. It'll be whisky or whisky.'

'Then I'll have a whisky.' She smiled, and as she sat herself down on the one and only chair she said, 'Thank you William,' with some emphasis.

'I haven't poured it yet.'

'I don't mean that. I mean for this.' She indicated the papers and the closed ledger. 'For taking it on. It's more than one has a right to expect. I don't remember asking you to do it.'

'Do you have it neat or with a dash?'

'Neat, yes, with a dash.'

He hesitated a moment and then splashed a drop of water into her whisky and placed the glass in front of her. 'You don't need to tell me what to do all the time you know, I'm a grown man.'

'I know. I'm very lucky to have found you.'

The comment hung in the air for a moment.

'There was so much that Thomas did around the place I knew nothing about.' She toyed with her glass. 'Is that bad of me?'

'Not unless you think it is.' He pulled up the one and only stool and sat down across the table from her.

'I'm sorry I ever doubted you, William.' She addressed this to her whisky.

'That's all right. I didn't know you did.'

'I felt so helpless. It served me right, I should have taken more interest when Thomas was alive.' Her voice shook slightly.

'Is that why you put the place up for lease?'

She smiled, feebly. 'It was my mother's idea. Hers and Sam's. You knew that of course.'

'I had an idea.'

'She wanted to take me off to the city and marry me off to some fine young man with prospects.'

'Of course.'

'She didn't seem to think it would be difficult to find someone to take on a widow with five children.'

'And property.'

'And property.' She paused for a moment. Perhaps now was the moment to broach the future. 'The property really belongs to Tom of course.' That was another thing, she never called her husband Tom except to his face. 'It was so much his place, he was in every part of it, he built the house – both houses – he felled the trees, he turned it from a tangled patch of chaos into a working farm. Almost single-handedly. It didn't seem right to stay here without him.'

'Pardon my saying so but that makes no sense at all.'

'Perhaps not.' She took a sip of whisky. 'Where did you get this?'

'You like it? It's pure Scotch.'

'Of course. What else?'

He lent with both elbows on the table, hands cradling his glass. They were beautiful hands, broad, strong, and surprisingly clean. A farmer is his hands, she thought to herself and, without quite knowing why, she reached across and laid one of hers on one of his. It looked tiny, and white, and rather silly, so she laughed.

'What's so funny?' He did not try to move away.

'My silly useless little hand on yours. It says everything really.'

He frowned, and then abandoning his glass he took hold of her hand with both of his, turned it over and appeared to study her palm.

'What do you see?'

He peered closely, as if her palm were a map. 'I see difficult times ahead. I see a smart young woman brought up in a smart house, with servants and fine clothes, transported against her will to a wild country peopled by felons, stuck on a farm, far from society, alone and helpless.'

'You make me sound like a convict!'

'So you are, in a sense. You did not choose to come here. Come to that neither did I. Come to that I was about the same age as you when I was forcibly uprooted from my home.' He let go her hand and placed it carefully down on the table. 'Fancy that then,' he said, and he stared across the table at her.

'I am not alone, and I am not helpless.' Elizabeth said gently, but firmly too. 'Thanks to you.'

'Is that an invitation?'

He may or may not have said that, she couldn't recall, maybe she just imagined he did. She felt suddenly choked, on the verge of tears. There was something inexplicably moving – bizarrely so – about the sight of a man used to acts of physical labour doing something so mundane, so *clerkish*, as keeping the books. She began to sob.

'What's up?'

She couldn't speak, so she gestured instead, at the table, at the piles of paper and the heavy ledger and the pot of ink – *ink* for God's sake! – that cluttered the table.

'All this,' she managed to splutter.

'Dear me. I'm sorry you find it upsetting. If I'd known you were coming I'd have . . .' he scratched his head.

'You'd have what, Will?'

'I'd have spruced myself up, for a start. And the place too. And I'd have hidden the books so you'd never find them.'

He puckered his cheek at her. And then without warning the sobs burst forth unchecked, and that's when he got to his feet – or maybe it was she who made the first move, she couldn't quite recall, as what happened next wiped what happened before right out of her mind. One way or another they came to be standing together right there by the table with the ledger and the two empty glasses and she felt his arms around her pulling her to him and squeezing her so tight she could barely breathe; and she burying her face in his chest, still sobbing fit to bust, and breathing in the warmth of his body and the smell of him – and oh Agnes, you have no idea how it felt to be held, to be cocooned, they must have stood there for, what, a minute at least, till he took a step back and gazed at her with those astonishing deep, chocolate, amused Scottish eyes.

'I'm so sorry,' she said.

He shook his head. 'That was a long time coming.'

'Yes.' She wiped her face with the back of her hand and stared at the floor for a moment. Then, 'I must go', she mumbled.

And she did. But she came back. If not the next night then the following week. And those nightly visits became more and more regular. Sometimes they talked about the farm, and the accounts, but more often than not they talked of other things entirely. As the visits became more and more regular so Elizabeth began to relax, and to smile again. So when it did eventually happen it seemed like the most natural thing in the world.

~

Of course the moment it was publicly known that Mrs Pitt was pregnant by her overseer, Agnes Pursip was on the doorstep before you could say *What do you think you are doing?*

'I'm not here to censure you dear, it's far too late for that. I just need to know one thing,' she said, perching herself on the hardest chair in the room; it being, Elizabeth surmised, her version of the hair shirt.

'No, we're not,' said Elizabeth. 'Before you ask.'

'Whyever not? The poor child – it's unfair on the poor thing to be born out of wedlock, it's bad enough as it is!'

Elizabeth shrugged. 'He'll manage,' she said. 'Or she. We love each other and we will love our children.'

'Children?'

Elizabeth shrugged again. 'Maybe, who knows?'

Who knows.

By then Will had moved himself into the house and into his mistress's bedroom and again, it seemed such a natural thing Elizabeth felt she hardly needed to explain to the children when their little brother John appeared. He was followed three years later by a sister, named Elizabeth, and then Augusta and finally Frances, with four and two years between them respectively. To young George the arrival of four step siblings may not have been a huge surprise, or even much of a shock; after all children only know what they know. William had always seemed like a brother to him, and the shift to stepfather only cemented the relationship. It would have delighted George to know William had become a permanent member of the family because otherwise, well, people are always moving on, aren't they? How could he have managed the farm without him?

It is a mystery why Elizabeth and William never married. The assumption is she resisted doing so to protect her children's inheritance, as at that time women were bound by law to hand over all ownership of property to their husband on marriage. It says something about Elizabeth that she was prepared to risk her reputation for the sake of her (legitimate) children. (One can only hope there was some kind of provision made for their half-siblings.)

It also says something for Will, that he stuck around when he had nothing to gain, financially speaking that is. Because stick around he did.

But what interests George's biographer most is the effect his mother's flouting of convention and total disregard for disapproving gossip from the likes of Agnes Pursip might have had on him. Because in due course he was going to flout convention himself.

Chapter 4

1822: The Hawkesbury

For those unlucky not to have made its acquaintance the Hawkesbury River – known by the original inhabitants of the area as Deerubbin – begins its 300-mile journey as a series of streams 50 miles south of Sydney. As the streams flow west they converge with others to form the Nepean river, before turning north and growing in size and momentum as the river picks up other waterways en route. Roundabout the town of Richmond it makes a sharp bend to the east and changes its name to the Hawkesbury, before it curves and twists its way through perpendicular cliffs to emerge at last into the Pacific Ocean 50 miles north of Sydney. It is one of the most beautiful areas in the whole of New South Wales and a very desirable place to live.

In the early days of European settlement it was called 'the granary of New South Wales', thanks to the fertility of its soil. In good years it kept the colony going. In bad years, when the Hawkesbury flooded – which it did frequently – the whole colony risked starvation.

~

We don't know for sure why Mary Pitt first made the decision to give up her cosy cottage in Dorset in 1801 to travel across the world to live in a penal colony. There were signs her husband

Robert, who had died thirteen years earlier – when Thomas was six years old, the same age as his son George when he lost his father – had left the family close to penniless. So mother, son and four dowry-less daughters scraped by thanks to the charity of the local landowner, Lord Rivers, who allowed them to stay on in their little cottage on his estate in Fiddleford rent-free, in return for which Thomas worked for him as a farm labourer.

But working for someone else in the comparatively dulcet climate of England was a far cry from what was to be expected of the twenty-year-old head of the Pitt family in New South Wales. Not only was this a very different country with an impossible climate and alien soil, it was Thomas's responsibility, with the reluctant help of two government servants, to first clear the thickly-wooded 100-acre plot of land granted to his mother near the Hawkesbury before building some kind of dwelling on it, from scratch, out of whatever materials could be found and with only the most primitive tools. And then to turn that and the second 100 acres next door, granted to him later that same year, into a working farm.

Yet unlike his father, Thomas prospered. He became a pillar of the local community, donating money towards a school – well before he was a father himself – and helping to found the local Benevolent Society, along with his brother-in-law William Faithfull. He saw his four sisters married before he found a wife for himself in young Elizabeth Laycock – daughter of the pioneer and eccentric Thomas Laycock of the New South Wales Corps and his long-suffering wife Hannah.

At the time of his death, according to his will, Thomas was in possession of 630 acres of land: the two 100-acre grants near Richmond plus another 30 acres nearby, currently rented out, and a further 400 acres across the river in Kurrajong, which he and Elizabeth had been granted in 1811 and 1819. Elizabeth may have felt herself alone and abandoned at a very tender age, but she was far from destitute.

By the time George was born the Hawkesbury district was a

settled community with two established towns on its southern banks, named by Governor Macquarie Richmond and Windsor, and others further downriver which he christened Wilberforce and Pitt Town (the latter named, I feel the need to add, after the British Prime Minister of the time).

The town of Richmond was a long walk or a short horse ride from the Pitts' farm, and it was here that in 1822, at the age of eight, young George went to school, along with his cousin George Faithfull, who was the same age. Early New South Wales rarely enjoyed the luxury of single-purpose buildings, so schools, churches and even courthouses often had to share premises, resulting in letters of protest from the likes of the Reverend Cowper that 'profane language and an abuse of the Creator's name and attributes are habitual on the same spot where at other times they offer up their petitions in the most solemn manner'. (The profane language belonging to the arguers in court rather than the children being educated, presumably.) The money for the school buildings, and for schoolmasters, was raised from local landowners via a General Order issued in 1804, which invited local settlers to contribute twopence for each acre of land they owned for a period of fourteen years to pay for a teacher who could double as a preacher. In the case of the original incumbent of Richmond School, a Mr Harris, sufficient contributions were unfortunately not forthcoming, which is why he found himself having to 'preach a free gospel and run almost a free school'.

The school the two Georges attended was built in 1813 and also served as a chapel. The Georges' fathers donated five guineas each towards it. It was a 'substantial two-storeyed' building, built by William Cox (who was also the first to build a road through the Blue Mountains), situated next to a burial ground on the corner of Francis Street and what is now Windsor Street. The schoolmaster at the time was Mathew Hughes, an Irish convict who'd been transported for life for being involved in a murder while serving in the Irish militia. (He had arrived in the colony in 1796 on the notorious convict ship *Britannia*, the same vessel that delivered fellow convict James Horse, who once worked for Thomas.)

By 1822 Hughes had been a teacher for some years, first at Kissing Point and then at Windsor, before he had received his absolute pardon. While at Kissing Point he had in lieu of a salary been allowed 'the privileges of His Majesty's stores' – meaning free food and victuals – an 'indulgence' which had been withdrawn following the deposition of Governor Bligh, when for the second time in its short life the colony was in the hands of the New South Wales Corps. When the status quo was restored in the person of Governor Macquarie Hughes was forced to write to the aforementioned Reverend Cowper asking him to plead with the governor for restoration of this indulgence, since he was otherwise compelled to take time out from teaching to 'labour in the field' to support himself and his wife. Despite his convict origins Hughes had a reputation as an upright citizen, a Methodist and a strict teacher of the old school, who apparently required his students to bow to him and pronounce 'Your servant, Sir' every time they entered the classroom.

Hughes was not the only convict schoolteacher. The Reverend Henry Fulton, one of the witnesses to Thomas Pitt's will, ran a private boarding school in Richmond set up in 1814 for the sons (no daughters) of wealthy landowners. Like Hughes he was Irish, transported for life for sedition. Unlike Hughes he had a top class degree from Trinity College Dublin and was regarded as one of the best-educated people in the colony. Hughes's successor at the school in Windsor, Joseph Harpur, had been transported for life for highway robbery. A later teacher at Richmond School, who delighted in the name 'Mr Hogsflesh' and who taught Elizabeth and William's four younger children (but who was not to my knowledge a convict), also moonlighted as a publican and a drover. It was a world of make-do and multi-tasking, you could say.

Education did not become compulsory until the 1870s, and in the 1840s only half the children in the colony went to school at all. So for George to have apparently only attended Richmond School for two years is perhaps not so surprising – his cousin George Faithfull quit after only one – and it is likely his education continued in other ways, at home in particular. It was customary among some families for parents to read to their children of an evening, once the farm duties had been taken care of. And William, brought up and educated in Scotland, may well have had a copy of Robbie Burns's poems about his person.

~

In 1822, the year after Thomas's death and according to the census, Elizabeth was in possession of 610 acres of land – the 200 acres at Richmond and 400 acres at Kurrajong – of which 30 acres were cleared. She had 93 cattle, 23 hogs, five horses, twelve acres each of wheat and maize, three of barley, one of potato and a two-acre garden and orchard. Resident on the Richmond property were Elizabeth, William Scott and his sister Margaret and a government worker named Richard Barker.

(I confess I'm puzzled about the '30 acres cleared'. It contradicts the notice Elizabeth placed in the newspaper after Thomas's death, advertising her 200 acres at Richmond with '150 cleared'. And with 30 acres under cultivation that suggests the rest of the farm was still woodland – so what were her animals grazing on?)

Six years later, according to the 1828 census, Elizabeth's holdings had apparently increased to 730 acres (probably a mistake), of which 200 were cleared and 70 cultivated. Her cattle had gone from 93 to 250, she'd got rid of the hogs and acquired twelve horses. Resident on her properties were Elizabeth and six of her seven children, including Elizabeth (Betsey) Scott and excluding Eliza, her youngest by Thomas, who had gone to live with her grandmother Hannah Laycock in Sydney. She had three servants – one serving convict, one free and one free by servitude – making a total, with William and Margaret Scott, of six adults and six children. The following year they were joined by another government servant called William Broggy (aka Brophy), and two years later by a founder and stockman.

So, in ten years the number of people working for Elizabeth had gone from three to nine, and included only one woman. If the list is complete it means Margaret Scott was acting as housekeeper and nursemaid for the children and possibly cook as well.

There's no way of knowing how many of these people, or animals, were living on the Richmond farm and how many at Kurrajong. Kurrajong is some distance from Richmond, across the river and fifteen kilometres further north. On a trip to the district in 2017 a descendant of GM's brother Robert, who has lived at Kurrajong all his life, showed us the boundaries of the old 400-acre property. The countryside around is beautiful, lush, green, and hilly, but not, he told us, as fertile as the alluvial soil on the Richmond properties. (All that now remains of the Kurrajong property is the original well, tucked into the corner of the garden of a modern house. The homestead itself, built at some point probably by Robert Pitt and named *Trafalgar*, was burnt down in a bush fire in 1944.)

For George these were the years that turned him into a resourceful, not to say ambitious, farmer and stockkeeper. There was still a good deal of the two properties to be cleared, and the size of the stock increased. This required a knowledge of breeding, which George would have acquired partly from William and partly from peering over his neighbours' fences, both literally and figuratively, and sharing information with fellow farmers. He became handy with a gun. He learned how to cope with infestations of caterpillars that appeared from nowhere and marched in formation across the paddocks devouring everything in their path, leaf by leaf and stem by stem, leaving 'not so much as a solitary standing blade', before vanishing into the earth again. Entire crops were annihilated, leaving both animals and humans with nothing to eat. There was a bad drought in 1824-25. But fortunately, and surprisingly, there were no floods. Between 1819 and 1857 the mighty and unpredictable Hawkesbury river chose to stay within its banks, the longest time in its history before or since.

GM also learned a harder lesson: as any farmer knows when it comes to dealing with animals or humans, it's the humans who are the problem. As a youngster, according to my speculative account, George had come to enjoy playing master of the house with the government servants, watching them jump to attention the moment they saw him and hasten to do his bidding whenever asked, or more to the point, told. He even tried bribery, playing one against the other, offering favours to the one who was quickest to, say, make him a cup of tea or fetch his hat from the veranda. Fortunately for his future's sake George's activities had a witness, and one day Will called the ten-year-old boy to his hut for a lesson on life.

'How would you like it,' said Will, 'to be told what to do by a whippersnapper a quarter your age?'

George did a bit of mental arithmetic. 'You mean by a two-and-a-half-year-old?' He snorted. 'I'd like to see him try.'

'Then take a look in the mirror.'

GM thought for a moment. 'What do you mean?'

'Do you think a convict is a lower being than yourself? Think before you speak now.'

GM did so. It was clear to Will he'd never done such a thing before.

The boy scratched his head, 'I think there are people who give orders . . .' He tailed off, then tried again. 'There are people who are bosses and there are people who are . . .'

'Bossed?'

'Yep.'

'And who determines this? What Godlike personage says to a person – you're the boss and to another – you're the underling?'

'Well,' George began, 'you know there have to be the people who decide things and the people who do what they decide.'

'On what grounds?'

'Otherwise nothing wouldn't get done.'

'Otherwise nothing would get done.'

George shook his head with annoyance. 'Anyway, they're convicts. They've done crimes.'

'All right. So listen to this. There are men working on this property who are government men, who've done crimes, as you say. They are fed and housed by their masters and given a certain wage per year to distinguish them from the common slave. Unlike the common slave once they've served their time they can go on their way. With me so far?'

George heaved a sigh and nodded.

'Don't you sigh like that with me, young man.'

George blinked.

'If for instance a government man goes off the rails and commits a misdemeanour – you do know what a misdemeanour is, do you George?'

George nodded again and studied his feet.

'If he happens to go off the rails for whatever reason that could set him back years. He might have to start at the very beginning and serve his term over, or worse, get sent off to do hard labour somewhere like Van Diemen's Land. Or Norfolk Island. On a chain gang. With irons on his ankles. Working on the roads. In the heat. Eighteen hours a day. Would you fancy doing that George?'

'No of course not!' George threw his weight onto one leg and stared at Will with studied boredom.

'Because that is what you are driving those men to do, do you see?'

'What do you mean?'

'I've had some complaints.'

'About me?' George drew himself upright. 'Like what?'

'I don't need to tell you, you could do that yourself. They were polite complaints, so far, because they are polite men. Unlike some others I could name.' Will looked idly round his hut. 'Decent men, on the whole, not bad workers if you treat them right.' His gaze returned to George. 'Do you think you're better than a convict, George?'

George pouted.

'Because in one sense you are, or so society sees you. Or you could just say you are lucky, as am I. So far.'

'It's you who told me to do it,' the boy mumbled.

'What's that? Speak up, I can't hear you.' Will cocked a hand behind his ear. 'What did I tell you to do, exactly?'

'You told me to tell them what to do. So I did.'

'And you did well. You did it with authority. That did not give you the right to treat those men like animals, or playthings. Authority is not authority if it is abused George.'

'Well how am I to know?'

'You're to know because they are human beings George, under the employ, and the care, of your mother and the family, which includes you. They're being given a second chance, which a lot of people are not. You could even say they are life's victims and if you had just a splinter of imagination,' he reached over and tapped GM's forehead with his finger, 'you could see yourself as one of them. Could you not?'

Will sat back and waited. 'Are you with me George?' he said. And after what seemed like a very long time, George nodded.

~

It was a useful lesson for George, and a timely one. To be given authority over the government servants, men several times his age, tough, defiant and as often as not resentful; to be able to tell them what to do, to be on the lookout for petty thefts and search their huts for stolen goods without warning, and to mete out punishment, would be a challenge to a man of any age. To quote an early settler, Peter Cunningham, 'To enforce his authority a man must go among [his men] . . . and beard them without timidity.'

George grew up fast, and authoritative, a natural leader of men.

Chapter 5

1827: The Aboriginal connection

Late on in my researches I made an interesting discovery: at the age of around twelve years old GM recorded the words of an Aboriginal song. It went like this:

Murring anna juriwanna,
Woodgeree wanna,
Geeli, geeli. Angi, Argo, Bah.
   (This sung many times)
Go at Poto Pah, coogee Mia-a.

The song appeared in the 1897 edition of *The Australasian Anthropological Journal*, passed down presumably by GM's son RM (my great grandfather), who was on the Council of the Australasian Anthropological Society at the time.

I hunted for a translation of the words but it was hard to find. So many Aboriginal languages have disappeared. I assumed it was the Darug language of the people of the Hawkesbury, and I remembered a production of Kate Grenville's *The Secret River*, which I'd recently seen in a quarry near Adelaide, in which the Aboriginal characters spoke Darug, thanks to one of the few Darug descendants who had retained the language. His name was Richard Green.

I managed to track him down, and after a bit of toing and froing, and quite a lot of work on his side, he came up with this:

    Belonging - *Nganna* (*Murring anna juriwanna*)
    We ask for me for you - *Wudgari wanna* (*Woodgeree wanna*)
    You and yours - *Giligiliangi* (*Geeli, geeli. Angi*)
    The young from far away - *Ngargu-ba* (*Argo, Bah*)
    To come eat with us - *Bada-ba* (*Go at Poto Pah*)
    Near the lavatory - *Guugi Coogee* (*Coogee Mia-a*)

So it's an invitation from them (the Aborigines) to the young from far away (whoever they may be – the white people perhaps?) to eat with them near the lavatory, if you please. ('*Coogee*' means 'stinking place' according to various online sources; referring in the case of Coogee Beach to rotting seaweed.) It took a bit of interpreting on the part of Mr Green to translate GM and RM's spelling into more colloquially-understood Darug.

Make of that what you will, my question is how did young George come to make the acquaintance of Aboriginal people? Were they working on the Richmond properties? In which case, why did they not appear on the census?

This is what you might call a loaded question requiring a loaded, as in carefully-researched, answer.

The original Aboriginal population of Australia before the whites moved in consisted of around 250 language groups, otherwise known as 'tribes' or 'nations'. Each nation inhabited a different part of the continent, and while they did not claim ownership of any particular part of it in the European sense – meaning they did not build houses or fences or other obvious physical symbols of possession – they did respect other nations' territories. Boundaries were marked on the landscape, on trees or rocks or the ground itself, and no one from one nation would venture onto the land of another without invitation. These physical marks were invisible to most Europeans, needless to say.

Governors of New South Wales were under strict instruction from the British government to respect 'the true proprietors of the soil' and to treat the Aboriginal people like

British subjects, which generally speaking they did their best to do, certainly in earlier times. However since they did not recognise or understand (deliberately or otherwise) the Aborigines' connection to their country the British Government declared it *terra nullius*, and therefore belonging to the British Crown.

How anyone, governors or other, were expected to respect a country's indigenous population while taking their land and feeding grounds away from them was never explained. Suffice to say one of the many effects of this contradictory policy meant the country's original custodians had no status, and while theoretically they were given the same rights as British subjects they did not appear on regular musters or censuses, and they were not even recognised as citizens or given the vote until 1969. They were, effectively, non-people.

The Europeans were not the first to recognise the richness of the land surrounding the Hawkesbury River. The Darug people had lived there for however many tens of thousands of years, fishing its waters and harvesting the yams and wildlife and other forms of sustenance. When the Europeans moved in there were skirmishes between settlers and Darug and many deaths on both sides. By the time Mary Pitt and her family arrived there in 1802 the Darug had been more or less pushed back from the Europeans' properties, and relative peace reigned, for a while at least.

The general view of contemporary historians seems to be that earlier governors and officials of the Enlightenment had a better understanding and relationship with the Aboriginal people than their later counterparts, products of the Victorian period. Governor Macquarie, who took office at the beginning of 1810, started out with a benign attitude toward the Aboriginal people but when they resisted or refused to obey his orders he came down on them like the proverbial ton of bricks.

For example in March 1816 a group of Aboriginal men plundered a settler's farm in Bringelly (west of Liverpool and south of Badgerys Creek) resulting in the death of five farmworkers. Macquarie's reaction was fearsome. He ordered three military detachments to scour the countryside from Kurryjong Brush in the north to Illawarra in the south (an area of around 80 miles) and to capture as many 'Natives' as possible and hold them hostage until the perpetrators of the crimes gave themselves up. Anyone who resisted should be fired upon and their bodies hung up on trees 'in order to strike the greatest terror into the Survivors'. This resulted in what became known as the Appin Massacre, in which at least fourteen Aboriginal people were killed by the militia, including many women and children and some who died trying to escape over sheer cliffs. It was what Macquarie claimed to be an 'unavoidable result'.

In May Macquarie declared that from the 4 June that year (King George III's birthday) no 'Black Native, or Body of Black Natives shall ever appear at or within one Mile of any Town, Village, or Farm, occupied by, or belonging to any British Subject, armed with any warlike or offensive Weapon or Weapons of any Description . . . on Pain of being deemed and considered in a State of Aggression and Hostility, and treated accordingly'. And any group of six or more Natives discovered loitering around a farm would be seen as the enemy.

By way of a carrot Macquarie offered any 'Black Natives' who were prepared to settle down and act like white settlers grants of land and victuals provided from stores. He also established a school for Aboriginal children, first at Parramatta and then Black Town, with the aim of turning them into good little Europeans. But while the pupils were quick enough with the learning they regularly absconded, and even the ones who lasted the course eventually went back to their families and their old ways in the bush.

Attitudes to the Aborigines were mixed, to say the least. Some settlers simply thought of them as savages and to be exterminated as quickly as possible. Others tried to learn their languages and get to understand them. Some individuals, mostly churchmen in the earlier days, 'adopted' Aboriginal children and brought them up with their own family; but again the children invariably escaped back to their own eventually, often after years of living with white people. Some settler families also adopted, or kidnapped, Aboriginal children, for whatever reason – for protection or exploitation, as servants or sexual partners, or for the purpose of 'civilising' them, it's not always possible to know. The one thing they all had in common was the certainty of their belief they were doing the indigenous people a favour.

We benefit from hindsight needless to say, but such was the assumed superiority of Victorian Europeans nobody seemed to appreciate the fact that the Aboriginal people, who had survived on the continent for upwards of 60,000 years, were perfectly happy as they were thanks very much and could see no advantage, or point, in learning European ways. And that no matter what enticements or inducements the colonists might offer them nothing could beat the strength and pull of family.

By way of illustration, I can't resist here recounting a story told by a local settler of the time called James (Toby) Ryan.

He was watching a couple of 'blacks'. The man was stretched out on the ground and the woman was nudging him for food, so eventually he got up, grabbed his tomahawk and went off, returning in half an hour with three possums, which he roughly skinned and cooked on a fire the woman had made. When it was partly done he tore into it and ate the best bits, throwing the rest over his shoulder to the woman, who ate what she wanted and threw the rest to the dogs. Having eaten his fill the man stretched out on the ground again. 'This was a common practice of the blacks, who never looked for food until necessitated,' said Ryan.

It was just this kind of practice that the whites found so hard to understand. Disregarding the obvious hierarchy of man over woman over dog: a man was meant to toil from sunup to sundown, not just saunter off into the woods every time he felt hungry. It is what earned the Aboriginal people the label 'lazy'. In modern terms you might call it Ultimate Mindfulness.

But to return to young George and his friendship with local Darug:

There is evidence that Aboriginal people, boys in particular, helped out on settlers' farms during harvest time in the early days, and I surmise this is when George made the acquaintance of some Aboriginal children of his age, hence the song. It's also said they used the river crossing at Yarramundi, just up the road from the Pitt farms, as a route from the Cumberland Plain to the Blue Mountains. In his thesis on the Darkiñung people Dr Geoff Ford claims GM's father Thomas may have taken part in bush exploring, which, if correct, means he had probably already made the acquaintance of local Aboriginal people as guides. He also claimed GM 'was to become known for his close contact with local Aborigines', though the only evidence he offers for this is George's recording of the songwords.

So my guess is George was used to the company of Darug people from a young age; that he played with them and worked alongside them, children and adults, that they were a regular part of his young life and that of his siblings. He may have learned their language, who knows. It would stand him in good stead in his later life, as there is no question any white person who took the trouble to make friends with the Aboriginal people in the early days of settlement stood a much better chance of survival. And there are signs that GM had more than a passing relationship with the Aboriginal people in times to come.

Chapter 6

1820s: At home

The simpler the house the less the work, said the writer Mary Gilmore in the latter part of the 19th century. Early frontier women had it easy as far as housework was concerned: no glass windows to clean, no tiled floors to wash, curtains to pleat and iron or furniture to polish. And perhaps more importantly, no particular standards to have to live up to.

That may well have been the case for the Pitt women on their arrival at the Hawkesbury in 1802. Their first house, thrown up in a hurry by Thomas, would have been pretty rudimentary: probably built of slabs (rough planks of wood) with a bark or shingle roof, a mud floor and strips of hessian covering the walls and roughly dividing up the living space. The kitchen such as it was would have been an open hearth with some form of chimney, and if they were lucky they'd have had a bread oven. Furniture would have been assembled from wood offcuts: wood blocks to sit on and a slab of wood supported on more wood blocks to eat off. With a shortage of metal everything was made, and held together, by wood – of which, in the earliest days, there was never a shortage. Mary Gilmore claims the women became so used to sitting on slabs of wood they felt unsafe perched on chairs.

The second house built on the property at Richmond was

made of brick – we know this from a later census (of 1841) and from a pile of them left on the property, which the current owner Margaret Betts says are the remains of house number two. (Margaret lives in house number three, built much later by one of GM's sons.) Nobody knows when house number two came into existence but my guess is it was before Thomas met and married Elizabeth, and certainly before she started producing children in 1814.

It was a 'capital' house, as described by Elizabeth when she was advertising it to let: probably symmetrical, following the Georgian fashion from the old country, with a tiled roof and with the ubiquitous and uniquely Australian addition of a veranda. There would have been – if not immediately, certainly as the years passed – a separate kitchen, a living room and at least three bedrooms: one for the master and mistress of the house and one each for the male children and the female. Glazed windows, with curtains, and bare wood floors, with perhaps a rug here and there for decoration and for colour. There would be proper furniture, made of wood of course, and a dining table made of rosewood maybe, or cedar, highly polished and kept covered at all times.

Servants, convicts or otherwise, slept in outhouses: women separate from the men, but convicts and free men, Protestants and Catholics, all mucking in together. Only the overseer had his own hut.

The women sewed. From an early age, even when thimbles had to be made out of cow hide, little fingers created curtains, adornments for the furniture, even their own clothes. When not sewing they tended the garden and the orchard. The Pitts probably grew peaches until the fruit fly got at them, at which point they switched to citrus fruit which they sold at the fruit markets at Agnes Banks. At mealtimes vegetables had to be picked and prepared just before cooking, so they kept their freshness. Water drawn from the well had to be 'aerated' to make it drinkable, which meant several bucketfuls would be drawn up and tipped back in until it contained enough air to taste like spring water. 'Flat water meant flat tea,' said Mary Gilmore.

By the time Thomas departed the world it's safe to assume he left behind a comfortable house, albeit one that would be improved and added on to as the years went by and Elizabeth's family grew.

~

As a widow living alone in relative isolation with small children Elizabeth would have been vulnerable, for sure. If, as I have speculated, her mother Hannah feared for her safety she had good cause. There were bushrangers, mostly escaped convicts, some of whom had absconded from working on the Great North Road a few miles downriver near Wiseman's Ferry. One afternoon in March 1825 Elizabeth's neighbour, a Mrs Crawley, was returning from a shopping trip to Sydney with her son and a cart full of purchases when she was held up and relieved of her property by three armed men on the Richmond Road near Windsor. On hearing of his wife's ordeal Mr Crawley set off before dawn the following morning in pursuit of the villains, along with an Aboriginal boy and three neighbours (one of whom was Robert Aull, who plays an important role later in our family story). Soon after daybreak they came upon three armed men on the Chain of Ponds on Richmond Road whom they rightly assumed to be the guilty men and a fierce gunfight ensued, resulting in the escape of one of the men and the capture of the other two and the wounding of Mr Crawley. Mrs Crawley's property was restored, minus the liquor, and the perpetrators were taken before the Windsor Court House and charged.

Another settler, Toby Ryan, was held up on a road near Penrith with his father and only released when he revealed his name. (It seems bushrangers only targeted strangers.) Ryan claimed bushrangers hid out at the Chain of Ponds and that robberies were committed there all the time. The most notorious of them was 'Wild' Jack Donohoe, who despite his customary uniform of velveteen jacket and waistcoat was described by Ryan as 'the most insignificant looking creature imaginable'. He used his pistol to light a fire to make tea and terrorised the countryside from Bathurst to Illawarra for eight years. After he was eventually shot dead by troopers a pipemaker made a fortune selling pipes made out of a mould taken from a cast of Donohoe's head, complete with the hole where the fatal bullet struck. He was also the subject of a song called 'The Wild Colonial Boy', which was sung in pubs throughout Sydney until it was eventually banned.

So without a male companion there would have been no shopping trips to Sydney for Elizabeth. Back then there was no such thing as a regular coach service between the Hawkesbury and the outside world, despite various attempts to set one up. Most enterprises failed thanks to the dire state of the roads, which were pitted with potholes and, in the wet, so muddy horses sank up to their knees. When a regular service was eventually established in 1832 the 50-mile journey took five hours and entailed four changes of horse.

But then Elizabeth had her hands full producing children. Between 1824 and 1833 she gave birth to four of them, one boy and three girls. Agnes Pursip continued to visit, less regularly now time was taking its toll on her, though the doughty woman's spirit was as vibrant as ever, as were her lectures on the stigma of bastardry: 'Not to mention,' she would add, 'the obvious perils of aligning yourself with a man without morals, and who's to know whether he might up sticks and vanish without trace one day and then where would you be?'

Elizabeth smiled calmly back and replied, 'Why should he? His home is here, his children are here, his children are his life. As am I,' she added for good measure, and she felt it. She had never had the slightest qualms about Will's loyalty. 'Not to mention,' she continued, taking the phrase from the older woman's lips, 'he and George make the perfect working team, they depend on one another just as I depend on them.'

Elizabeth was immovable, and as even Mrs Pursip herself was bound to admit the years had given her increasing maturity and confidence. And so the redoubtable Agnes was finally forced to admit defeat. She kept going until Elizabeth's last child was born in 1833, and then, as if the point of her life – and in my story – had disappeared, she faded from the scene.

At some point in the 1820s Eliza, Elizabeth's youngest daughter by Thomas, went to live with her grandmother Hannah Laycock in Sydney. She was recorded as living there in the 1828 census when she was eight years old. Three years later Hannah, one of the colony's early pioneers and widow of ex-Quartermaster Thomas Laycock, died at the age of 72.

Her will makes interesting reading.

Having outlived her husband by over twenty years Hannah had accumulated a good deal of property, including four houses in Pitt Street in the city, which she left to her two surviving sons, a grandson and Elizabeth's daughter Eliza. Putty Farm, her property north of the Hawkesbury, she bequeathed to another grandson. All she left her only surviving daughter was the smaller family bible, a 'dressing glass', a portrait of her grandson Thomas WEB Laycock and one of the Pitt Street houses on the demise of her son William.

What should the family historian make of that? It looks to me like a family rift, and it is not outlandish to assume this had to do with Elizabeth's liaison with William Scott; especially if, in my version of events, Elizabeth had defied her mother's suggestion she remove to Sydney and marry again.

Despite this apparent snub there is every sign that Elizabeth and William and their children – by 1833 numbering eight, including Elizabeth's and Thomas's four (excluding Eliza) and her four by William – were thriving, as was the farm. In 1831 William's sister Margaret left to marry Edward Inall.

The only blot on the family happiness at that time was the death in 1834 of Elizabeth's son William Henry, aged 15. The lack of information as to how he died suggests it was from illness or disease.

Apart from that tragedy they were good days for the Pitts and Scotts. But they weren't to last.

Chapter 7

1834: Distraction

And so GM grew up. And up, until he reached well over six feet. At the age of twenty he was an imposing young man with black hair, an impressive nose and a beard that, throughout his life, he confined to beneath his chin – more of a ruff than a beard you could say.

He'd been working shoulder to shoulder with his mentor William Scott for twelve years now, along with his brother Robert, younger by three years and even taller than GM. The three men worked the two farms at Richmond – which GM renamed Bronte, after the family's patron Admiral Nelson, Duke of Bronte – and at Kurrajong.

There was work to be done on the house too, with Elizabeth and William's expanding family. Extensions had to be added to accommodate all those children, ruining the (assumed) symmetry of the original house with a (possibly) bulging extra bedroom on one side and a larger kitchen on the other.

GM had, ever since his father had died and before even that, been a hard worker. It was what his life was, he'd been used to slaving from sunup to sundown – and later, if there were books to be kept – it was what every farmer has always done and always will. But lately, his workmate and stepfather couldn't help but notice, he was becoming distracted.

'Just off for a stroll,' he'd say to William, as he set off down the track towards the river, whistling, of a late afternoon. Now as anyone knows, farmers don't 'take strolls', strolls are for idle city people. Moreover Scott couldn't help but notice how GM made a point of sprucing himself up before his strolls, changing out of his muddy moleskins into spanking clean flannel and slicking down his hair. He also watched him pluck a rose from the garden which he placed in his lapel and which, Scott also observed, was not there when he returned.

From the time of day and the direction of his perambulation it didn't take a genius to realise GM was off to the pub, which could only mean one thing: like so many others in the colony he was becoming a Drinker.

This came as a surprise to William, as GM had never shown undue interest in grog, nor shown any signs of having over-imbibed. So one late afternoon as he was heading off in his usual manner and direction Will caught up with him and said he'd accompany him on his strolls, if he didn't mind.

GM hesitated for just a moment before grinning and nodding and slapping his stepfather on the shoulder and sauntering off, whistling a Scottish air.

The pub was called the Governor Darling and it overlooked the Yarramundi Lagoon. It was a cute spot, Scott knew already. He knew the owner, Robert Aull, and his wife Mary, both convicts and both of them on their second marriages.

'No surprise eh, Scotty?' said GM cheerfully as they came within sight of the lagoon and the simple slab structure on the far side.

'I never took you for a drinker George,' Will replied, mildly.

There were at that time a lot of pubs in New South Wales, roughly twice as many as there are now, believe it or not – at least 40 of them in the Windsor district alone. Pubs were not just for drinking however, they were where people convened to gossip, compare prices, exchange news and organise petitions to the governor. They were community halls and minor seats of parliament combined. The Governor Darling would have been GM and William's local, just a spit away from Bronte. But it didn't take long for Will to clock the reason for GM's increasing absences wasn't, after all, the booze.

She was a demure little thing, quiet, pleasant-looking, dressed in black with a lace collar and her hair tied back neatly away from her face. She reminded William of a novice nun. She stood behind the bar like a sentry, but the moment the two men entered and she set eyes on GM her face lit up like the sun.

'Well now!' she said, as GM edged his backside onto a stool. 'See you've brought your stepfather with you today. Hello Mr Scott, how are you?'

'I'm grand Miss Johnson, thank you.' Will looked from one to the other and nodded slowly.

'What's that?' said GM.

'Nothing,' said Will. 'I was just wondering what was going on and now I know.'

'So you can go home again,' said GM.

'I could.' William put his hand in a pocket and fingered some coins. 'But now I'm here, I'll have whatever you're having George.'

'That'll be two whiskies then,' said the young woman, whose name – as both men knew – was Julia.

There was a pause as she turned her back to attend to the drinks and the men stared straight ahead of them, without speaking. William was frowning.

'What's up Scotty?' asked GM.

Julia returned with two glasses of liquor. Then she looked from one to the other of them and said, 'So what's the gossip now?'

'I was going to ask you the same thing,' said William. 'I think perhaps the gossip is right here in front of us.'

'I'm sure I've no idea what you mean, Mr Scott.' She stared at him wide-eyed, then she flushed, and dropped her gaze and began scrubbing violently at the wooden bar in front of her.

'I'll leave you two lovebirds to it then,' said William, and wandered off in search of more neutral company.

GM didn't get back to the farm until late. Will was sitting on the veranda smoking his pipe, alone.

GM paused at the top of the steps. 'Where's mother?' he asked.

'Gone to bed.'

'Did you tell her?'

'Tell her what?' William removed the pipe from his mouth and tapped it on the side of his boot to settle the tobacco.

'You know.'

'Of course I didn't. I don't know what there is to tell.'

George sat down next to his stepfather. He couldn't keep the grin off his face.

'What do you think of her then Scotty?'

William squinted at him. 'She's all right. She's not particularly pretty, and she looks as if she's in mourning, or about to join a convent, and serious, and very young.'

There was a silence. GM's grin faltered.

'Is that it?'

'Why? What does it matter what I think?'

'I've asked her to marry me.'

Will nodded slowly, and then he said, 'Her mother and father were convicts. And her stepfather. You do know that, don't you?'

'Of course I do. Does it matter?'

William shrugged. 'Your mother might have some say in it.'

'I don't think . . .' George broke off.

'You don't think she has a leg to stand on, is that what you're saying? Not to mention your stepfather, so-called. Well you may be right. But it's your life. And there are some people around here who might disapprove.'

GM squinted into the darkness. 'What about the two of you? There are people around here who might disapprove of you.'

'Well that's their lookout. For me, I don't give a tinker's cuss, and nor I believe does your mother.'

GM looked back at his stepfather *de facto*. William didn't

smile often, but he joked a lot, and it wasn't always easy to tell when he was and when he wasn't, even after all these years.

He knew all about his potential in-laws. He knew that both Julia's late father John Johnson and her stepfather Robert Aull had been transported for forgery, which was not a big crime in his view, and her mother Mary for stealing. He also knew they'd made good, that Mary had owned property in Sydney and elsewhere, as did her husband Robert, who was a landowner and a publican. What else a person had to do to make themselves respectable he was darned if he knew.

'He's Irish,' said GM, for no particular reason.

'Who is?'

'The – you know – stepfather.'

'So?' Will stuck his pipe back in his mouth and turned to look at him. 'There are plenty of them in this country.'

'I wouldn't want to cross him, tell you the truth.'

'He'll be on cloud nine. He and his missus.'

'Why?'

'Well look at you. Fine young man with perfect pedigree. What more could a father want? Especially an Irishman.'

GM pulled himself upright and puffed out his chest.

'He already had a house-full of children of his own before he married again and took on however many more,' Will went on. 'He'll be delighted to get rid of one of them at least. Is how I see it.'

'Is that your blessing, given in your own way?'

'You don't need my blessing,' said GM's *de facto* stepfather 'It's your mother you should be thinking of.'

'I'm nearly twenty-one.'

'Are you indeed. How time flies.'

They sat there for some time, the two men, in the darkness, in silence. Listening to the call of the willie wagtail and the chirrup of distant bullfrogs, lost in their individual thoughts.

PART TWO

London 2015

Chapter 8

The convict stain

I'm leaving GM for the time being to contemplate his future while I traverse continents and centuries in order to investigate his future in-laws, my great great great grandparents John Johnson and Mary Moore.

I became aware of their existence only recently. Convict ancestry was kept a dark secret in my family, and in many Australian families apparently, until a couple of generations ago. As Babette Smith says in her book *Australia's Birthstain* colonial Australia's beginnings as a penal colony were rarely mentioned in public and much of convict history was not made accessible to family historians until later in the last century. It's different now of course. What Australian doesn't want to lay claim to a 'legitimate' ancestor? It not only tells the world how far back their Aussie ancestors go – transportation in New South Wales ended in the 1840s – it adds a touch of spice to tales of humble beginnings that led to better things.

We all know the early Botany Bay convicts were petty criminals, guilty at the most of minor theft or forgery or at the worst highway robbery, but very rarely – if at all – of acts of violence. Some were transported for political reasons – such as the Tolpuddle Martyrs, from the Pitt family's home county of Dorset – and others, from Ireland in particular, for activities generally labelled 'sedition'.

It's also well known that the prisons in England were bursting at the seams in the late 18th century, not just because of the poverty that drove some people to new levels of lawlessness, but because of new and stricter laws that deemed the theft of an item such as a handkerchief punishable with a prison sentence.

Of the 160,000 or so convicts who were transported over the 70-year period 80 percent were men, half of them carried sentences of seven years, mostly for crimes against property, and three quarters of them could read and/or write (compared with 58 percent of the people in Britain who were able to sign marriage registers at that time).

John Johnson and Mary Moore were tried in Assize Courts for, respectively, being in possession of forged banknotes, and stealing items of clothing include a petticoat. I know this because I'm lucky enough to have had the initial research done for me, mostly by my aunt Barbara Lamble. I know where, when and what my convict ancestors were convicted of and when and how they were transported. What I don't know is *why* they committed their crimes in the first place.

Mary Moore was apprehended in Gatton in Surrey, which no longer exists. But working backwards from the age she claimed to be on her arrival in Sydney in 1809, which was nineteen, my searches reveal a Mary More [sic] born in Banstead, Surrey on 15 March 1789 to parents John and Sarah.

As for John Johnson: he was described in 1810 as 39 years old, a native of Derbyshire, a potter by trade, 5ft 5¼ins tall, of fair to ruddy complexion with grey to brown hair and hazel eyes. Searching on the Ancestry website throws up several John Johnsons born in Derbyshire around 1770, including one whose middle name was Potter (a nice coincidence, but more likely to do with a family name than an occupation, unless his trade had been decided for him at birth). I'm plumping for the John Johnson who was baptised in Church Broughton in Derby on 5 March 1769.

There is a fly in the ointment: on his marriage certificate in Sydney some years later John Johnson is described as a 'widower'. So he had a wife, and dead to boot (although it was not unknown for convicts in the new colony to claim a dead spouse back home who was not actually deceased). So what happened to her?

Again I have my aunt to thank for discovering an Elizabeth Johnson who was part of an official Removal Order in 1809 sending her and her daughter Mary from Hartington to Taddington. A quick look at the AA road map shows these to be two small villages around six miles from one another, close to the towns of Buxton and Bakewell, but crucially, in different counties: Hartington in Derbyshire and Taddington in Staffordshire. Hence, I imagine, the removal from one county authority to another.

A brief exchange of emails with a helpful person at the Derbyshire Record Office tells me that had Elizabeth been left destitute when her husband was transported the local parish would have had her removed from wherever she had been living back to the parish in which she was born. And while there is nothing to prove this Elizabeth Johnson was John's wife, the timing fits. It also fits with the fact that John was apprehended for his crime on the streets of Leek, which is around ten miles from Hartington across the border in Staffordshire.

~

So it's off to the National Archives in Kew in south London to investigate my ancestors' crimes.

The NA are housed in a large brutalist building, set behind an ornamental lake that adds a feeling of tranquillity to the surroundings, which is most welcome because these places can be quite intimidating. I enter the Archives with some trepidation because while I've been here before in the past I cannot remember a) whether my card is up to date, b) what the procedure is or c) where to find anything.

I said once in a blog that research is a bit like having your second baby: you forget how to do it, you dread what it entails, but the end result – assuming all goes well – is so exhilarating you wonder why you ever had any fears to begin with.

I'm not sure that analogy is ideal, but in this case it all comes back to me in a flash: the cloakroom procedure (see-through plastic bags provided; no pens, no food or drink), the helpful staff who take you through the system line by line so even an idiot like me can follow it.

Crimes and punishments are beautifully preserved in the National Archives. (Details on how to negotiate them are laid out in the chapter notes.) In no time at all I am actually perusing the original Gaol Books containing details of all the crimes judged in particular sessions at the Staffordshire and Surrey Assizes.

'The Assize Courts were where the most serious criminal trials were heard twice a year by judges appointed by the monarch,' I read. That being knowingly in possession of three forged banknotes and stealing items worth a total of one pound thirteen shillings and sixpence were deemed serious crimes shows how low the bar was in those days.

The Gaol Records for John Johnson's trial is an ancient book with no index, but since it is in chronological order beginning in 1805 it doesn't take long to find Stafford Assizes Lent 1808. There, painstakingly written in copperplate, it says:

'Staffordshire Lent Assizes – 48th Geo: 3rd 1808

'Whereas John Johnson and John Baddeley were at this assizes severally convicted by their own confession of feloniously and without lawful excuse having in their custody Bank of England notes knowing the same to be forged and counterfeited for which they were sentenced to be transported to parts beyond the seas for the term of 14 years . . . It is therefore (and Justices John Sparrow Esq and John Lane Esq.) By the Court Pugh'

The next document is the Gaol Record for Mary Moore's trial at Surrey Lent Assizes in 1808.

On the page headed 'Surrey Lent Assizes 48th Geo 3rd 1808 at

Kingston upon Thames' it states the trials began on Thursday 24 March before Sir Archibald Macdonald Knight and John Heath Esquire, Justices, and the Grand Jury comprised 15 Baronets and 8 Esquires. On the relevant page it states:

> 'Mary Moore – House breaking daytime (no person therein) of Thomas Cunningham and stealing therein his goods value £1.13.6.'

Above this is written:

> 'Puts herself jury says not guilty of breaking and entering the 'Dw. Ho' [dwelling house] say guilty of stealing the goods, no good To be transported beyond the seas for the term of seven years to such place.'

The legal tradition of eschewing punctuation does not make this easy to follow, but I take it that 'Puts herself' means Mary represented herself, and the fact that the jury found her not guilty of breaking and entering but guilty of stealing the goods suggests that she had access to the empty 'Dw. Ho.' of Thomas Cunningham, which means she may have been working for him.

So there in its original primary-source form is evidence of the trials of both John and Mary, which coincidentally took place at the same time, Lent 1808. However for details of their crimes, the when and the where, I need to look at the original indictments. This is where it gets truly interesting.

In all my family history researches I have usually had something to go on by way of information provided by previous family genealogists. And though it may seem as if I am reinventing the wheel, by investigating these primary sources for myself I am not just checking their facts – which are invariably true, if not complete – but by being able to lay my very own hands on the original documents I am getting far more of a feel for the lives of my ancestors and the context in which they lived and, in this case, committed their crimes.

John's indictment, to take a case in point, is a bulky, unwieldy collection of randomly-sized parchment scrolls loosely held together with wool. When I untie it it springs open like an animal released from a cage, spewing parchment all over the table and causing me to take a step backwards.

It's an intimidating object, you could say. The parchment is stiff and partly creased and the scrolls relating to John are at least six feet long, so it is virtually impossible to unravel them completely and I haven't enough room – or hands – to hold them flat and prevent them from springing back into the tight roll they've been sitting in for over 200 years. Eventually I find some weights in the form of small sandbags and weighted bits of rope (it feels wonderfully medieval) and I'm finally able to tame the beast sufficiently to make out what's there.

At the top of scroll one it says:

> 'Staffordshire to wit The Jurors for our Sovereign Lord the King upon their oath present that John Johnson late of Leek in the County of Staffordshire labourer [the word 'labourer' was used to cover a number of trades] heretofore to wit on the twentyninth day of September in the fortyseventh year of the Reign of our Sovereign Lord George the third by the grace of God of the United Kingdom of Great Britain and Ireland King defender of the faith with force and arms of the parish of Leek in the county of Stafford feloniously knowingly and unwittingly and without lawful excuse had in his possession and Custody divers forged and counterfeited Bank notes that is to say one forged and counterfeited bank note the tenor of which said forged and counterfeited Bank note is as followeth that is to say'

This is followed by eight carefully drawn facsimiles of a banknote stating,

> 'Bank No 13632
>
> 5 April 1806
>
> I promise to pay to Mrs A^{bm} Newland or bearer on Demand the Sum of One Pound London the 5 day of April 1806
>
> For the Govr and Comp^r of the BANK OF ENGLAND
>
> G Gordon C Phillips'

and alternating with them, repeated virtually word for word four times:

> 'with intent to defraud the Governor of the Bank of England . . . And the Jurors aforesaid upon their oath foresaid further present that the said John Johnson . . . feloniously did dispose of and put away a certain forged and counterfeit Bank note'

Halfway through the written excerpts the Governor of the Bank of England is replaced by a 'John Radford'.

The next two (even longer) scrolls relate to John's colleague John Baddeley and the one after that shows three more facsimiles of John's banknotes. Another scroll headed 'Staffordshire Wednesday the thirtieth day of March 1808' lists the defendants, their pleas and sentences. There are two entries for John:

> 'John Johnson – feloniously forging a one pound bank of England note with intent to defraud the Governor and Comp^r of the Bank of England . . . Person confesses – To be hanged
>
> John Johnson – for feloniously having in his possession a bank of England note – Not guilty. (vide above)'

The death sentences for both Johns were immediately commuted, as the final declaration states that John Johnson and John Baddeley 'were sentenced to be transported to parts beyond the seas for the term of 14 years . . .'

~

And now for Mary. It's another not quite so bulky bundle tied with tape and labelled on the outside: 'ASSI 94/1616 Lent Assizes, 48th Geo 3^d 1808, Surrey, Felony File'.

Again this is made up of several lengthy parchment rolls, among which is one listing 42 prisoners and their crimes, including:

> 'Mary Moore – Committed on the 19th October 1807 by the Rt Honourable Lord Leslie charged on the oath of Elizabeth Cunningham with feloniously stealing at Gatton, one red cloth cloak, two muslin aprons and

divers other articles of wearing apparel the property of Jane Cunningham.'

Another list states Mary's and others' sentences, thus:

'committed of Felony let them be transported beyond the seas for the term of seven years each to such place as his Majesty with the advice of his privy council shall think fit'

On the same page above Mary are several other 'felons' convicted of crimes such as stealing a sheep price £4 or stealing goods value £2.12s, and against them the ominous words: 'let them be severally hanged by the neck until they are dead.'

Then on a separate scrap of parchment it states:

'The Jurors for our Lord the King upon their oath present that Mary Moore late of the parish of Gatton in the country of Surrey Singlewoman – on the twentieth day of August . . . about the hour of three in the afternoon of the same day with force and arms at the parish aforesaid in the County aforesaid at the Dwelling house of Thomas Cunningham – there situate – feloniously did break and enter (no person in the same dwelling house there being) and one cloak of the value of fifteen shillings two Handkerchiefs of the value of three shillings two aprons of the value of five shillings one pair of stockings of the value of sixpence one Frock of the value of five shillings and one petticoat of the value of five shillings of the Goods and Chattels of the said Thomas Cunningham . . . then and there feloniously did steal take and carry away against the Peace of our said Lord the king his Crown and Dignity.'

On the back of the same portion of parchment is written 'Thomas Cunningham, Jane Cunningham, Elizabeth Cunningham, 3 Sworn in Court. A True Bill.'

~

So there we have it.

John Johnson, a potter, possibly married with a possible child, was apprehended on the 29 September 1807 in Leek and found to be in possession of three forged banknotes. He admitted his crime and was sentenced first to hang and then to be transported for fourteen years.

Mary Moore was committed on the 19 October 1807 at Gatton in Surrey on the oath of Elizabeth Cunningham for entering the empty house of Thomas Cunningham and stealing items of clothing valued at £1.13s. 6d. She was sentenced to transportation for seven years.

We have the who, what, where and when, if not the why John and Mary committed their crimes.

In light of what happened to them subsequently, and to their eldest daughter Julia, what at the time must have felt like the lowest point in their lives would in due course turn out to be the first step on their path to transformation.

Chapter 9

1807: Crime and punishment

One of the joys, and potential hazards, of family history is the side-track.

In order to get to grips with the context in which John and Mary were tried and sentenced I've found myself probing the world of the early 19th century criminal justice system, and it's surprising what an eye-opener that has turned out to be: how different it was, how random, how – by modern standards – *unfair*, and so weighted against the defendant.

If you committed a crime in 1807 you were far more likely to get away with it than you would have been twenty years later, when there was an established police force; but in the unhappy event of being caught and tried your chances of being proved innocent, or escaping a heavy sentence, were pretty slim.

What policing existed was in the hands of the local parish constable, who was an untrained volunteer working in his spare time and not always diligently, so most crimes were reported by the victims of the crimes. As a victim of theft you had the option of letting the culprit go with a reprimand, or demanding the return of the stolen goods or, if the culprit was in your employ, dismissal. As a last resort you could take him or her to court, via the local magistrate, so long as you didn't mind the cost in money, time and inconvenience.

It cost from £1-£3 to take a case to the Assize Courts (more than the cost of the stolen goods in the case of Mary, and over £1,000 in today's money), and you not only had to provide your own witnesses you had to make sure that they, and you, turned up at the court on the relevant day, which involved travelling often some distance to the town in question and then hanging about waiting for the case to be heard. So it's not surprising that many victim-prosecutors chose the cheaper and easier options.

The accused meanwhile spent the intervening time between arrest and trial, which in the case of both John and Mary was over six months, banged up in the local gaol, sometimes in irons (for serious offenders, probably not for John and Mary) and often in filthy, overcrowded and downright dangerous conditions. Come the trial itself it was up to the defendant to prove his or her innocence of the charge; in other words she or he was considered guilty until proven otherwise – the exact reverse of the way our western law works now. Very few defendants could afford legal representation and there was no such thing as legal aid.

After the prosecution had presented its case the defendant was then allowed, with the aid of witnesses if they had any – which was unlikely as they'd have been hard put to arrange for anyone to attend while languishing in gaol – to give their side of the story. Courtrooms are intimidating places (I know, I've been there – as a jury member not a defendant I hasten to add), and since most of the accused were not of the privileged classes they would have had their work cut out to convince a jury of their innocence. What's more, again unlike today any previous convictions were made public before sentence was passed.

In the early 1800s private property was considered so sacrosanct that the theft of a few items of clothing was thought serious enough to be tried in the Assize Courts, and if the jury valued the stolen items at more than 40 shillings the sentence was technically death. That inevitably led to a practice called 'pious perjury' where a jury would deliberately undervalue stolen goods – in one case from the 23 guineas valued on the indictment to 39 shillings in court – so the defendant could escape the death penalty. And nobody appeared to bat an eyelid.

Nor were sentences consistent. In 1778 a young woman called Elizabeth Colley was sentenced to fourteen years' transportation with the First Fleet for receiving stolen goods worth thirteen shillings. Twenty years later my ancestress Mary Moore was transported for a mere seven years for stealing items worth £1.13s.6d.

What's more the judge could both overturn the jury's verdict and commute death sentences at will. In the early 19th century 80 percent of the people convicted of capital offences were reprieved or had their sentence commuted, as often as not to transportation. (Which makes you wonder why the law was what it was in the first place.) Bearing in mind all this it's not surprising that, according to the authors of *Bound for Botany Bay*: 'the surgeon Alick Osborne, who sailed on no fewer than nine convict voyages, said that most of the prisoners on his ship did not deserve the punishment inflicted on them'.

So looking at the case of Mary Moore the question that leaps out at me immediately is why did Thomas Cunningham take the poor woman to court rather than opting for easier solutions such as dismissal or the return of the cloak, the aprons and the stockings etc that presumably belonged to his daughter?

Of course that is making the assumption first that Mary was working for the Cunningham family, and that she was indeed a 'poor woman' with no previous convictions. If she was a repeat offender that would surely have shown up in the records. But what if they'd had a falling out? What if they had already dismissed her and this was her way of getting her own back? If the Assizes were for 'serious' cases only there must have been something more to Mary's crime than the face-value theft of a few items of clothing, mustn't there?

The British Library has a digital newspaper archive which I scour for mentions of a Mary Moore getting up to no good in

Surrey in 1807. I come up with a blank.

Then there's John and his forged banknotes.

In 1807 the £1 and £2 banknotes had only been in existence for ten years, and they were notoriously easy to forge. Penalties for being knowingly in possession of, passing on ('uttering') or creating forged banknotes were the same, and were harsh, as the volume of forged notes in circulation threatened to unbalance the economy.

John's apprehension, unlike Mary's, does get a mention in the local press:

> 'Committed to our county gaol, John Baddeley, charged with having uttered at Hanley, a forged and counterfeit two pound note of the Bank of England, knowing the same to be forged and counterfeit, and also with having twenty-nine forged notes of the Bank of England in his possession; and John Johnson, charged with having uttered at Leek, a forged and counterfeit one pound note of the Bank of England, knowing the same to be forged and counterfeit.'

John Baddeley and John Johnson appeared to be partners in crime in this respect, apprehended together on the same day in two different places. (Hanley is one of the 'Six Towns' known collectively as The Potteries in the Midlands, and Leek is around ten miles northeast of it.) They both received the same sentence of fourteen years' transportation despite the fact that Baddeley, in addition to his £2 note that he was attempting to utter, was in possession of no fewer than 29 other forged notes, which would be worth thousands of pounds now. Their sentences were reported in the *Stafford Advertiser* on 2 April the following year:

> 'The following prisoners were tried yesterday . . . John Johnson and John Baddeley, severally charged with uttering false notes, pleaded guilty to having them in their possession, and will be transported for 14 years.'

John Johnson was a potter, and he was literate – we know this as he signed his marriage certificate in Sydney some years later. If the Elizabeth Johnson who was subject to the removal order with her daughter Mary two years later was John's wife it suggests she had been left destitute. And yet records say that when passing sentence a judge would take into consideration such mitigating factors as age, circumstances and, bizarrely, whether or not the defendant was drunk at the time of the crime. So on the face of it it seems unnaturally harsh that someone like John should be transported from the country of his birth for fourteen years – with very little chance of returning – leaving behind a wife and a small child.

It's time to pay a visit to The Potteries to get a flavour of the environment my great great great grandfather lived in.

~

It starts badly. I spend several minutes wandering aimlessly around the car park at Stoke on Trent station before realising I've taken the wrong exit. I then ask for directions to the Potteries Museum and am sent in precisely the wrong direction. I spend the next hour walking in a circle before I eventually find a bus that will take me to Hanley. I realise, too late, that there is more than one pottery museum and that Stoke and Hanley are quite separate towns.

The Potteries Museum is impressive but not that useful. Next door in the library the helpful staff guide me to the local history section, where I discover that the Baddeley family goes back to the '10th Year of the Reign of King Ed^d the 4$^{th'}$ (by my calculations 1452), and that there was a John Baddeley of Sheldon – another of the 'Towns' – who was a well known pottery manufacturer. He died in 1772 however so he was not 'our' John Baddeley, though no doubt he was of the same family.

I read that the population of the Potteries doubled in the late 18th century, partly thanks to the newly built Trent and Mersey Canal, and that there was 'no scarcity of money [and] a good business was done . . .' I also discover that at the time John was apprehended in Leek the town was a dismal, dark and dirty place, with no streets lights and open sewers running down the side of the street; where crimes such as burglary and theft were rife and law and order was in the hands of a single constable in the daytime and 'three or four old watchmen, or "Charlies" as they were called, at night'. That's about the sum of it.

Elsewhere I read there was a high population of child labour in the potteries and it was not uncommon for a potter to begin his working life at the age of seven and to work a twelve-hour day five days a week. Testimony taken in 1840 tells of terrible working conditions. Potters generally were pale-faced, unhealthy-looking, and subject to colds and breathlessness from the exposure to extreme temperatures and dust. This goes some way perhaps to explaining why John Johnson did not live to old age. Otherwise, lacking comprehensive records of an industry that paid its workers in cash, at a time when there were no such things as income tax or pensions, it's impossible to find out who John was working for or in what capacity.

It's fair to assume he was, like most potters, working on the kilns from a tender age, having attended school up until then. Why he found himself on the wrong side of the law one September day in 1807 has to remain a mystery, for now at least.

~

John spent the next five and a half months in the local prison before being transferred to a prison hulk called *Captivity*, moored off Portsmouth; at which point there doubtless would have been times he wished his death sentence had not been commuted.

Prison hulks came into use in the 1770s originally as temporary holding places for prisoners where there was no room for them elsewhere. The vessels were usually ex 'men-o'-war' that had been stripped of their armaments and sat there, in the water, rotting along with their inhabitants. It was thought cheaper and more effective to confine wrongdoers in ships moored offshore, or on the Thames, than to build new prisons, which is why the hulks were still in existence until the middle of the 19th century.

On arrival the prisoner was stripped of his clothing and washed in a large tub of dirty water before being given a suit of 'coarse slop clothing' and clapped in irons, in which he remained for the duration of his stay. The fetters were placed on each leg with a chain linking them that tied around his waist or his throat. The ship he was assigned to might have been built for 200 but housed two or three times that number. If he was lucky he'd have a hammock to sleep in, otherwise it was the bare floor of the deck. At Portsmouth the hulks were moored close to a 'foul marsh', which stank. The portholes were either blocked off or barred to prevent escape, which meant ventilation was almost non-existent and after a long night's confinement there was often not enough oxygen to light a candle.

The prisoners, if they were lucky, were put to work on the ship itself or on docks on land, where they became objects of fascinated curiosity from the general public. On the Thames boats were chartered to bring sightseers alongside the hulks, and the occupants were allowed to climb onto the quarter-deck and gawp at the poor wretches below. There were often children among the convicts, living 'cheek by jowl' with hardened criminals and first-timers, though later on the convicts were divided up and separated into groups according to their behaviour and placed on one of the three decks: from the worst offenders in the bowels to the best on the top deck. When there wasn't enough work to go round there was another problem: idleness. And a man had to keep his eyes open at all times in case he might be robbed by someone he thought was his friend.

It was in such conditions that my three times great grandfather spent the year from September 1808 to August 1809. Why a forger like John had to endure this kind of extreme punishment is not clear, but after all that time he would have assumed he was condemned to serve out his sentence on board *Captivity*. So when he was eventually transferred to the convict ship *Anne* to be transported to New

South Wales he must have heaved a sigh of relief. His friend John Baddeley was not so lucky: he died on board *Captivity* a month earlier, on 8 July 1809.

John's conduct on leaving was logged as 'g', or 'good', which was the second highest accolade – one down from 'v.g'. One can only hope for his sake he spent most of his time on the upper deck.

By the time John Johnson was preparing to leave Portsmouth for Botany Bay Mary Moore had already been living in Sydney for six months.

PART THREE

Bound for Botany Bay

Chapter 10

1808: Mary and John

Mary Moore only had to wait three months to be transported. She left England on 2 July 1808 on board the convict ship *Aeolus*, in convoy with the *Admiral Gambier* and other vessels en route to Sydney via Rio de Janeiro.

Convict quarters in the bowels of these roughly-converted merchant ships was cramped, dark, smelly and crowded. It was not a place for privacy or peace, but during the seven month voyage (the *Aeolus* for some reason stayed put in Rio for two months) the one thing the 79 female convicts had was time. It's said they made their own entertainment, singing, carousing, playing cards, and avoiding (or encouraging and enjoying) the attentions of members of the crew. No doubt there was time spent in contemplation, and anticipation. Only one thing was certain: the prospect of any of those ladies ever seeing their native country or their loved ones again was virtually nil.

Many of the convict women on board *Aeolus* and other transports may have been given seven year sentences for minor offences, but while for the men there was the possibility of working their passage home once their sentence had expired, for the women transportation was effectively a sentence for life.

The only other certainty facing these women was the uncertainty of the future that awaited them. Convict assignment had always been a lottery: a man or a woman might be assigned more or less at random to a settler, or an emancipist, who might treat them well or, disregarding official guidelines, like chattel. She or he might find her/himself working for the government in some capacity, which might or might not be preferable. There would have been tales circulating the bowels of those female convict ships about how on arrival they would be lined up while male members of the local community were allowed to come on board to inspect them and take their pick among them and haul them off to become their servants or their mistresses, or both. And while it's hard to believe such pimping sessions could take place under the eye of the authorities there's plenty of evidence to show that such things did take place. Lord Castlereagh (Secretary of State for War and the Colonies) was appalled at the manner in which female convicts were 'given into the possession of such of the Inhabitants, Free Settlers, and Convicts, indiscriminately, as made a demand for them from the Governor'. Another commentator declared the lack of any official method of assignment or accommodation provided not only caused the women huge distress, it rendered 'the whole colony little better than an extensive brothel'.

The *Aeolus* docked on 26 January 1809, coincidentally twenty-one years to the day since the arrival of the First Fleet and one year exactly since the incumbent governor, William (*Mutiny on the Bounty*) Bligh, had been ousted from his position in a military coup organised by the New South Wales Corps, who at that time held the reins in the colony. Official documents show the current commander-in-chief, Colonel William Paterson, was too busy coping with the shortage of grain caused by flooding at the Hawkesbury and trying to get ex-Governor Bligh to actually quit the colony to pay any attention to the assignment of new convicts.

The only record of what might have happened to Mary and

her fellow passengers appeared in the *Sydney Gazette*, which announced the arrival of the *Aeolus* 'with 79 female convicts, all in good health; the principal part of whom have been sent to Parramatta'.

'Parramatta' could only mean one thing: the Factory above the Gaol.

Parramatta is twenty odd kilometres up the Parramatta River west of Sydney town. It was settled early on by Governor Phillip and it was home to the original – now Old – Government House, built by his successor Governor Hunter. It also housed what later became known as the Female Factory, constructed under the orders of Governor Macquarie to provide accommodation, employment and shelter for female convicts 'from corrupting influences'.

In 1809 however this building was not yet in existence. The original Factory above the Gaol, built in 1804 by Governor King, had fallen into disrepair partly due to a fire the previous year. Pictures of the time depict a forbidding-looking two-storey stone structure situated next to a bridge across the river. It comprised two rooms 80ft by 20ft – built for 60 but accommodating up to 200 – in which the women worked in the daytime producing cloth, and slept at night. Records imply the Factory went out of business for a couple of years until May 1809, when the *Sydney Gazette* announced that it was open and operating under new management. So the reference to Parramatta in the *Gazette* in January is a bit of a mystery.

For her sake I hope Mary did not end up in the Factory; it might have provided accommodation and shelter from the wicked outside world, but the world inside was just as wicked, if novels and accounts written of that time can be believed. The work was tough and relentlessly repetitive, and the women were incarcerated within the Factory walls just as they might have been back home. The only way out was for the best-behaved, later known as the First Classers, who if luck was on their side might be allowed the privilege of being lined up and picked out, again by members of the male community, as assigned servants or, more likely, wives or concubines.

Female convicts had a particularly rough time of it in the new colony. Successive governors complained they were more of a nuisance than the men, who at least served a useful purpose as labourers. The otherwise tolerant Governor Hunter said there was 'scarcely any way of employing' them and too many were taken up with looking after infants. His successor Governor King described them as 'the refuse of London' and worse than the men, and effectively endorsed the pimping sessions as a way of shifting the responsibility for their welfare onto the private sector, so to speak. Even Governor Macquarie, who arrived a year after Mary did, complained that the 'Female Convicts are . . . as great a drawback as the Males are useful', that they cost too much and were 'difficult of Appropriation'.

All of which prejudice, as one might dare to call it, placed these women in a worse situation than they would otherwise have been. So it's worth bearing in mind that most of them were first offenders, that three quarters of them had 'some level of literacy' and that between them they did have skills and were not necessarily incorrigible layabouts and prostitutes.

The fates of these women convicts varied hugely. Some, such as Margaret Catchpole – perhaps the most famous of the early female transportees, mostly because of the plethora of books, films, plays and debate her story inspired – made good lives for themselves. But her letters home were full of a desperation common to many convict women: how she missed the old country and her friends, how it was solely the prospect of hearing from them that got her through the days. It pays to be reminded that no matter how well these women did, how hard they worked and how much they succeeded in making new lives for themselves, the dreadful banishment from everything and everyone they had ever loved remained the ultimate punishment.

~

There are no records of Mary Moore on her arrival in Sydney, so once again we are in the land of speculation.

The first sight of that glorious harbour has taken away as many breaths as there have been new arrivals to behold it, and I'm sure Mary was no exception. Convicts, and sometimes passengers, were usually kept on board for the first few days after arrival, and whether or not this allowed for the women to be lined up and appraised by potential masters and husbands there would have been time for Mary to have breathed the sweet air and taken a long look at the strange little settlement sprawled in higgledy-piggledy fashion across the banks of the harbour. How tiny, and makeshift, it must have looked to a woman used to living among centuries-old buildings in England. I like to think that Mary's spirits were lifted by the sight of her new home. It looked manageable, almost toylike.

Sydney was then a mass of colour and noise. It was January 1809, the height of the antipodean summer. Trees and shrubs were in full bloom, windows and doors were adorned with cages of brightly-coloured parrots, the markets and street stalls were piled high with peaches, nectarines, melons and other exotica. The people were a strange and startling mix of formally frock-coated gentry and servant women in improvised garments and home-made straw hats, the scarlet livery of the military contrasting with the grey and canary-yellow of the surly government men. There were gigs and chaises, phaetons and chain gangs, the racket of street traders singing the praises of freshly-harvested seafood, the pervading smell of animal dung and brick dust.

It was a crazy world. It had none of the order and certainty of the old country. It was terrifying and thrilling and unlike anywhere else in the world.

~

Half a year later, on 16 August 1809, John Johnson was at last transferred to the vessel *Anne* for the voyage to New South Wales along with 199 other prisoners, a handful of free settlers – including the Reverend Samuel Marsden, who officiated at the marriage of two of my ancestors and was on his way back to the colony after a two-year break – and a detachment of the new Governor Lachlan Macquarie's 73rd regiment, some with their families.

The ship, captained by Charles Clarke and carrying a cargo that included Irish butter, cheeses, hams, coffee, sugar, molasses, rice, soap, tobacco, shoes, tools, glasses, Madeira wine, barrelled port, rum and various assortments of brandy, sailed on 25 August and arrived at Port Jackson via Rio de Janeiro on 27 February the following year.

The *Sydney Gazette* reported the convicts were healthy and expressed 'the highest satisfaction at their treatment on the passage'. Three days later Captain Clarke received orders to disembark the prisoners and they were taken by boat to the Hospital Wharf and placed in the hands of the Principal Superintendent Mr Nichols.

What a difference a year makes. Governor Macquarie had only arrived in the colony two months earlier but already he'd expressed his determination to restore 'Harmony and Union' to a colony beset by the recent outrageous disturbance caused by the mutinous New South Wales Corps – for which purpose he had brought his own military regiment (the 73rd) with him. Moreover as mentioned already the new governor's attitude to the male of the convict species was a good deal more positive than to the female.

'Men are very much wanted in the Colony,' he wrote to Lord Castlereagh. 'I have distributed the greater Number of the last arrived Convicts [from *Anne*] among the Settlers here, and I sent Sixty of them to the Derwent for the use of the Settlers there, reserving only a few of them who are Mechanics for being employed in carrying on the Government Public Works at Sydney.'

So which group did John fit into?

The Derwent is in Van Diemen's Land (now Tasmania), so it's unlikely he went there. 'Mechanics' were defined not as men who worked with machinery but 'bakers, boat-builders, brewers, combmakers, farriers, hatters, plumbers and glaziers, printers, shipwrights and weavers' among other trades including, presumably, potters.

The Government Pottery was first established back in 1791 in what was then known as the Brick Fields area of Sydney – what is now south George Street. Its fortunes fluctuated depending on how many skilled potters there were in the colony at any given time. At the beginning of the century there were several potteries operating in the 'Brick Field' village, so John may have begun his convict life either working in the Government Pottery or for one of these independent potters, and the lack of skilled labour was probably one reason why barely four months after his arrival he was granted his ticket of leave, with the instruction: 'Potter to remain within the city of Sydney.'

Tickets of leave entitled hard-working and trustworthy convicts to sell their labour to whoever they wanted, though as the document states they were confined to a particular area and had to report regularly to the local authority. It also meant they were no longer on government stores and had to fend for themselves. The following year Macquarie tightened up on the guidelines and stipulated minimum sentences that had to be served before they could be issued, but John was lucky: he was given his first taste of freedom just over two years into his fourteen-year sentence. It's possible his year spent on the hulk had something to do with it; it's also possible that in those early less-than-organised convict assignment days the powers that be were anxious to get as many convicts off the stores as soon as possible in order to save money.

So a year went by with no record of either John Johnson, potter, or Mary Moore, trade unknown, both living in Sydney. The only thing we can be sure of is that both of them kept out of trouble – or there would surely be some record of their misdemeanours.

Time again to dip into my imagination.

PART FOUR

Sydney

Chapter 11

The little brown jug

A person with enterprise, some capital, a willingness to work their socks off and put up with a primitive life style might well have thought of New South Wales as a genuine land of opportunity, even as far back as 1809. To begin with the government, even the rebel version, was eager to do all it could to aid free settlers to make their fortunes; and there was all that free labour.

The quality of that labour was variable of course, not to say unpredictable. When, in my (entirely invented) version of the story, a Mrs Landstaff first set eyes on her convict assignee her first words were 'I have an inventory'.

Mary Moore may or may not have understood the meaning of that word, let alone its connotations. At this stage in her convict career she was still reeling with relief at not having been sent to the Female Factory, so the prospect of working for even such a wooden-faced individual as Edna Landstaff was bearable, even something to look forward to.

'And I've made out an indenture,' the good lady continued. She thrust a piece of paper at the younger woman. 'Read through it please and tell me if it is acceptable.'

Mary stared blankly at the document before handing it back with, 'I can't read madam'.

Mrs Landstaff gave a heavy sigh and proceeded to recite aloud from the document, rapidly, occasionally stumbling over a word, which led Mary to believe the lady did not wholly understand everything that was in it; which in itself suggested it had been drawn up on her behalf by someone with legal knowledge, all of which – to the sharp-witted Mary – told her a good deal about her future employer.

'This indenture witnesseth that I, Mary Moore, do put herself Servant to Mrs Edna Landstaff from this date until the Full Term of her Sentence is Expired, unless it is the Wish of Mrs Edna Landstaff to Terminate her Services Prior to this Date. The said Servant shall serve her Mistress; her Secrets keep; her Lawful Commands every where gladly do; the Goods of her said Mistress she shall not waste nor damage nor take or lend unlawfully to any; Taverns, Inns, or Alehouses she shall not haunt; at Cards, Dice, Tables, or any other unlawful Games she shall not play; Matrimony she shall not contract; nor from the Service of her said Mistress Day or Night absent herself; but in all Things, as a faithful and Assigned Government Servant, she shall behave herself towards her said Mistress and all her Family. In return for which the said Mary Moore, Government Servant, shall be Provided with sufficient Clothing, Meat, Drink and Lodging during the said Term.

'AND for the true Performance of all and every the said Covenants and Agreements, each of the said Parties bindeth herself the one to the other, firmly by these Presents. IN WITNESS whereof the Parties above-said to these Indentures have interchangeably set their Hands and Seals at Sydney in this His Majesty's Territory of New South Wales the 14th day of May in the forty-ninth Year of the Reign of Our Sovereign Lord King George the Third of the United Kingdom and Great Britain, King, Defender of the Faith, and so-forth, and in the Year of Our Lord One thousand eight hundred and nine.'

Once again she held out the document to Mary, along with a pen.

'Do whatever it is you can, make a mark or something.' And

when Mary appeared to be hesitating: 'Is there something wrong?'

'No madam, nothing at all.'

Mary took the document and against what she recognised as her name at the bottom she wrote a cross. Her hesitation had to do with nothing other than a terrible urge to collapse into giggles at the ridiculously exaggerated formality of a document that, her instinct told her, had more to do with her prospective employer's naivety than anything that was decreed by officialdom. She was also puzzled at the lack of the word 'convict' anywhere on the document. 'Government servant' sounded almost respectable.

She handed back the document and the pen with a smile, which was returned, albeit tentatively, by her employer; though in the circumstances perhaps 'slave-owner' was nearer the mark.

'And now I will show you to your room.'

Because that is what I am, thought Mary, as she followed her mistress up the creaking wooden staircase to the loft at the top of the little stone house: a slave. Still it could be worse. I have a roof over my head, and a room that – Lord help me – back home we might call a cupboard. There was barely space for the skimpy mattress that Mary assumed was to be her bed, and a small cupboard for her 'things', such as they were.

Mrs Landstaff cast Mary a slightly nervous look, which confirmed the girl's suspicions that she might be the first 'government servant' her mistress had ever taken on.

'And when you have made yourself at home please attend me downstairs and I will explain your duties.' She hesitated in the doorway for a second, then vanished back down the stairs.

~

Mary's instincts were correct. She was the first convict to be assigned to Mrs Edna Landstaff, shopkeeper of George Street, wife of Harold Landstaff, mother of little Harold and infant Ida. The (fictional) Landstaffs were free settlers, encouraged to emigrate by an acquaintance who'd travelled to the colony some years before and set up what was turning out to be an extreely successful business. The Landstaffs had been in the colony for less than a year and it was Harold's idea that with such an abundance of free female labour his young wife should open up a shop and get a convict to run it for her, and the household and the children while she was at it. Edna, who at 22 was only three years older than her assigned servant, had never run a shop before, let alone employed a young girl serving a seven year sentence for theft. She was both daunted and excited at the thought of managing a business in such a makeshift environment as the infant Sydney, but the prospect of having a convict in the house acting as her servant, nursemaid, housekeeper and pretty well anything else terrified her. Hence the indenture, which was the idea, needless to say, of her husband; and which even she thought slightly over-the-top in these unfamiliar circumstances.

Thus a relationship based on the blind leading the blind – which, had Mary been the sort of person to exploit, might have led her in a quite different direction – developed more quickly than it otherwise might have done into a form of partnership. Since Mary could not read it was Edna who perused the pages of the *Sydney Gazette* for sales of linen, needles, buttons, lace, tallow or anything else that took her fancy, while Mary ventured to the markets and came back with peacock feathers, glass beads and a number of other exotic and unusual trifles. She found she had an eye for what might sell in 1809 Sydney. And it did not take Mary long to realise the real reason behind Harold Landstaff's keenness to encourage his wife's commercial endeavours, which was that he himself wasn't finding it as easy to make his own fortune as he'd hoped.

Come 1810 and there was an air of renewal in the township of Sydney. After the fractiousness of the Bligh years and the chaos of the interregnum there was now a new governor who no longer talked about the colony in terms of survival but seemed to view it as a place of bounty and expectation. He had already laid plans for a proper layout of streets, named after –

who else – dignitaries from the old country and previous governors of the new, including, of course, himself. He had disbanded the New South Wales Corps, for so long regarded (though not by everyone) as the scourge of the colony. He had set up an ambitious building programme including a new hospital, built by emancipists in return for being allowed a monopoly on the import of spirits – which meant Governor Macquarie was a pragmatist as well as a visionary.

~

It was perhaps in pursuit of something like soap – because Mrs Landstaff and her servant had by now expanded her shop to include such useful things in addition to the knick-knacks and general household goods – that John Johnson found himself face to face with a young woman across the counter of the little shop in George Street, bartering.

Mary was used to bartering. It was how people conducted business back in the early days before there was a proper currency established; in many ways it was a safer form of transaction than promissory notes, or the odd piece of foreign coin that nobody quite knew the value of.

John drew from his pocket a piece of cloth, which he unwrapped to reveal a small clay jug. Placing it with exaggerated care down on the counter he looked up at the sombre-faced dark-haired girl behind it and grinned.

'What's that?' Mary asked after a moment, with what sounded like scorn.

John removed his cap and scratched his head. He was searching for a smart retort to an obvious question in order to throw the girl's scorn right back at her. But as tends to happen in such instances nothing came to mind, so he said, 'It's a jug'.

'I can see that,' she said.

'I made it,' said John.

'I thought you might've,' she said.

'So, what's it worth? Two ounces of soap? Three?'

Mary picked up the jug and wrinkled her nose. She turned it this way and that and shrugged. It was all part of the game.

'We don't do bartering here,' she said, placing the object back down on the counter.

'What d'you mean you don't do bartering? How d'you sell anything if you don't do bartering?'

Mary shrugged again. It was an odd gesture, done with one shoulder as if she couldn't be bothered to use two. 'It en't my shop,' she said. 'Besides,' she picked up the object again and peered at it. 'It en't got no shine on it.'

'That's because it en't got no glaze on it. It's as naked as the day it was born.' He snorted. 'There en't nothing to glaze it with unless you use salt.'

'If it en't glazed,' said she, placing the object back down again, 'how d'ye stop it leaking?'

John stared at her for a moment. 'It don't leak,' he said.

The young woman seemed to think for a long time. She hadn't smiled once since he'd entered the shop. She'd barely shown any animation at all, come to that. John shifted from one foot to the other.

'How much do you want for it?' she asked him eventually, in a bored fashion. She looked straight at him for the first time. Her eyes were a very dark brown, like her hair.

'I'll settle for four ounces of soap,' he grinned. He was beginning to feel outfaced and uncomfortable. 'Eight and a half pence should do it.'

'Six,' she said, automatically.

John's eyebrows shot up. 'You're a smart one, en't you? Seven.'

'Six,' she persisted. 'We mark them up double. We'd have to sell it for fourteen.'

'Then six it is.' He hesitated, wondering if he ought to seal the deal with a handshake and deciding not. He started to make for the door. 'And there's more where this came from.'

'Course there is,' said the young woman.

As he reached the door John turned to say, 'I'll be back in a couple of days.' But she had already turned her back on him.

Chapter 12

The smile

Mary's brain was buzzing. It was coming up to two years since she'd begun working in the shop and by this time she was running it almost single-handedly while her employer busied herself producing babies. The more babies the less attention she paid to her business, which suited Mary just fine. She'd learned how to label the goods and invented her own form of keeping accounts, which the Landstaffs seemed to trust even if they didn't totally understand them. Through it all she was careful not to put a foot wrong and not to assume; if she had a suggestion she thought it through carefully before voicing it out loud, and the strategy paid off. By now she no longer had to ask permission to change the stock or the display, or adjust the prices. She was allowed far more freedom than most people in her situation and she was aware of it. She took her work, and herself, seriously, as anyone could see.

The appearance of the strange-looking ginger-haired man with the little brown jug had got her thinking of new ways she could enliven her shop's front, with pretty and unusual objects bearing the proud stamp: 'MADE IN NEW SOUTH WALES'.

John could not produce the stuff fast enough. For various reasons – no, truth to tell for one reason only – he pretended it took him longer than it did to produce the cups and saucers and bowls and plates, which he bore to the little shop on George Street item by item, sometimes more than once a day.

It took countless visits before he managed to get the girl behind the counter – whose name he had by now established as Mary – to crack a smile. It was not accidental.

'I got something a bit special here,' he said. He'd brought a canvas bag with him this time and, as was his manner, he made great play of digging into it and bringing out yet another linen-wrapped item and placing it down on the counter before her.

'Guess what,' he said.

Mary screwed up her face. 'Teapot.'

John shook his head. She reached over and felt the object all round, prodding it gently here and there. She frowned. 'Feels like a face.'

''Tis a face.'

'It is?'

He removed the covering. Mary stared, and then let out a hoot of laughter.

'What's that, it's . . .'

'Yep.'

'It's . . .' she pointed at herself. 'Is it?'

''Tis,' said John. 'Good likeness, don't you think?'

Mary picked up the tiny bust and held it in the flat of her hand. She was staring and shaking her head and when she spoke it was with something approaching wonder. 'It's perfect.'

She was too busy still gazing at her clay-formed likeness to notice John blushing to the roots of his ginger hair. When she did look back at him she was smiling from ear to ear. It was a lovely smile, it transformed her.

'You're a clever one,' said Mary. 'How much are you wanting for it?'

'It's not for sale, it's for you.'

'Oh.' For a moment she seemed nonplussed. 'Well how much are you wanting for it, from me?'

'You paid for it already.'

'How come?'

'With your smile,' he said.

That wiped it from her face immediately. She looked at him steadily.

'Are you coming on to me?'

'Course I am.'

She seemed to think for a moment. She did a lot of that. She looked away from him and down at the floor and John couldn't be sure, though he was really, but it seemed she was trying not to let him see she was trying not to smile. So he took his chance.

'I been coming on to you ever since I entered your shop six months ago and four days. And it's taken me this long to get a smile out of you. Carry on like this and we'll be in our old age before I even get to hold your hand.'

She was leaning on the counter with her arms spread and her head so far down he couldn't see her face, but he could see she was shaking – with anger perhaps, or . . .

She looked up at him then. She was laughing.

'You've got a cheek, en't you?'

'You call this cheek? After six months and four days and I'm coming in here once a day and sometimes more just to try to get a squeak of a smile out of you? I call that the patience of a saint.'

'Well then, what can I say?'

'You don't need to say anything. 'Tis enough.' With which he took another chance, knowing this time there was no turning back, and reaching across the counter and with his finger he softly traced the smile on her face, as if to see if it was real. Which it was. And when the smile remained, steady, he knew he was home and dry.

~

On 27 February 1811 John Johnson, widower, married Mary Moore, spinster of the same parish, at St Phillip's Church in Sydney. The minister was the Reverend William Cowper and the witnesses were Catherine Briscoe and John Hopkins. (There was a convict called Catherine Briscoe who arrived in the colony in 1797 who may or may not have been Mary's witness. John Hopkins, a lifer, arrived in the colony on the same ship as John.) Mary was the only one of the four who signed with a mark.

Who can begin to imagine the feelings flooding through John and Mary's hearts on that day? How could they have dreamed their now long-ago petty misdemeanours – the product of possible pique in Mary's case and opportunism in John's – could have led them to this: to marriage and freedom and a new life, with prospects, in this new country? How could John throughout his hellish year on the hulk, from which he must have thought he would never escape, have pictured the sheer joy and the possibilities that lay ahead of him in the alien country he'd been forcibly removed to?

Three days after the wedding Mary was given her ticket of leave, as was customary for a married partner. She was free now to work for whoever she wanted, or for herself, or not at all. In my speculative version of events she bade a sad farewell to the Landstaffs – now she was free the 'indenture', that pompous and by now long-forgotten bit of legal nonsense, was rendered redundant – and concentrated on the business of making babies.

On 29 October 1811, eight months after marrying, Mary produced her first child, John. Eighteen months later little Charlotte arrived but survived barely one year. Julia, their first child to grow to adulthood, came along on 14 January 1815 and two years later Mary Ann. Little John died in 1819, aged just eight, and was replaced by another John, born in 1820. Sarah born in 1822 completed the family.

Meanwhile in the 1814 muster John was listed as C (convict), off stores, TL (ticket of leave), employment potter, and Mary as simply 'wife to J Johnson'. Two years later John was given his Conditional Pardon, which removed all the restrictions upon him except the freedom to leave the colony.

He was also given a grant of 40 acres at Airds, south of Sydney near present-day Campbelltown, though what he did with it is not on record.

In 1822 John received his Absolute Pardon and appears on the muster as 'FBS' (Free By Servitude), employment 'Licensed Victualler'. It seems he had decided that becoming a publican was more lucrative than making pots.

As for what else Mary and John and their family got up to I'm relying on official records. And here I'm up against a problem.

There are dozens of entries for a John Johnson, or Johnston, in the colonial secretary's papers of that time, but whether or not they refer to my ancestor it is virtually impossible to establish. For example in 1822-1823 alone there are six convicts assigned to a John Johnson 'Of York Street, later George Street, later Pitt Street'. Of those, two – Thomas Rowland, Pipe Maker, and William Tibbitts (otherwise known as Tibbitt or Tibbles) also appear on the 1828 census working for Mary. Then there are no fewer than nineteen 'convict mechanics' assigned to a John Johnson, including another Pipe Maker called James Milwood.

Convict mechanics, as I already explained, were skilled craftspeople. But nineteen mechanics would only be assigned to someone running a substantial business, or one with an extremely rapid turnover of staff. And why John should be assigned Pipe Makers – makers of clay pipes – is a mystery; unless he was continuing to make and sell pottery in addition to running a pub, if such a thing was possible.

There are other references to a John Johnson 'publican and builder' regarding requests for allotments of land and money paid and sometimes unpaid 'on accounts of rents' for assigned convict tradesmen. In one memorial it states he had purchased an allotment at 52 George Street in 1822 on which he built a two-storey stone house. A further memorial sent from Upper Pitt Street asks for 'indulgencies' to help with building expenses.

At this point the family historian has to draw a halt and admit defeat, or at least acknowledge that she will never quite get to the bottom of which John Johnson was which. The only thing she can be sure of is that Mr and Mrs Johnson did acquire land and that at the time of John's death, on 10 June 1825, from causes unknown, they were living in George Street.

~

So yet another young woman was widowed and left to bring up several young children alone. John had lived till he was 55, which for someone who had probably spent their childhood and youth working twelve-hour days inhaling toxic substances is not bad going. Mary was 37 when she became a widow with children aged ten, eight, seven and three. She appeared to have had three convicts working for her.

They were resourceful, those early pioneering women. Who would someone like Mary have to turn to at a time like this? At least she had a trade.

She had spirit, too, and maybe there was someone around to advise her, because on 21 November, five months after John died, she petitioned for a grant of land; and on the strength it seems of the four convict workers listed as having been in her late husband's employ she was granted 160 acres next to Reedy Creek in the parish of Millah Murrah, County Roxburgh – just north of Bathurst – to add to the 40 already granted to John back in 1816.

Three years later Mary crops up on the 1828 census, which for the first time included all the inhabitants of New South Wales – free, convict, emancipist and all shades in between – and listed women by their married names. It takes some interpreting, but from it I glean that Mary 'Johnston' [sic], aged 40, was living in George Street with her four children, her employment Shopkeeper; and that she had two or maybe four convicts working for her, including Thomas Rowland.

So in a remarkably short time Mary had gone from convicted felon to landowner, shopkeeper and employer. She was what you might call an interesting marriage prospect.

Chapter 13

1829: Robert Aull

Julia Johnson, Mary's eldest, had just turned fourteen years old when Robert Aull came into her life.

Fourteen is a tricky age to find your life turned upside down. It was three and a half years since the death of her father and the family had just about settled into what seemed to Julia to be a happy existence. She was of an age where she was beginning to take on more responsibilities in the shop and leave her sister Mary Ann, not quite twelve, to look after the two youngest children. Her mother seemed content, the shop was doing well, she couldn't see any need for the upheaval they were about to face.

She was a little afraid of Robert. He was Irish, and tall, and her mother said he'd kissed the Blarney stone, whatever that was, which gave him the gift of the gab. That was partly the trouble, the gab. She didn't trust him, and the more he gabbed the less she believed what he said.

For example not long after he came onto the scene he sat the whole family down to tell them the story of his adventures on the convict ship that brought him to New South Wales. *Francis & Eliza* had sailed from Cork in southern Ireland with both male and female convicts on board (already Julia found that hard to believe). One day, off the coast of Madeira and a month into the voyage the convicts were huddled in their dungeon in the bowels of the ship when they heard the crack of a cannon and their first thought was – War! This was followed immediately by a God-Almighty judder as the ship slammed against something solid, obviously an enemy ship, which they assumed to be French. They heard shouting, and another cannon shot, and then the thud of running feet on the upper deck, and the timid among them must have felt some fear, said Robert, as there they were locked into the hold of the ship with little chance of escape if the vessel happened to catch fire. Eventually the bolt on the hatch door scraped open and an unfamiliar face appeared in the opening and said something like 'Say, what have we here?', which didn't sound very French. The face having then vanished leaving the hatch door open the convicts made a run for it; or as much of a run as anyone can do with leg-irons.

They discovered chaos and mayhem on the upper deck. The ship was being stripped of its rigging and the captain and the surgeon were held captive with ropes. The vessel that had rammed them was an American privateer – he could tell by the flag – and as they watched so their captain and the surgeon were forcibly removed onto the pirate ship, which was appropriately called *Warrior*. Meanwhile the Americans were ransacking everything they could find and removing boxes and cartons of maps and provisions and medicines, while the soldiers on board *Francis & Eliza* – who were there precisely to stop such a thing happening – looked on and did nothing.

After several hours Captain Harrison and Surgeon West were returned to the ship looking the worse for wear and the Captain without his uniform. Then just before the privateers departed they cut off the convicts' fetters and threw them into the sea and went on their way. And here is where in Julia's mind it became too fantastical for words.

'So what do you think happened next?' said Robert, smiling at each of them in turn.

'You escaped?' ventured Mary Ann.

Robert laughed. 'If we'd have escaped,' he tapped the tip of the young girl's nose with his finger and she flinched, 'we'd not be here, would we? We did not escape. We took over the boat and we formed watches, in turn, and sailed her on with what rigging they'd left us.'

'Why didn't you escape?' Julia frowned. It was all very well, these tall stories, she could see right through them. But she didn't like to see her younger siblings hoodwinked.

It wasn't the convicts that absconded, it was the crew, Robert went on. A bunch of them had deserted and left to join the pirates. Then the first mate and his cronies broke into the grog and drank themselves into a stupor and proceeded to set the ship on fire, not once but several times. Captain Harrison could do nothing. The rest of the crew, the ones who were still there and still sober, stood helpless. So seeing as how they were all going to end up drowned or burnt or both, not to mention what might become of the poor helpless females on board, the male convicts set about organising themselves into a watch; they took it in turns to restore some kind of order and get the ship to the nearest piece of land, which turned out to be Santa Cruz in Tenerife. Here the troublemakers among the crew were taken off the vessel and dealt with, and new rigging and supplies were produced and a new uniform for Captain Harrison, and the ship sailed safely on.

'That's not quite all.' Robert raised a finger to forestall interruption. 'In Sierra Leone there was a fever the like of which you cannot imagine. It killed the entire crew of the *Wilding* and it did for most of us as well. Not me, mind. It takes more than a tropical fever to set me low. A good half of us was sick with it when we arrived here. The captain and the surgeon told the governor about us and the governor said we'd all get our pardons, right away.' He paused, and shook his head.

'And did you?' Mary Ann picked up her cue.

'Not right away, but we got them in the end.'

'What did you do?' This was nine-year-old John.

'Do?' Robert turned his dark eyes on the little boy. 'What do you mean by 'Do'?'

'He means,' Julia explained, as if to a child, 'what did you do to get yourself transported.'

She knew it was not a question you asked of convicts. She'd learned that from her parents, but the message had not filtered down to the younger ones, and besides, she wanted to know the answer herself.

'If you really want to know,' said Robert, with a hint of steel, 'I was sentenced to death for uttering forged stamps. Commuted to transportation, for life.'

Four pairs of eyes stared at him. It seemed to Julia to be pretty far-fetched, to be given the death sentence for talking about forged stamps. She realised there must be more to it but she was darned if she was going to give him the satisfaction of asking him.

'There's another nice anecdote to do with *Francis & Eliza*, do you want to hear it?' said Robert.

'Yes please,' piped the little ones.

'Well now.' Robert leaned forwards and made a play of looking over his shoulder to see who might be listening. He dropped his voice to a whisper. 'There was a lady on board *Francis & Eliza* who'd had connections, so the story goes, with the aristocracy. She told the pirate captain she'd been falsely convicted of swindling and the fool was so smitten he gave her sanctuary and several thousand dollars and other trifles. It wasn't till he got back to port he realised it all was a hoax, but by then the lady in question had eloped with a sailor and was suing the captain for payment of a promissory note of $5,000. So he got his come-uppance and more.' He leaned back. 'I tell you it's a true story. Or so they say.'

The four faces continued to stare at him with differing degrees of comprehension. For Julia that was the final straw. He was not just a liar, or a fantasiser, he was a scandal-monger.

There was a matter of more personal significance that chanced to Robert on board *Francis & Eliza*, which he may or may not have divulged to the children on that occasion.

Among the female convicts there was a 28-year-old Dublin woman called Jane Thompson, a 'straw bonnet maker', transported for seven years for a crime unspecified. Despite the fact that on arrival in Sydney on 8 August 1815 they were sent in different directions – she to the Female Factory in Parramatta and he to Liverpool (or possibly Windsor) – their first child was born the following year, in 1816. The year after that he sought to marry her, first at Parramatta (where presumably Jane was still living) and then at Castlereagh, where they finally tied the knot on 18 March 1817.

How Robert first found himself in the Richmond area I haven't yet managed to establish, though it is possible he was sent there rather than Liverpool on his arrival. His occupation both back in Ireland and in the colony was listed as 'labourer', which could mean anything. It is interesting to note that he was a Protestant and Jane a Catholic (though since her first child was born out of wedlock it can be assumed she was lapsed), and that their five children were all listed on the censuses as P for Protestant.

In the ensuing years between his arrival in the colony and the day he cropped up on the doorstep of the Johnson household in early 1829, Aull – otherwise referred to in official documents as Aule, Awl and even Hall – managed to acquire a fair amount of land, most of it in the Evan district near Windsor. He was also appointed constable and pound keeper for Evan for two years and on the 1822 & 1825 censuses he is listed as a 'landholder', with a Conditional Pardon. He aided with the capture of a convict who'd escaped from a road gang, and apprehended, with a colleague, the three armed bushrangers previously mentioned – for which he petitioned for a reward. In 1828 he was charged with misusing a convict servant and breaking an agreement with him (he'd allowed the convict to farm some of his land independently in an attempt, he claimed, to get him to work harder) as a result of which the convict was removed. That same year according to the census Robert was in possession of 300 acres in the Evan district, with

40 cattle and eight horses, and he had two male convicts working for him and a female free settler.

All of this suggests to me a man of ambition with a nose for opportunity and a dash of derring-do. I am making the assumption therefore that Robert Aull was not displeased to find himself taken from the courts of Londonderry with a death sentence to a new world where he was able to get his hands on considerable stretches of land; plus, at some point along the way, an Absolute Pardon.

But then on 21 December 1828, Robert's wife Jane died, aged 42, probably in childbirth. She left him with five children, the eldest of whom was twelve, two years younger than Julia.

Four months later, on 5 May 1829, he married Mary Johnson at St James's Church in Sydney. They were both 38 years old.

Mary's family had increased from five to eleven. It was time for them to relocate.

Chapter 14

1829: Upper Richmond

In the days before women's magazines and popular songs an adolescent like Julia may have been aware there were multifarious reasons for a man and a woman to marry, other than for romantic love.

There was finance, which included property, which – as Julia was less likely to know – on marriage a woman automatically handed over to her spouse lock, stock and barrel; there was status, convenience, business acumen, a parent for their children or simple companionship.

Of all of these it was Mary's business acumen that might have proved most useful to Robert, in addition maybe to companionship and as a mother for his five children; of whom the youngest, also Mary, was three years old. There was also Mary senior's 200 acres of course, though I have yet to discover what happened to them. The year after they married Robert took out a publican's licence for a new inn at what *The Australian* called 'Yarrow Monday's Lagoon' near Richmond, where 'Mrs. Aull, formerly Mrs. Johnstone, of York-street, Sydney, is well acquainted with business, and no doubt will ensure custom.'

The pub was named the Governor Darling, after the departed governor, and it lay on the banks of the Yarramundi

Lagoon. The 'lagoon', so-called, was a freshwater lake that ran parallel with the Nepean River (and was the site of the first sighting by a European, Governor Hunter, of a platypus). It is a beautiful spot now and I've no doubt it was even more beautiful then.

It would have been a huge upheaval for Mary and her children however, to have been uprooted from the bustle and excitement of Sydney, where the air was thick with brick dust and the foul stench from the nearby tannery (owned incidentally by James Wilshire, who unbeknownst to Julia was to later become her uncle), to the relative peace and health-giving surroundings of Upper Richmond.

By this time I like to think that Julia, having discovered that what her stepfather had told her about his adventures on the high seas was true, and that uttering forged stamps meant passing them around rather than talking about them, was more or less reconciled to her stepfather, and to her new siblings. And that waking in the morning to the warble of magpies and the curious cackle of the kookaburra was preferable to the cacophony of heavy industry and the racket of city street life.

As for her mother, I imagine with her business acumen and experience as a shopkeeper Mary would have rather enjoyed being the *maitresse d'* of a public house. She and Robert did not have any children together, even though Mary was only 38 when she married – which in a country where women were often still producing children in their forties was not regarded as beyond childbearing age. Perhaps they considered they'd produced enough between them.

Come 1832 Robert was still expanding his farming properties around Upper Richmond, Kurrajong and Bilpin, much of it rented. On acquiring the lease of 280 acres east of the Yarramundi Lagoon he placed a fierce notice in the *Australian* warning that any CATTLE or PIGS found TRESPASSING on his land bordering 'Yellow Monday's lagoon' would be IMPOUNDED by his good self, and that any persons trespassing would be prosecuted according to law.

This is ironic bearing in mind that many years later he would be made bankrupt and owing rent to the owner of that same piece of land, the wonderfully-named Sir Digory Forrest, of Exmouth, England.

Two years after that, in 1834, Robert bought another pub called The Pilgrim Inn, this time at what used to be known as Emu Plains on the Bathurst Road, which he leased out. And so up until the 1840s, when the colony suffered its first serious depression, he continued to acquire more and more land, including, in 1838, the lease of over 1,000 acres of Crown Land in the Kurrajong/Bilpin area (next door to Trafalgar, home to GM's brother Robert and his family).

He was also occasionally in trouble with the law. In 1833 he was accused of assaulting a police constable by riding over him (found not guilty), and in 1838 a neighbour William Farlow took him to court for 'illegally impounding Swine' belonging to him (case dismissed for want of evidence). In 1839 he was brought before the Petty Sessions to answer a complaint of ill-use from his housekeeper, a Jane Vassall-Brown, and was ordered by the presiding magistrate William Cox, JP (who coincidentally had endorsed Robert's application for a publican's licence back in 1830) to pay all wages owing to her, and she was removed from her position.

In 1842, at the height of the depression, Robert was declared bankrupt, owing £57.1s.3d, partly to the said Sir Digory Forrest. This despite the fact that he had in the previous two years been getting rid of his property as rapidly as he'd acquired it, including selling a good deal of it to his daughter and son-in-law. Four years later he received his certificate of discharge.

But what of his wife Mary throughout all these years? As a married woman who since 1825 had acquired no land in her own right, nor broken the law nor applied for a publican's license nor petitioned the governor for anything, she seems to have disappeared, typically, from official records.

My guess is that with all that accumulation of land Robert

was focusing his attention on his farming activities and leaving the running of the Governor Darling to his wife and daughters. But there are a couple of niggles forming in my mind, one of which emerged in the 1841 census.

The census – the first since 1828 – required 'every householder, employer of servants and proprietor and occupier of land to complete the census schedule on the second day of March 1841'. Only the householder was named but all occupants living at the property were listed under their age group, gender, marital status, 'civil condition' (born in the colony, came free etc), religion, occupation and whether their house was brick or stone, finished and/or inhabited.

Robert Aull is listed as an emancipist and landholder aged between 45 and 60, living in a finished wood house, with a female of the same age (so far so good), who was single and came free to the colony.

Well now: either Aull was being misleading, or there is an error on the record, as Mary was neither single nor did she come free to the colony. The other possibility is that he and Mary were no longer living together. Since the only person named on the census is the householder it's impossible to know who this other female was.

And what of Robert's children? In 1841 his youngest, Mary, would have been 14 and his eldest, Elizabeth, 25. The only boy, William, does appear in the census, just beneath his father, one of two males living in Richmond, both 'aged between 14 and 21' (William would have been 16), both single and born in the colony, occupations 'Gardeners, Stockmen and Persons employed in Agriculture' living in an unfinished wood house. The second young male is not named.

The plot thickens. We now have one missing wife, three missing children, a mysterious woman and an unnamed adolescent male. I suppose it is possible that William was living with his father, albeit in a separate house, and the other male could have been working for Robert. It's pretty clear the woman living with Robert was not his wife.

The other niggle is the fact that Mary Aull was later buried (in Richmond in 1867) not under her second married name but under Johnson. Of course this could have been her children's idea, but it's beginning to look as if the Aull/Johnson marriage did not survive.

Then the miraculous happens.

Anyone who's travelled the rocky road of family history will be familiar with those hours, days, months spent trawling through documents and newspaper items for nuggets of gold, or even brass, and rarely finding anything. I've already spent the best part of yet another day searching for Robert Aull on Trove and getting to the stage where all that's emerging is endless Roberts and the odd 'aull' in place of a mis-scanned 'all'. I am on the point of giving up when I come upon a notice placed by Robert Aull in several newspapers in February 1839. It goes some way towards solving the mystery of what happened to Mary, but in doing so it creates another. But that must wait till later as I'm getting ahead of myself.

It's back now to 1835: Robert is still the licensee of the Governor Darling on what was popularly known at Yellow Monday's Lagoon and his 20-year-old stepdaughter Julia has recently made the delighted acquaintance of the not-quite-21-year-old George Matcham Pitt; a relationship which I have no doubt Robert Aull, and Mary, encouraged. GM was after all that precious commodity: a landowner, born in the colony of free settlers, distantly connected to Admiral Nelson, with not a trace of the convict stain on him. Who, particularly an emancipist, would not want such a desirable person as a son in law?

Chapter 15

Interpreting our ancestors

How can we really know what our ancestors were like? With no diaries or letters or oral memories, all we have to go on are public records and mentions in the press, and not everyone gets mentioned in the press, especially the women.

In my case other family genealogists have already laid much of the groundwork for me. But that groundwork, even if accurate – which in the case of my aunt Barbara and the family biographer Janelle Cust it reliably is – can be incomplete, and what I would call 'uninterpreted'. It's one thing to lay down the facts and another thing to figure out what they mean. This is where the amateur historian has to turn not just detective but psychoanalyst as well.

As I was working my way through the Pitts and Scotts and other branches of the family bits and pieces of information came dropping into my lap at unexpected times and from unexpected sources. Some of these sources were in the public domain, on the Australian National Library's appropriately-named website Trove; others came from distant family relatives who contacted me through the family website I set up several years ago.

Trove, for those unfamiliar with it, contains digitised editions of official publications such as government gazettes and newspapers going back to the very first edition of the *Sydney Gazette* in 1803. To say it's invaluable is an understatement. It has a smart search engine that lets you browse for particular names or events on specific dates. The slight snag is the newspapers have been scanned electronically and are often indecipherable until some patient user (myself included) takes the time to correct the text and make it readable. This means that 'new' information appears to crop up all the time.

As each new piece of information arrived I had to stop and rethink, and as often as not to start all over again.

The first time this happened was when I discovered that the property Elizabeth advertised for lease after her husband Thomas died was not, as I had initially assumed, part of her 400-acre grant in Kurrajong but the farm on which she and her family were living. It put a quite different complexion on Elizabeth and what must have been going through her mind in the early days of her widowhood. I had to find, or invent, reasons why she decided to lease the farm in the first place and uproot her entire family from the only home the children had ever known, and then reasons why she appeared to change her mind.

Then there was Mary Johnson. My discovery of her grant of land came as a surprise, since it seemed to have been given for no other reason than that she was recently widowed and she employed convict servants. Since it was outside Sydney and presumably farming land I assume it was meant as an investment, but I have no idea what Mary did with it. What is interesting is that it raised Mary's status from emancipist and shopkeeper to landowner and Woman of Property. More broadly, it also went to show that Macquarie's controversial favouring of time-expired convicts – which his successor Sir Thomas Brisbane was on strict orders to countermand – lived on well after his 'reign' (it was Brisbane's secretary Frederick Goulburn who gave Mary her grant). It is in these details of daily life that appear sometimes to contradict 'official' policy that the family historian can serve a useful purpose.

The next surprise came in the form of GM's contact with the Aboriginal people as a child. It was just a few words of a song, recorded by ear in GM's version of the original Darug language. That is all it was. But what a story might lie behind it?

Later still I was to discover another connection between GM and, this time, the Kamilaroi people of north west New South Wales. There was even a possibility I have distant Aboriginal relatives, which is intriguing to say the least (if unlikely). Both these contacts were exciting discoveries and an opportunity to explore Aboriginal history, which is something I do with trepidation. This is sensitive territory: authors of the calibre of Kate Grenville have publicly stated they do not feel qualified to write from an Aboriginal point of view, so who do I think I am? (It is a modern sensibility: authors like Eleanor Dark, writing in the 1940s, had no qualms about recording the arrival of the Europeans from the point of view of pretty well everyone from governor to convict to Aboriginal onlooker, and with great insight and sensitivity.)

Perceptions and attitudes change all the time of course, particularly in Australia and its growing consciousness of the country's pre-colonisation past. Post colonial guilt and political correctness cloud the issue in many ways as modern writers succumb to a kind of self censorship. One even has to be careful about language. 19th century words such as 'native' (not to mention 'savage') are totally out of course – except when it refers, as it does rather confusingly in history books of yesteryear, to whites born in the colony. 'Aborigine', coined by Governor Macquarie, is dubious; even 'indigenous people' is frowned on; 'blackfellow' or even 'blackfeller' has the right friendly connotations but only for people who've made real friends with the blackfeller; the only acceptable term to use to refer to the Aboriginal people is the Aboriginal people, which sounds cumbersome and, so it seems to me, rather formal. But there we are.

So while I regretfully realise I cannot or should not

dramatise an Aboriginal character in my story the fact that GM made friendly contact with the local Darug people, and later with the Kamilaroi, is important. Settlers, squatters in particular, were characterised partly by their attitude and relationship with the Aboriginal people. GM's cousin George Faithfull had a fearful run-in with a group of armed Aboriginal warriors on the Broken River (near the NSW/Victorian border) in 1838. In a letter to Governor La Trobe of Victoria he wrote of his experiences, ending with: 'The fight I have described gave them a notion of what sort of stuff the white man was made, and my name was a terror to them ever after.' (In George's defence, he was fighting for his life and the survival of his men and his stock.)

As a postscript to this: when I pondered on the problem of how to present the Aboriginal people in my book to a Wiradjuri man called Mark Saddler in Wagga Wagga he responded with words of some wisdom: 'Whatever you say or don't say you are bound to offend someone.' Enough said.

Then there was the Scott family. I had them down as Irish – after all they arrived, as free settlers, on the convict ship *Surry* from Cork on 20 December 1816. I was even rather proud of myself when I came upon this in the ship's log:

> 'Remarks on Sunday 20th October: At 2¼ am Mrs Joan Scott / Passenger / departed this Life after a short Illness leaving three small Children on board.'

The three small children being, I assumed, William (16), Margaret (11) and young James (4). Three years later seven-year-old James is admitted into the Male Orphan School by his 'parent/guardian' Thomas Pitt, and three years after that William and Margaret crop up on the census working for Thomas and Elizabeth.

Then I am contacted out of the blue from a descendant of William's sister Margaret (called Gail Sutton) with proof positive the three siblings were born in Peebles in Scotland and were travelling to Australia to be with their father James, who had been transported for life. When their mother died they were placed under the care of their father, and then removed from it when he reoffended in 1818 and was sent to the Coal River in Newcastle. How they ended up working for Thomas is anybody's guess, as are his reasons for 'adopting' young James.

Further research on my part tells me *Surry* began her voyage in London before sailing to Cork to pick up their allocation of Irish convicts. So Joan Scott and her three children must have travelled down from Scotland to join the boat at Tilbury.

So I now have a William Scott who rather than being an Irishman taken on by the Pitts as a jobbing labourer in 1822 is a Scotsman who had been effectively adopted by them in 1818, along with his sister and younger brother. By the time Thomas Pitt died in 1821 William had been with the family for three years. It means not just a change of nationality but a change of status. William was not just an employee, he was pretty well part of the family. It meant extensive rewrites and a complete re-evaluation of William and of his subsequent relationship with Elizabeth.

Finally, and most crucially, came my late discovery of letters written by GM to the press in his old age; which, if true, threw a whole new light on his personality.

Lacking evidence to the contrary I had chosen to depict GM as an enlightened man who treated everyone – settler, convict or Aborigine – equally. To realise another side to him at such a late stage in proceedings was, not to put too fine a point on it, a shock. But that is in the nature of biography. In writing, as in life, it takes time to get to know a person. First impressions are not the full story.

It is ultimately what makes family history so all-absorbing. There is always something new to discover, and it is often those unexpected insights that add spice and credibility, and substance, to the old cliché that truth is not just stranger than fiction, it can be darned inconvenient. It is also what gives any story that unexpected smack of authenticity and makes the whole business of researching one's family history so endlessly, infuriatingly fascinating. The story is never over.

PART FIVE

New South Wales

Chapter 16

1835: Death & marriages

On the first day of 1835 Elizabeth Pitt died, of unrecorded causes.

GM had never felt grief like it. It was a physical pain, like a knife had cut right through him. It was not the slow pain of realisation he felt when his father died – a pain then part-dissipated by his immediate need to prove himself through hard work, and the bewilderment of a young child with little understanding of death. It was not even the intense sadness he felt when his brother died the year before, aged just fifteen. This was an angry pain at the loss of a mother, a still young woman of barely 38 years old – almost the same age as his father when he died, as it happens.

William and GM stood side by side by the grave, dressed from head to toe in unnatural black. William's face was grey, his expression inscrutable. He had barely spoken a word since Elizabeth's death.

Julia slipped her slim hand into GM's and he felt its coolness and its comfort. He held onto it, tightly, as if it was a lifeline.

On the far side of the graveyard of St Peter's Church he glimpsed the figure of a black-haired woman he knew to be Julia's mother. He'd met her, on the odd occasion, exchanged the odd word of greeting, not much more, as she was a shadowy figure – something that may or may not have had to do with her convict background. She was responsible for the day-to-day running of the Governor Darling, that much GM knew, while her husband Robert, though absent for the most part working on his properties, or working to acquire more of them, was only too happy to clap GM on the back on the rare occasion when they came face to face, as if he was an old acquaintance. Some people may have taken exception to such bonhomie, but not GM.

The funeral and the wake that followed would have seen a gathering of the clans, the two great pioneering families of Pitt and Laycock, and by extension of Faithfull, Wood, Jenkins and Wilshire. If even half the cousins had turned up – and chances are many of them did bearing in mind the close families ties – Bronte would have been full to bursting point.

~

Of the older generation of Pitts, born in England, there were GM's three surviving aunts Lucy, Jemima and Hester, now in their 50s or very nearly so. They had migrated to the colony back in 1801 with their mother Mary and now deceased siblings Thomas and Susanna. Other 'Sterlings' included 60-year-old William Faithfull, the late Susanna's husband, who lived nearby, and James Wilshire, Hester's husband and businessman, now 63, who had founded Sydney's most successful tannery – the emissions of which Julia and her family would have inhaled every day when they lived in the city. Of the Laycocks only Elizabeth's brother William, now 50, was still alive in 1835.

At the wake they spoke of Elizabeth's death as the passing of a vanishing generation who knew the old world. For the elders among them it seemed important to hold onto something of a past that was beyond the understanding of GM and his cousins. The old country was far away and of no particular interest or relevance to the lives of the Currency generation, born in the colony. They were Australians now.

For a man as gregarious as GM it would have been

impossible to remain too sad for too long in the company of his extended family. He moved from aunt to uncle to cousin, introducing them in turn to the young woman at his side. It was the first time Julia had been exposed to the full clan of Pitts, Faithfulls and Wilshires and it must have been quite overwhelming. So many of these people GM had spoken of and here they were in the flesh. His aunt Lucy, a widow, pale and attired in layers of slate grey and deep purple, appraised her quite openly from head to toe and finally nodded in what Julia hoped was mild approval. Jemima, twice a widow, her skin coloured chestnut by a life spent working outside, gave her a cursory glance and welcomed her heartily to the 'Pitt madhouse'. Hester, the youngest, mother of more children than GM could keep track of, gave Julia a sweet smile and pressed a cool cheek against hers. If any of them knew of Julia's convict parentage they gave no sign of it (although she may have been aware of aunt Lucy casting her a curious glance across the room from time to time.)

There were GM's siblings: his younger brother Robert, seventeen years old, taller even than his brother but as quiet as GM was garrulous. His sister Mary was wrapped around a young man Julia discovered to be Mary's and GM's cousin Thomas Laycock, Elizabeth's nephew. With them was Eliza, now fifteen, who'd spent much of her younger life living with her grandmother Hannah Laycock in Sydney. Of GM's half-siblings only the eldest, John, aged ten, was present. The others, Julia assumed, were considered too young to attend such a grownup gathering. Of their father William there was no sign.

She observed William Faithfull, GM's uncle and mentor in times past, grey-haired and grizzled but still holding himself ramrod straight, slapping a hand onto GM's shoulder and telling him 'talk to me any time you need to'. There was William's younger son George, GM's cousin and ex schoolmate, who gave Julia a cheery welcome before he went on to chat to GM about his farming activities in the Goulburn area where, Julia gleaned, he was helping out on the property of his elder brother William Pitt Faithfull. GM listened with total concentration, for once barely interrupting. Julia noticed how the faces of these young men lit up whenever they got to talking of farming in far-off places. It was not like the enthusiasm of her stepfather, who counted his land acquisitions in numbers of thousands of acres. It was more a spirit of adventure at the prospect of seeking out the undiscovered wonders of a country that nobody yet knew the limits of, and which these young men could not wait to get their hands on.

For an outsider the Pitt / Laycock / Faithfull *milieu* might have seemed a bit like a closed shop. Not only did they work for one another, they inter-married and named their offspring after one another. The legacy of the Matcham and Pitt names was firmly established in this extended family; a way of honouring the memory of the matriarch and pioneer Mary Pitt, *née* Matcham.

~

The following month, on 16 February 1835, Governor Bourke named Port Phillip after the Whig Prime Minister Lord Melbourne, and George Matcham Pitt turned 21. True to his father Thomas's will he inherited the 200 acres on the Hawkesbury, now named Bronte, and his brother Robert took charge of the 400 acres at Kurrajong.

Six months later GM's younger sister Mary Matcham Pitt married her cousin Thomas WEB Laycock at St Matthew's Church in Windsor. Shortly after that, on 22 September, GM married Julia Johnson in the same church. The Reverend Mr Styles officiated and the marriage certificate was signed by Robert Aull, Hannah Polack and an 'A Mair' of Sydney.

GM and Julia's wedding breakfast, in my story, was hosted with some aplomb by Robert Aull at the Governor Darling. It was a merry affair, attended by many of the pub's regulars and including William Scott, who had at last emerged from self-imposed solitary to toast the happy couple. Ever the onlooker at such events he observed how Julia's mother Mary had to be extricated from the kitchen in order to join in the celebrations, and how she still kept in the background, as far away as possible it seemed from her husband, smiling broadly and, just perhaps, weeping quietly.

Later that same day, according to the *Sydney Gazette*, 'the happy couple set off for the interior to enjoy the honeymoon'.

Julia Pitt (Elders Ltd)

Chapter 17

1835: William Scott

It was a cool late September evening. William rested his hands on the railings of the veranda and gazed out over Bronte farm. GM and Julia had left on their honeymoon and William was thinking back to the time GM's mother, so young and so uncertain, had called him to this very spot to tell him she was thinking of leasing the farm. She'd looked so vulnerable, almost childlike, so he'd done his best to sound casually reassuring while struggling to contain the panic at the thought of losing her, and her children, who were the closest he'd known to a family since his arrival in the colony as a bewildered sixteen-year-old.

It was also sixteen years since he'd come to live with the Pitt family, and you could say Elizabeth's death meant there was no real reason for him to continue living at Bronte. In some of his gloomier moments he might have thought there was no real reason for him to continue living. Except of course for the children. And the farm.

Back then William had been a single man with no ties. This time he was the 34-year-old widower and single father of four young children aged between eleven and two years old. However hard he found it getting up in the morning a farm and children do not look after themselves. It was the daily routine of animal and child husbandry that got him through the day, but as he stood there watching the sun disappear behind the mountains he realised it was time he took a good hard look at himself.

He had no security at all. He did not own any land in his own right, he had always been dependent on one or other member of the Pitt family, and now his future lay with GM. And while he knew and trusted GM he also sensed the young man had ambitions, and an ambitious man can be unpredictable. However much his *de facto* stepson relied on him, however much he knew and appreciated what he'd learned from him, that did not make William irreplaceable.

But if it takes a crisis to make a person re-assess his situation that is no bad thing. To William Bronte represented hard work and happiness and a sense of security he could not have dreamed of when he first arrived in this strange country motherless, hunting for his father. His memories of his native Scotland were fragmentary. It hadn't been an easy upbringing, there was always want (why else did his father turn to crime?), and yet a child only knows what a child knows, so the early years for William and his siblings were manageable, even enjoyable, up until the moment his mother announced their father was to be transported across the seas for a crime she refused to tell them of. He recalled asking her innocently how long he might be gone for and receiving no response other than a pursed lip and a frown. And then there was his mother's preoccupation with, he later realised, the business of raising enough money to transport the rest of the family to this unknown place across the seas to join their father; who was, even William realised, a *prisoner*, living behind bars – so really what was the point of travelling all that way in the first place? Then when he was told New South Wales was a penal colony with no prisons, and that his father would in due course be a free man, his spirits lifted, and that pleasant thought sustained him throughout the voyage on that strange convict ship stuffed full of Irishmen, right up to the point where his mother, who had been gradually ailing throughout the journey, died, just two months before the three children arrived at Sydney in the height of the summer of 1816.

It couldn't have been a worse introduction to Australia for William, Margaret and young James: to arrive in this strange, hot country knowing no one, still mourning the loss of their mother. What happened next we don't know. However happy they might have been to be reunited with their father, would a convict with a life sentence really be in a position to care for three young children, one of them only four years old? At whatever point they ended up in the care of Thomas and Elizabeth Pitt – temporarily in the case of young James – it must have been, for both William and Margaret, like finding a home again.

At Bronte right now there was just William and his four children, the eldest of whom, John and Betsey, went to the same school in Richmond that GM and his cousin George Faithfull had attended over ten years previously. Sister Margaret had married Edward Inall in 1831. Whether or not GM's youngest sister Eliza, then fifteen, returned to Richmond after her grandmother Hannah died is not known; though since she eventually married her cousin Austin Forrest Wilshire, who was brought up in Sydney, she probably didn't. In addition to the farmworkers there would have been a housekeeper, and hopefully a gentle nurse to look after the young Scott children, deprived of a mother at a very tender age.

How ambitious was William? Can one assume that after sixteen years of living and working for other people on Bronte and Trafalgar that he was now looking towards his own future and a property of his own, if only for his children's sake? If not here on the Hawkesbury, where there was barely a free square foot to be found, then further afield? What of all those rumours of the country in the far beyond that was for the taking? The settlement was growing fast, a man could get left behind if he wasn't careful. There's only so long a widower with four children to support can remain a hired hand, spending his time and energy on behalf of someone else. No matter how much the prosperity of the Pitt family at Bronte relied on him it's difficult to believe a capable man like William Scott was not turning his mind to a future life elsewhere. There was only one problem: he needed capital.

Chapter 18

1835-1838: The land of golden soil

It took the best part of twenty years for the colony of New South Wales to establish itself as a permanent settlement with an assured future. It wasn't really until Governor Macquarie's time (1810-1821) that both governors and people were able to turn their attention away from the day-to-day business of survival and look around to see what else this new country called Australia had to offer.

What it immediately had to offer was an unknown quantity of territory, which the British government through its colonial representatives declared 'Crown Land' and therefore rightfully theirs. The fact that it was in the custody of Aboriginal people did not deter either the authorities from giving it away or the colonists from taking it up, whether or not they were officially authorised to do so.

When Mary Pitt arrived in New South Wales in 1801 the settled mainland colony consisted of Sydney Town, Parramatta to the west, patches of land around the Hawkesbury River to the north and the Shoalhaven River to the south. (Not forgetting Van Diemen's Land and the convict settlement on Norfolk Island.) The northwest was then blocked by the Blue Mountains, but when that barrier was eventually breached in 1813, revealing fertile acreage spreading to the horizon, the newcomers were quick to spread through it and take up land beyond. No matter that official land grants had always been at the behest of the governor and may be given to certain people so long as they lay within the 'limits of location', the more ambitious colonists travelled themselves and their stock as far as they could physically go, in the knowledge that officialdom could not catch up with them. They were called squatters, or as the *Sydney Gazette* described them, 'bush rangers with a base'.

The squatters were not medieval barons and squires but ordinary people, albeit with access to money (or a healthy dose of audacity). Many of them were Currency lads, born in the colony, unencumbered by the memory of past hardships and all too aware they were occupying what was probably no more than a mere corner of a continent of unknown limits and unimagined promise. The European population in the eleven years of Macquarie's governorship trebled, from 10,000 to more than 30,000. By the late 1820s migrants were beginning to pour in, lured by the prospect of becoming landowners – beyond the wildest dreams of anyone back home in the old country. They vied with the locals to occupy the outer limits and they often had an unfair advantage over them because they had money, which more than made up for their lack of experience or knowledge of local conditions.

At that stage land within the Nineteen Counties – which stretched from the Manning River in the north to the Murrumbidgee in the south and inland as far as present-day Dubbo and Orange, comprising around 22 million acres – was still being officially granted free of charge, but only to people with capital. For one square mile an applicant had to prove he was in possession of £500, in cash or stock or farming equipment, or £2000 for a maximum of four square miles. The rationale being there was little point in giving someone land if they hadn't the wherewithal to farm it properly and fund it for however many years it took to produce an income. Then in 1833, under Governor Bourke, the niftily titled 'Act for protecting the Crown Lands of this Colony from

Encroachment, Intrusion and Trespass' introduced Land Commissioners whose job it was to control the unauthorised occupation of land.

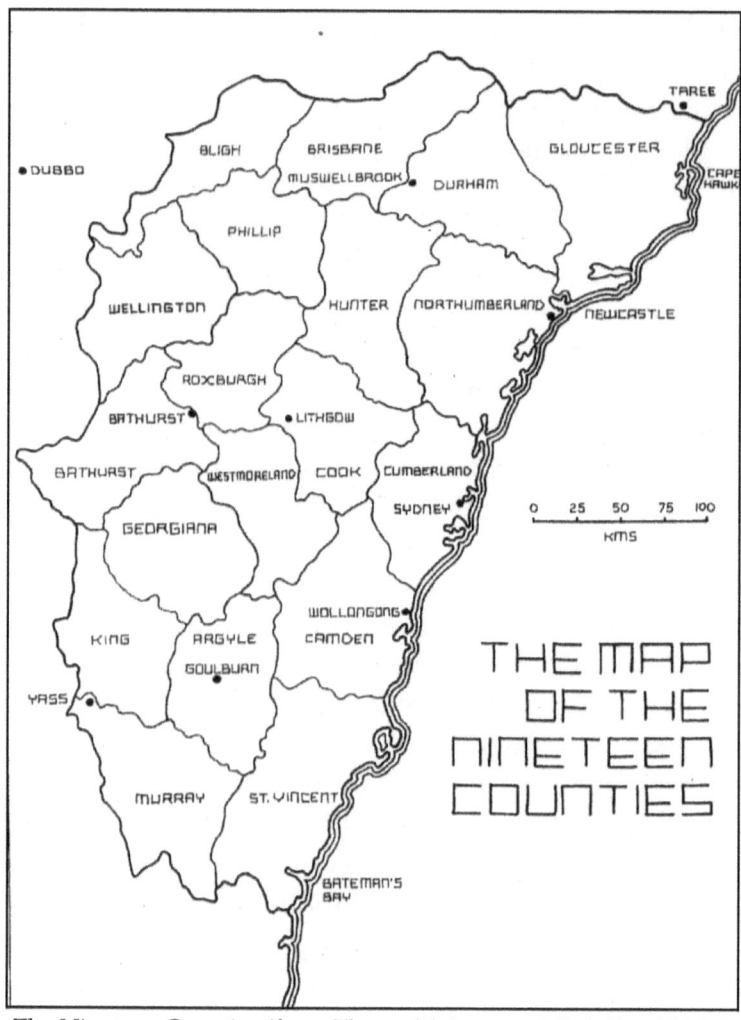

The Nineteen Counties (from *Thomas Livingstone Mitchell and his World*, Sir William Foster, Sydney Institution of Surveyors, 1985)

It was a game of cat and mouse, the governor and his officials running to catch up with the squatters and in the end bowing to the inevitable. So in 1836 Bourke introduced another Act allowing anyone to take up unoccupied land of any size anywhere for a payment of an annual licence fee of £10, the only stipulation being that sufficient stock should be grazing on it. The boundaries of the runs were agreed between the settlers. There was no security of tenure however and the licences could be revoked or sold off at any time, so very few squatters attempted to erect permanent buildings on their land or make substantial improvements. It was the responsibility of the Land Commissioners – one appointed for each of the nine districts – to collect the licence fees and issue fines for breaching the Act (£10 for the first offence, £20 for the second, £50 thereafter). They were allocated small groups of mounted constables, known as Border police, to help keep the peace between settlers and the Aboriginal people..

~

Meanwhile back in 1835, GM returned from his honeymoon in full newly-wedded bloom, too busy regaling his stepfather with wild and whacky stories of the adventures he and Julia had met on their travels to allow William to voice any misgivings about his future. GM's enthusiasm was infectious, not to say overwhelming. A person who did not share in it could quickly feel like a curmudgeon.

So life went on. Will and GM worked together on the farm just as they'd always done. In 1836 GM and Julia's first born, Thomas, arrived, and survived just three months. A little over a year later, in October 1837, George Matcham Pitt junior was born.

One evening, after Julia had retired to bed with the new baby, GM sat Will down and through the smoke from his pipe asked him if he had ever thought about acquiring some property of his own.

Will laughed briefly. 'And how would I do that?'

'Well now,' pronounced GM with a hint of smugness, 'it's not as if there's a shortage of the stuff. It all depends where of course.'

'And how much.' Will squinted at him.

'How much have you got?'

Will scoffed.

'You think we could cobble together a tenner between us?' said George. 'Because that's all it takes. For a year's licence.'

'A year's licence? Where?'

GM chuckled. 'At the Gwydir.'

'And where the devil's that?'

'It's quite a way. About three months overland, give or take. With the cattle.'

'With the cattle?'

'Best to take it with us because you won't find anything up there.'

GM gave Will the biggest grin.

The following year, in early 1838, he and William set out for the great unknown. They took with them a mob of cattle and a young drover called Jack Timmins.

Chapter 19

1838: The big journey

> 'As a young fellow he [GM] left the Hawkesbury, which had cradled so many of our pioneers, and on foot drove a number of cows and calves all the way to Moree . . . It was such stuff that the founders and builders of Australia were made.' *Stock & Station Journal*, 13 December 1932.

The first bit of evidence GM and Scott made the journey to what was then not yet Moree appears in Janelle Cust's book, where she says, 'In April 1838 George Matcham Pitt and William Scott took possession of Crown Land on the Lower Gwydir (Moree district), leaving George Bull in charge'. (Her reference is Treasury, Letters received 1847, SRNSW 4/2788, Wm Scott 47/4126) I also have a copy of a licence taken out by William Scott in 1839 for a a property on the 'Big River' in the region of Liverpool Plains.

However on a previous visit to Moree I could find no mention of GM in the area until ten years later, in 1848, when he applied for a licence for a property called 'Coorar'. According to censuses he was still living in Richmond throughout the 1830s and '40s, fathering children among other things. Of course he could have been an absentee landlord. And Scott may well have made the journey without him and simply included GM's name when applying for the licence.

But then another significant piece of information falls my way courtesy of a young Aboriginal man named Clayton Simpson Pitt: that's 'Simpson' as in the desert, and 'Pitt' as in Tom Pitt, born in the Gwydir area in 1838.

Neither Tom nor Pitt is an Aboriginal name needless to say. And since there are no signs of any other (white) Pitts in the area at that time it's fair to assume the name came somehow from GM – whose father and whose firstborn, who had died two years earlier aged just three months, were both Tom.

I put out a plea for information on Tom Pitt in the local *Moree Champion* and receive a healthy pile of responses from Aboriginal Pitts, some of them still living in the area, all of them descended from Tom Pitt and mostly through his son Arthur.

What can this mean?

The most obvious answer is that either GM was in the area the previous year and had a fling with a Kamilaroi woman; or – and more likely – Tom Pitt's father was working on GM's property in 1838. It was customary for Aboriginal workers to adopt, or be given, the name of their employers, partly because no white man could get their tongues around the original tribal names. The Pitt clan, so Clayton and his cousin Dorothy Tighe-Pitt tell me, is now one of the biggest family 'Gamilaraay' (aka Kamilaroi) groups in Moree.

In 1838 GM was 24 years old and had been married for three years, which is no guarantee of fidelity of course. The photo I am sent of Tom Pitt's son Arthur shows him to be what looks to me full-blood Aboriginal. So I think we can assume the name was innocently acquired, presumably by Tom Pitt's father.

The timing is interesting: Tom Pitt was born in April 1838, the very month that GM apparently took up land on the Lower Gwydir. Yet records show it was William Scott who paid the licence on the Big River property – which begs the question why it was not Tom Scott.

Tom Pitt, father unknown, was quite a character in the area and lived into his seventies. Unlike many other Aboriginal people in the district he stayed put in the area of his birth, while the white man effectively built the town of Moree around him. He was a much respected elder of the local community and was 'an occasional police tracker', according to one report. He was also the victim of a shooting in 1910, when a white man walked into the settlement where Tom and his family were living and started to maul the women. When the attacker turned his attention to his elderly mother, Tom, no spring chicken himself by then, hit him and drove him away, but the man returned later and shot Tom in the arm, as a result of which it had to be amputated.

The Kamilaroi connection ostensibly establishes GM's presence in the area in 1838, if not before. Records at that time are sketchy and Aboriginal history is passed down orally, so we may never quite get to the bottom of it all. Investigations are, as they say, ongoing.

~

The first whitefellers to set eyes on the outer reaches beyond the settled areas of New South Wales were more often than not convicts on the run. A convicted cattle stealer called Richard Craig was the first European to reach what came to be known as the Clarence River (also known as the 'Big River', confusingly), and on being caught he tried to trade his freedom for information about the cedar that was growing there. George Clarke, aka The Barber, escaped from a farm in Singleton on the Hunter River northwest of Sydney and went north, hooking up with a group of Kamilaroi on the way and teaching them how to rustle cattle and sheep in return for becoming a part of them. On his recapture he told the authorities about a 'Big River' the locals called the Kindur, which was believed to flow northwest right across the continent to emerge into the 'gulph of Van Diemen' – now the Timor Sea – on the north coast.

It was partly with this in mind that the surveyor general Sir

Thomas Livingstone Mitchell set off from Sydney in 1831 to explore the regions beyond the Liverpool Plains, in the hopes of discovering not just the Big River (there are a lot of Big Rivers in Australia) but the inland sea that so many early explorers were convinced existed since so many rivers appeared to flow west, away from the coast. He took with him an assistant surveyor, fourteen convicts, twenty bullocks, three drays, three carts and nine horses. At that stage the country beyond Tamworth, which is around 200 miles due north of Sydney, had not yet been officially surveyed and so was, to most whitefellas except The Barber, *terra incognita*.

I mention Mitchell because he very usefully kept detailed diaries of his expedition to the country where my ancestors took up land. And I have now reached the point in my family history adventure where, thanks to a grant from the Royal Australian Historical Society, I am about to embark on my second pilgrimage to the town of Moree, along with my Australian cousin Libby and in her car, in order yet again to research GM and William Scott's exploits in the outer regions of northwest New South Wales. We are hoping to replicate as far as possible the route they might have taken; but since unlike the surveyor general they did not keep a diary of their journey we are planning as far as possible to follow the route of Sir Thomas Mitchell.

But before setting out on the literary version of our journey I feel the need to describe what to this hitherto ignorant Londoner has turned out to be one of the most fascinating and quintessentially exotic Australian topics: droving.

.

Chapter 20

The drover

He is a central feature of Baz Luhrmann's film *Australia*, as played, and somewhat glamorised, by Hugh Jackman. He is the rather more authentic star of the 1945 film *The Overlanders*, played by a young Chips Rafferty. His wife is the subject of the Henry Lawson short story *The Drover's Wife*, and of the Russell Drysdale painting of the same name. He is Banjo Paterson's *Clancy of the Overflow* and *Saltbush Bill*. He is the archetypal Australian legend, even if his roots did begin in America.

I can remember one day driving through the Australian countryside with my brother and thinking I really should get my eyes tested. I am pretty myopic so I rely on contact lenses but even so, on those long, long straight roads I fancied I was seeing mirages. I realised in time it wasn't my eyesight that was faulty, it was those massive distances. We just don't have them here in lil' ol' England.

In a country where people think nothing of driving a hundred miles to have dinner with friends, and where the corner shop is – to bush people – fifty miles away, droving, otherwise known as travelling a mob of sheep or cattle overland from one place to another, often across thousands of miles, is a complex and understandably much revered skill.

Despite the invention of trains and trucks and road trains the practice still exists, albeit with motor vehicles or motorbikes instead of horses (though horses are also used in modern times apparently as they don't tend to break down or run out of fuel in the middle of nowhere). I believe tourists can pay a small fortune to go on one.

Needless to say droving was not a subject I had hitherto given much thought to, but having spent some time looking into it I became sufficiently fascinated to want to share my findings with my readers. Here, for the equally ignorant therefore, is some of what I have learned:

All cows are not the same. They have distinct personalities, much like people. There are the pliant ones, the contrary ones, the lazy ones and those for reasons of their own like to walk in a diagonal direction. There are the leaders and the stragglers, and each animal being a creature of habit is likely to take up the same position each day throughout the drove.

Despite their calm appearance cattle are prone to panic if not treated gently. They need to be woken quietly in the morning for instance (as do we all) and the slightest sudden sound or flashing light, or the smell of water after a long dry patch, can cause them to 'rush', crushing everything in their way.

There are rules that existed in the old days, and still do, as to the minimum distance an overlanding mob was supposed to travel in a day. Since journeying vast distances inevitably involved crossing private land it was a way to prevent the travelling mob from encroaching for too long on local landowners' properties, eating their grass and drinking their water and so forth.

Banjo Paterson wrote about it in his poem *Saltbush Bill*:

> 'Now is the law of the Overland that all in the West obey,
> A man must cover with travelling sheep a six-mile stage a day;
> But this is the law which the drovers make, right easily understood,

> They travel their stage where the grass is bad, but they camp where the grass is good;
> They camp, and they ravage the squatter's grass till never a blade remains.
> Then they drift away as the white clouds drift on the edge of the saltbush plains.'

(For what happens next, read the poem. It's a very funny story.)

I don't know when this law was first introduced: none of the accounts I've read of other early droving expeditions mention it. Besides, speed, to GM and other overlanding drovers, was not the priority. The priority was to get the cattle or sheep to their destination in as good a condition as possible, which meant keeping them fed, watered and free from stress. Some mobs had to be slowed down in order to encourage them to feed.

Typically, the drovers would arrange themselves around the animals and walk at their pace. Depending on how many were in the party there would be one man riding in front to keep the mob steady, two on either 'wing' and three behind, one on each corner and one in the middle. They would have had dogs with them.

But the real challenge came at night. There were no fences, so the men would light a circle of fires around the cattle and camp outside it and take it in turns to keep watch. (When Mitchell's bullocks became restless he constructed 'a temporary stockyard of ropes tied between trees'.) The night watchman might have had the use of a 'night horse' who could see in the dark and whose sole job it was to sniff out any straying cattle and bring them back. If they lost any stock overnight they would not move on the following morning until they found them. Later on there was another hazard: wild cattle, escapees from previous excursions who roamed the countryside and could appear unexpectedly, unsettling the animals and the men alike; which is why on setting up camp for the night one of the first things the drovers would do is make a mental note of nearby trees that were easy to scamper up if necessary.

I don't know how GM and his team travelled or what they took with them. Mitchell had bullocks and drays to carry his supplies, but they caused problems – axles broke and the wheels got stuck in mud, and they were tricky when it came to negotiating dense wood. On one occasion when crossing a mountain Mitchell's men had to completely offload the drays so the bullocks could negotiate the climb unencumbered, and the men had to carry the contents themselves. And he did not have cattle to contend with. My guess therefore is that GM and his team took packhorses rather than drays or carts.

A drove inevitably involved crossing water. In GM and William's case they would have been used to this as they drove cattle from Bronte on the south side of the Hawkesbury to Trafalgar on the north, there being no bridge across the river at that time. Looking at the mighty Hawkesbury now this looks like a well nigh impossible task, but in the old days there were crossing places. Cattle can swim, even I know that, though given the chance they'd avoid it unless coerced. Coercion could take the form of using a dairy cow to lead the mob, since dairy cattle are that much more domesticated apparently and likely to do as they are told. Some landowners had a 'decoy' cow which they would bring out whenever they spotted overlanders, to lead them and their cattle over the water and on their way as quickly as possible.

Our journey, my cousin and I, in her nearly-new Subaru, took us one and a half days.

Mitchell's party consisted of around twenty men, and his journey from Sydney to the Gwydir took him five weeks.

GM's team most likely comprised around half a dozen men, including himself, William Scott and Jack Timmins. There's no knowing how long their journey took.

~

According to a Timmins descendant young Jack made his first appearance at Bronte back in 1832 when at the age of fourteen he rode from his home at Yarramundi, where he lived with his convict parents, and presented himself to the lady of the house to ask for a job. The man who was to become a legend in his later life as a drover and dog breeder was already an accomplished horseman and had accompanied his father on several cattle droves between Sydney and Bathurst. He was nervous his convict background might work against him but it seems Elizabeth offered him work immediately. It marked the beginning of a long association between Jack and the Pitt and Scott families.

It's said Timmins accompanied GM and William on their trek north, which makes sense as there's nothing to say that either of the two men had ever driven a mob of cattle any further than their property across the river at Kurrajong. Timmins claimed he could cross mountains with a mob of cattle and only his dogs to accompany him; dogs he had trained to such perfection that, so the unlikely story goes, when he camped overnight one of them would herd the cattle, one would bring him firewood and another water, so all he had to do was 'sit there and direct them'.

~

I've no idea what route GM, Will and Timmins took. I don't even know if they themselves knew precisely where they were heading or what they were expecting to find beyond the Liverpool Plains. All they had to go on was what they had gleaned from their neighbours George Bowman and Robert Fitzgerald, who had already taken up land in the area. So I'm going to assume that for some of the way at least they followed the route northwest, laid out, and so minutely described, by the surveyor general six years earlier.

Chapter 21

1830s & 2015: Three expeditions

Sir Thomas Mitchell left Sydney on Thursday 24 November 1831. Ahead of him lay a journey of 300 miles before he could arrive at 'the vast untrodden soil' that lay beyond white settlement. He took with him a team of convicts and assistant surveyors and enough provisions to last them for several months, including flour, boned pork, tea, tobacco, sugar and soap. They also carried muskets, pistols and a small stock of ammunition including 'skyrockets' (presumably their version of distress flares). The following day he arrived at the Hawkesbury River, which he crossed in a ferry boat at Wiseman's Ferry – where he noted the river was 280 yards wide – and then proceeded north along the Great North Road, otherwise known as the Convict Trail.

My cousin and I set off from Sydney by car at 9.30am on Saturday 21 March 2015, carrying water bottles, suitcases and not much else. Since the Convict Trail appears on the map as unmade we decide to cheat a bit and start off on the Pacific Highway, through the increasing rain and traffic. It takes us around an hour and a half to get to the Brooklyn Bridge across the Hawkesbury.

Starting out from Bronte GM and his team would have begun by swimming the cattle across the river, and from there it's said they travelled along the oddly-named 'Bell's Line of Road' north to Kurrajong and thence along what's now known as Comleroy Road. They would then have had to negotiate their way through dense forest, although at this early stage of the journey there would presumably have been a quite well-established stock route.

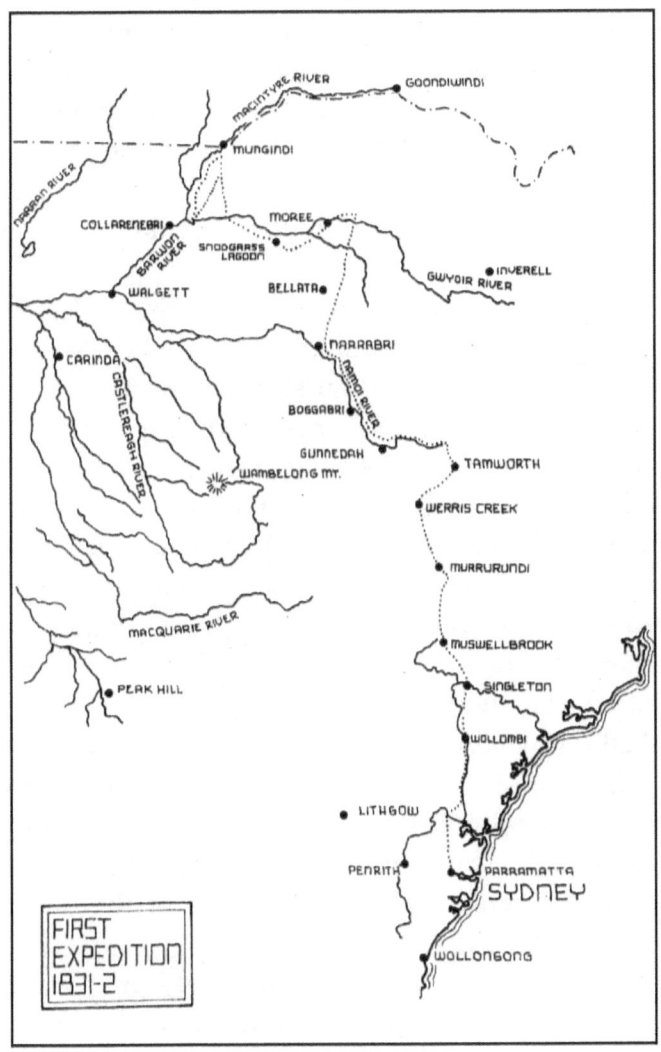

Sir Thomas Mitchell's first expedition (*Sir Thomas Livingstone Mitchell and his World*, Sydney Institution of Surveyors, 1985)

All three groups would have then converged on the small town of Wollumbi – aptly the local Aboriginal word for 'meeting place' – which is set in a fertile and often-flooded valley that even in Mitchell's time was well populated by local farmers. Here Mitchell stopped for his third night on the road at an inn, and it's likely GM did the same. We stop for lunch at one of the many delightful cafés and pay a brief visit to the local museum, where we happen to come upon several pieces of information concerning GM's sister Mary Laycock, including the illegitimate birth of her daughter's daughter in 1875, followed some months later by the wedding of the same daughter to the son of the drover Jack Timmins; proving yet again how small a world it was in the early days of New South Wales.

From Wollumbi the road north more or less follows Wollombi Brook to the town of Broke, named by Mitchell after a friend of his, not the financial situation of its inhabitants. It was around here that Mitchell passed the night on one of the 'many large and thriving establishments' belonging to John Blaxland. It is possible GM and Scott did the same. Whether or not they were acquainted with the Blaxlands, Australian bush hospitality is legendary: from the grazier to the humble shepherd everyone was expected to provide shelter and food for the night for passing travellers, no questions asked. They often shared a bed with them.

Mitchell's travelling day began at sunrise and finished at around 2pm, after which while his men made camp he continued on on horseback looking for a high point from where he could survey the surrounding country. He then returned to the camp and spent the rest of the day making detailed notes of the day's journey.

GM and Scott's day would also have begun at sunrise, and continued on until dark or until animals and men had had enough, which depended on the kind of terrain they were crossing at the time. For some reason both they and Mitchell made their trip at the hottest time of the year – in Mitchell's case between November 1831 and January 1832, in order, he said, to have the job done before the arrival of Governor Bourke – and they suffered terribly from 100^0 plus (F) temperatures, even at night-time. Mitchell also had a problem with mosquitoes, flies the size of bees 'with a hum almost as musical as the tones of an Eolian harp' and actual bees that made their home in the barrel of his rifle, filling it with honey. We encounter none of these, though we do drive through plagues of grasshoppers, as the devastation on the bonnet of Libby's car later shows.

Beyond Broke we pass an open-cut and underground mine called 'Bulga Newcoal', and it's round about here that I record a stark contrast in the surrounding countryside of the Great Dividing Range, from a lush green to an austere brown and, conversely, the appearance for the first time today of the sun. Beyond Muswellbrook is prosperous wine-growing and horse stud country. We're on the New England Highway now, travelling due north to Scone, where I make a note of the startling fact that 'the road finds a way through the mountains, of course. But it undulates, to say the least'.

Thomas Mitchell did rather better. Beyond Scone he came upon and closely examined the mysterious 'burning mountain' of Wingen. The mountain has probably been burning for thousands of years and, we now know, is due to a seam of coal some metres beneath the surface. Exactly what makes this coal continue to burn is beyond the ken of this writer. Unfortunately I only heard about it after our trip was over, or we would have stopped and given it our own close examination.

Which leads me to another interesting point:

Sir Thomas's mission as a surveyor was to take precise measurements wherever he was of heights and distances and to make detailed notes of the lie of the land, the soil, the nature and appearance of the rock, the nature and direction of waterways, the wildlife, flora, encounters with indigenous people and so on. GM's mission was to get from A to B with cattle; which meant for the most part he was looking for the easiest route through which to steer his animals and the nearest source of water. Driving in my cousin's new car with cruise control – a flick of a switch on the steering wheel and the vehicle cruises at a steady 110 kph so all you really have to do on those largely empty roads is steer – I barely have time to make general notes such as 'horse-stud country . . . beautiful plain . . . Great Dividing Range on one side, unidentified mountains on the other . . .' This is partly down to my paltry powers of description of course, but zipping along at speed doesn't give you the chance to feel and smell the landscape as both Mitchell and GM would have done.

For example around Murrurundi, just north of Wingen, Mitchell and his team found their path blocked by the Liverpool Ranges, a bank of mountains lying east to west between the Barrington Tops to the east and the Warrambungles to the west. It doesn't look like much on the map and driving along the highway you barely notice you're crossing them, but it provided a major challenge to Mitchell's party, who found themselves having to attach thirteen bullocks to each cart and draw them up one by one, and even then the axle broke on one of them and he had to abandon it. Then having reached the far side he was greeted with the distressing sight of Aborigines lying on the river banks dying of smallpox.

How the Aboriginal people came to contract smallpox is a puzzle as no Europeans succumbed to the disease in Australia; though it was not the worst thing the whitefella did to the black over the centuries. (There is a theory it may have been used by the whites as a form of 'biological warfare' in the first days of settlement.)

Mitchell relied hugely on local Aboriginal people, following paths laid down by them over the centuries and using them as guides. He described being led at night-time by young boys from the neighbouring tribe 'who ran cheerfully before my horse, alternately tearing off the stringy bark which served for torches, and setting fire to the grass trees . . . to light my way.'

He found his 'sable companions' friendly, funny, skilful and happy to help without expecting anything in return. He also drew a distinction between those who were already acquainted with white people and 'myalls', who were not, and were terrified of him.

On arriving at the Peel River, just north of present-day Tamworth, Mitchell declared he was now entering *terra incognita*. Here he paused to remind himself of the responsibility of 'commencing the first chapter' of the country's history as he put it, and that by opening it up he was enabling 'civilised man . . . to extend his dominion over some of the last holds of barbarism'.

It's difficult for us to fathom nowadays but it seems Mitchell's friendly encounters with the Aboriginal community did nothing to alter his notion of them as savages. There is no way, and Mitchell would have been the first to admit it, that early explorers would ever have been able to get from A to B without the help of the local people and their unerring ability to find a route through what to white eyes looked like impenetrable scrub, or to find sustenance in featureless landscape. What white man was ever able to run up the trunks of sheer trees, where the branches did not begin until 60 feet above the ground, in order to pull a possum from his hole in the trunk? What white man was able to find water where there was none to be seen, or knew that the muddy water of the rivers of the black soil country was pleasantly drinkable if filtered through grass?

Come to that, what white traveller in the 1830s was not aware there were boundaries between the territories belonging to different tribes, marked by natural features in the landscape such as a ridge or a watercourse or a marked rock, which should not be crossed by the black or the white man except by invitation? When Mitchell's guide 'Mr Brown', who had led him and his party across the Liverpool Plains over several days, suddenly disappeared, the surveyor general knew it was because he realised they were entering 'myall' territory and he had no permission to be there. ('Myalls' did not have the use of the tomahawks the whites periodically gave to Aboriginal helpers by way of thanks.) Mitchell and his team would have known they were being watched by invisible eyes as they proceeded. As, presumably, would GM. Two of Mitchell's men, left behind at one point to look after the stores, were killed by Aborigines, and their camp ransacked.

Once across the Liverpool Ranges Mitchell was able to stop and marvel at the calm beauty of the land that lay before him. This was the Liverpool Plains, a huge expanse of flat country stretching north as far as the horizon and remarkably clear of trees, where cows grazed contentedly and the grass was so tall in places that when Mitchell set his dogs to catch kangaroos they disappeared in it. The owners of those cows were not the same in 1831 as they were two years later however, after the Australian Agricultural Company moved in and ousted the squatters from their land.

It is in Tamworth that my cousin Libby and I stop for our one overnight break in what turns out to be an unprepossessing chain motel. But at least we have a proper roof over our heads, which is probably more than Mitchell would have had.

As for GM, I would imagine he was well acquainted with the Australian Agricultural Company, and that even if he was not personally known to the superintendant of their 250,000 acres on the Liverpool Plains he would have been warmly received by their local representative and gained valuable information from him. He and Will may have been invited to remain at the overseer's homestead for a few days to rest the men and the cattle. They would have learned, had they not known it previously, that they had some considerable distance to go before they reached the outer limits of 'occupied' land. They would have acquired useful knowledge of the black soil country, where the earth was 30 to 40 feet deep in places and which, when wet, turned into heavy mud that clung to the feet of animals and men and the wheels of carts and drays, and when dry opened up cracks several feet wide. They would have picked up useful gossip about local squatters and the relationship between them and the Kamilaroi – those proud, intelligent people who suffered so much in the hands of the whites over the years.

Then, onwards in a north-westerly direction into Mitchell's *terra incognita*. Past the Namoi river, on the banks of which, Mitchell noted, trees grew in straight lines as if planted by human hand. When we passed it in 2015 it was dry, but a little further on the Namoi creek was flowing full and fast, due, we learn from the lady in the Narrabri information office, to the river having been diverted to bring it closer to the town and more accessible for tourists. My sharp-eyed cousin also noticed the trees by the side of the road had received a battering, and we learned from the same lady there had been a hailstorm the night before with hailstones the size of tennis balls. (She showed us pictures on Facebook to prove it; and I thought, though I shouldn't, 'So they have Facebook out here, do they?')

Now all three teams are travelling due north. Mitchell awoke one morning to find the whole country ablaze, the air so thick with smoke he could not see his way. This was no doubt due to Aboriginal controlled burning, deliberately carried out to regenerate the undergrowth and flush out the wildlife – a regular feature of indigenous land management. Christmas Day came and went without a mention. By now he had been on the road for a month and it had rained just once. Both men and animals were suffering so badly from lack of water two of his team were unable to walk and had to be left behind temporarily. At one point a storm threatened to break but the rain appeared to evaporate in mid-air.

GM and William should have encountered fewer problems, thanks partly to Mitchell's survey. But waterholes, creeks and even rivers can appear and disappear in a matter of days, or even hours, in 100 degree temperatures. Mitchell eventually did find water, needless to say, and on 8 January 1832, 44 days after leaving Sydney, he at last came upon a series of ponds of the purest water and drift matter high in the trees, and his spirits lifted as he realised he was approaching what had to be the Big River, also known as the Kindur.

But it was not. It was a river for sure, or as he described it at the time, a stream, though the width and depth of the channel indicated it usually contained a much larger volume of water. He realised however from the latitude this was none other than the 'Gwydir of [the explorerAllan] Cunningham', as he called it. The grandeur of the scenery and the magnificence of the trees seemed to compensate for what must have been to the surveyor general a massive disappointment: no Big River reaching right across the continent to the northern coast. No inland sea.

Mitchell crossed the river quite easily – the water only came up to his ankles – though he had some difficulty manoeuvring his horse up the steep bank the other side. As he continued on in a westerly direction following the flow of the river, we bid him a grateful farewell and part company with him.

Chapter 22

1838: The squatter

The squatter is another character from Australian legend. He may not have the unqualified approval of people like Banjo Paterson – unless, like 'Old Kiley', he lived on the premises and devoted his life to the care of his property and had respect for the people who worked for him. He was first and foremost a capitalist.

According to George Farwell, author of *Squatter's Castle*, the squatter was Everyman:

> 'Impoverished English gentry . . . redundant officers from the Napoleonic wars, scholars and scoundrels, adventurers, gully-rakers and remittance men. [His world] was sketched in bold and sweeping outlines against the massive canvas of the Inland, and he made it a source of legend.'

He was the man who dared to step out into the unknown, following in the steps of the early explorers and surveyors – or on occasion preceding them – searching for unclaimed pockets of land to pitch his tent on. Often he failed, sometimes he physically perished, from hunger or thirst or from Aboriginal spears. He was a capitalist, yes, in pursuit of wealth and prepared to take huge risks in order to achieve it. At best he loved working the land and was prepared to roll up his sleeves and get stuck in alongside his workers; a man who was happy to invest in his property, financially and emotionally, for as long as necessary. In the very early days he may have been considered a crook or a thief, but as time went on the term squatter became, thanks to the pioneers, respectable, even noble. In boom times some of them became ridiculously wealthy and built themselves grand houses which they filled with expensive imported furniture – including the ubiquitous grand piano – and acquired luxuries such as fancy carriages, fine wines and French champagne. According to the writer Anthony Trollope these outward trappings were a good indicator of a squatter's wealth: 100,000 sheep or more required a male cook and a butler, 40,000 could not be shorn without a piano, 20,000 was the lowest number rendering 'napkins at dinner imperative', and 10,000 indicated plenty of meat – mutton or beef – tea, brandy and colonial wine, but not champagne, sherry or 'made dishes'.

Meanwhile, GM and Scott were not the first Hawkesbury residents to arrive at the Gwydir. In addition to George Bowman and Robert Fitzgerald, Hannah Dight – the same Mrs Dight who was rescued along with her children from the Big Hawkesbury Flood of 1806 by Margaret Catchpole – also appears in early records in the region, along with her sons and members of the Howe family (whose offspring married her offspring). The other inhabitants seemed to have been largely squatters displaced from their runs in the Liverpool Plains by the Australian Agricultural Company; men such as Otto Baldwin and William Nowland – the first white man to find a way through the Liverpool Ranges in 1827 and after whom 'Nowland's Gap' is named – John Onus and Thomas Parnell, another Hawkesbury resident.

Whether any of these fine people were actually living in the Gwydir district at the time is another matter. Most if not all of them seem to have already taken up land elsewhere, especially in the Hunter Valley, so it is more than likely they were absentees, dividing their time between their various properties, as GM was to do later. They would have hired a reliable overseer, and it is a representative of this profession to whom in my story GM and William paid a visit on arrival to find out how the land lay, literally.

The building the Overseer occupied was basic, and temporary. It may have been a bark hut, it may even have been canvas, with a bare board to sleep on and if he was lucky, a table and a couple of stools. At that stage with no security of tenure it was unlikely to have been much more.

Our Overseer was a source of crucial local information, not just about the availability of nearby land but of other important considerations such as relationships with the Kamilaroi. There had been several incidences recently of attacks on both men and stock and several squatters had been forced to abandon their properties because of them.

~

It is important at this point to emphasise the significance, and the challenges, of being the first to farm what the European considered virgin land. No matter how much information a squatter might glean from his neighbours, until he had actually taken possession of his run and moved his stock onto it and stuck at it for several years, he had absolutely no way of knowing whether or not he had done the right thing. Australian countryside can turn from luscious green to stark, dust-blown brown in no time at all if there is no rain. Running rivers can turn to waterholes and then dry up completely, for years on end. Nowadays water can be imported, as can animal feed, but not then.

So the first thing the squatter would be on the lookout for on his potential run was a source of water, preferably a river, a creek or at the very least a waterhole. If it was dry, or the water level was low, he'd be looking for a high water mark to determine how full it'd be likely to get in good times, if there were any. He'd be hoping for a run with not too many trees that needed to be cleared before he could put his stock on it. An experienced squatter would be able to tell a good deal about the soil from the trees – mature trees implied the soil was good, small and spindly meant the opposite. The most reliable guide of all however was the cattle themselves. Cows have a natural ability to find the best feed and the canny squatter would follow their lead, and then keep a close eye on their condition as it would be obvious within a couple of weeks whether or not they were thriving.

The squatter also had to have enough money to be able to stock his farm and pay his workers for at least a year before he could expect any kind of return. If he was an absentee landlord he'd need at least two men: an experienced overseer and, for cattle, a stockman.

The stockman is another Australian legend. A skilled horseman, he had to be capable of riding great distances, over rough terrain, and staying in the saddle all day. His most prized possession, after his horse, was his saddle; it may have been made for him, it was certainly handmade, and he'd cherish it and care for it like a newborn baby. Likewise his stock whip, which he would wield with dexterity and restraint, as no station owner wanted a show-off for a stockman. He considered himself superior to the shepherd because he was on horseback, and because the rounding up of cattle, especially if they were unused to being with men, let alone a man on a horse, is not a job for amateurs. One stockman could look after 1000 head of cattle if he knew what he was doing.

Mary Gilmore described them as 'the world aristocrats' in the early days of settlement – equal to any man and answerable to none. If asked to do something menial he'd be off before you could blink. For example:

'Why did you leave the Sandersons, Bill?'

'He asked me to cut the wood!'

It was not a life for anyone. These men might go for days, weeks, months without seeing another soul other than their employer or their fellow workers. The routine was unchanging, and it's said they developed unbreakable habits; a stockman would put his saddle on the same branch of the same tree every day for instance. Many of them went faintly mad, or became deeply eccentric. They might lose the power of speech if they spent too long not using it.

Meanwhile, once he'd decided on his run the squatter would create some kind of a boundary, in agreement with his neighbours, using marks on trees and rocks and other landmarks, or creeks or gullies. There was no such thing as wire fencing in those days so he'd have had to construct something else to keep the stock from straying – tree trunks laid horizontally on top of another was one method. And he'd have had his cattle branded without delay.

All that done, he'd have set about building himself some kind of shelter, probably from bark and possibly no more than a humpy in the initial stages. That achieved, he'd have allowed himself to sit down, heave a large sigh of satisfaction, pour himself a tot of rum, light his pipe and contemplate the future. For some this calm, still window of meditation would turn out to be the best moment of the whole enterprise. His life as a squatter was just beginning.

Chapter 23

2015: Moree

It's 2015 and Libby and I have arrived at the Moree library bright and early on a Monday morning. We have just spent an extremely comfortable night in our spacious room in a caravan park with no fewer than five swimming pools, four of them thermal and at temperatures ranging from 38 to 42 degrees Celsius. Moree sits on top of an artesian basin, the biggest in the world apparently, a vast well of pure, hot, mineral-rich underground water which lay hidden from European discovery until way after GM and William visited the area.

Moree is famous for its artesian pools, which are a major draw for tourists. It was also famous as a target of the Freedom March of 1965, when a bunch of Sydney University students toured New South Wales drawing attention to injustices suffered by indigenous people, and in the case of Moree the fact that Aboriginal children were barred from the local swimming pool. When I told people we were going there they warned us not to park on the road if we wanted to retain our wheels. But it always seemed to us, not just this time but on our previous visit, an exceptionally friendly town with extremely helpful people. It is also one of the few places where we encounter Aboriginal people, many of them in the library.

I remembered the library as an old building with a separate, and extensive, family history section which you had to sign in and out of. But this library is a spanking new construction and on arrival we are told the family history section is not open to the public and we will have to wait until the president of the Family History Society arrives, which he may or may not do today. A number of thoughts flash through my mind to do with travelling across the world for this moment and what am I going to tell the Royal Australian Historical Society? I am politely told I should have emailed ahead of time, which I had done of course but received no response. Fortunately on checking my email on the library computer there is a reply sitting in my spam box from a Michael McNamara from the Historical Society (not the same as the Family History Society), promising to be in at 1.30pm. So all is not lost.

We spend the intervening time visiting the Lands Office, where we are lucky to find two helpful people, Vicky and Celedia, who photocopy some old local maps for us. We then wander up to the Information Office where another friendly and well-informed lady called Tian, who is a member of both historical societies and also runs guided tours of the area, tells us the sad story of Charles Dickens's youngest son Edward Bulwer Lytton (named after Charles's friend, a famous 19th century novelist). Young Edward was sent out to the colonies like so many before him by his father, following his elder brother Arthur d'Orsay Tennyson who had emigrated before him. (The literary naming habit ran in the family evidently.) Edward, known within the family as 'Plorn', began by managing a station – from where he was dismissed for criticising his boss – married the daughter of a local landowner and founded a stock and station agency with his brother called EBL Dickens & Partners. He lost money on his land investments and never managed to repay a loan to his other brother Henry, for which the family never forgave him. He held a seat on the Legislative Council for a time before he eventually fetched up in Moree, working in the local Lands

Office. By then his career was on the skids, his wife had left him, alcohol and debt had got the better of him and he died, alone, penniless, and estranged from his family back in England. He is buried in Moree Cemetery.

By the time we return to the library the president of the Family History Society has arrived and, munching on a meat pie, he invites us up to the family history section to have a poke around.

We spend some time doing exactly that and discover precisely nothing. We cannot even establish that the area we are in was once part of the Liverpool Plains district, or that the Big River could have referred to the Gwydir. There is no mention of either William or GM in this area as early as 1838.

Fortunately when Michael McNamara turns up he is able to confirm the Big River was indeed the Gwydir and that it could well have been part of the district of Liverpool Plains before it became known as the Gwydir district. We are edging forward millimetre by millimetre. However despite the vast knowledge of both local historians and the plethora of pamphlets and log books on the shelves we can still find no trace of our ancestor.

It has been said that Australians take an inordinate amount of interest in their local history. It seems pretty well every country town has at least one local history society and Moree, population circa 9,000, has not just two of them but a number of publications devoted to the town's history and a local newsletter called *Yilaalu*, edited by Michael McNamara. The knowledge of and interest in Australia's local history would seem to be out of all proportion to the length and extent of that history, until you look a little closer.

For instance Mr McNamara is able to tell us that Coorar Creek, where we know GM took up land in 1848, is now called Carolle Creek and has been known over the years as Coorah, Curragh or Carolle. This is the kind of local knowledge which is worth travelling a long way for, as we have done. He also downloads for me an electronic version of the Boughton Papers, all 237 articles of it, written by a local landowner called

Charles Boughton, which covers Moree's history from Major Mitchell's time until the end of the 19th century. I also buy a book called *The Rising Sun*, by R J Webb, published to celebrate Moree's 100th anniversary in 1962, another locally published booklet called *The Watercourse Country* by Kath Mahaffey, one-time president of the Historical Society, and the first edition of *Yilaalu*, dated 1977.

I reckon that's enough to be going on with. We retire to our room in the caravan park with its thermal swimming pools. Tomorrow we will venture out once again to where we know GM took up land in 1848.

The next day we drive north along a sealed road for 49 kilometres, to the township, if that's not an exaggeration, of Garah. There's a pub, two churches, a school, a general store (closed) and a number of houses in varying degrees of dilapidation, including one that looks as if it might have had an important past. We take the turning left past the police station and follow the road round in what I term the Garah Triangle. We are looking not for the piece of land GM and Scott allegedly took possession of in 1838 but for a property called Coorar, which GM acquired ten years later.

To say the countryside around Garah is flat is the greatest understatement. There is not the smallest hillock to be seen in any direction, it's as if some supernatural hand has ironed out every bump, every feature. There's not a tree, not a shrub, nothing discernible growing anywhere but brown scrub. No fences, so no livestock. It could not look more desolate. What there is however is a very well made road, so obviously something happens here, goodness only knows what.

GM, we say, we have you surrounded. Somewhere here-abouts you farmed 72,000 acres – or square miles, depending on which report you read. But that was not until 1848. What happened before then?

We leave the pleasant town of Moree the following morning none the wiser. There is only one place that might have the answer: the State Records of New South Wales.

Chapter 24

The puzzle explained

The State Records of New South Wales are not very conveniently placed way out in Kingswood, which is the far west of Sydney, not a place I have ever visited before. Sydney, for those unfamiliar with it, is a vast sprawling city whose 'centre', or CBD (Central Business District), is actually nowhere near the centre but towards the eastern fringes. Since the ocean blocks any further spread east it can only go west, and go west it does.

So here we are at this unfamiliar building, arriving quite late in the afternoon as we've driven from Windsor, where we spent the morning in the Hawkesbury library, one of my favourite places. There is barely time to dig out the documents that I hope will tell us something about William Scott's property on the Big River. It's a folder containing around a dozen handwritten documents, so I take hasty photographs before the building shuts up shop and we continue on our way to my cousin's place in Canberra.

The following morning I am about to start transcribing these documents when I become distracted by the funeral of Malcolm Fraser, live on television. Fraser was the Liberal (what we in the UK would term Conservative) Prime Minister of Australia from 1975 to 1983, which is quite a long reign by

Australian standards. I was not living in the country then but I first heard of him as the man who ousted Gough Whitlam, the great Labor leader whom most of my Australian friends regarded as the Great White Hope. For the second time in its history the country's leader was the victim of a coup, although this one was carried out by Her Majesty's representative the Governor General Sir John Kerr. It had to do with a deadlock between the Senate and the House of Representatives, but what's important is that Malcolm Fraser's Prime Ministerial career began in controversy, and it took a long time for the truly liberal-minded in Australia to forgive him for what they viewed as an act of treachery.

(The Dismissal, as it came to be known, was regarded as the biggest constitutional crisis in Australia's history. There was no precedent, and it's believed the Queen herself had no idea what Kerr was about to do and would not have sanctioned it, as interference in politics lies outside the boundaries of British constitutional monarchy.)

Fraser became one of those older statesmen – like Jimmy Carter and, more recently and closer to home, John Major – who come into their own once they've left office, perhaps because they are able to say what they truly think. He constantly criticised his own party for their policies on asylum seekers and foreign affairs, in fact he seemed to find more common ground with the man he displaced and the man who displaced him, Labor Prime Minister Bob Hawke. Fraser's legacy is as a great humanitarian and a passionate defender of human rights. He resigned from the party when Tony Abbott, a climate change sceptic, became its leader, declaring it was 'no longer a liberal party but a conservative party'.

So while the late and great Malcolm Fraser is being laid to rest accompanied by eulogies from his family and a sweet song from his granddaughter, and outside the church a cluster of grateful Vietnamese boat people express their gratitude for the man who welcomed them into the country, I at last turn my attention to my new findings.

The documents consist of a series of letters written between 1845 and 1847 from and to William Scott, GM, the colonial secretary, two land commissioners and two govenors. The story they tell is a sad one, though probably not uncommon.

It's time to go back to the Gwydir in 1838.

~

It is early in the morning in April 1838, my story goes. Our friendly Overseer has promised to take GM and William to a piece of unoccupied land he knows of on the Gwydir, aka the Big River, opposite Thomas Hall's place at Weebollabolla, at the very limits of settlement. The cattle meanwhile are left in the safe hands of Jack Timmins and are even now calmly grazing on the Overseer's land. It has taken them a few days to settle in this strange black soil country, and to get used to the fact that for the first time for months they are not being made to travel large distances.

The three men cross the Big River, which due to the recent dry times is not currently that big. Mr Overseer assures them it is an exceptionally dry time, being April and autumn and the end of a hot summer. As he points out, you only have to see from the high water mark on the river bank how full the river usually is.

He shows them an excellent piece of unclaimed land with two natural boundaries: the Gwydir to the south and a branch of the Gwydir to the north. To the east is occupied by the Baldwin brothers, Otto and Harvest – one of the many runs they have taken up since they were displaced from the Liverpool Plains by the Australian Agricultural Company – and to the west is unknown. In due course they will discover the extent of the run is 15,680 acres, not huge by pioneer squatters' standards (Thomas Hall's station on the opposite side of the Big River for instance is nearly three times the size), but quite big enough to be going along with. And it has a good river frontage, on two sides. This is a lucky find.

It would be good to think that William's heart, and GM's, are swelling at the prospect of this piece of land being truly theirs. Or rather relatively theirs, since nobody outside the Nineteen Counties is allowed to actually *own* anything. It will be William's and GM's for one year only and maybe beyond that, who knows, at this stage GM's optimism would be paramount.

They will mark out their boundaries to the west and the east in some form and in negotiation with their neighbours. They may even build some form of humpy out of bark stripped from a nearby tree, dried over a fire and weighted down to straighten it, then arranged over saplings to form a crude hut. This will act as a temporary shelter for them and for their overseer when they've found one, and he can build himself something more substantial as and where he sees fit. Next they will need to clear enough timber to make room for their cattle to graze and from that timber construct some form of paddock to keep them penned. Newly born calves will need to be branded pretty quickly as there are thieves everywhere.

Meanwhile they will be on the lookout for a reliable and experienced overseer, as neither William nor GM has any intentions of living on the property. Very few landowners in that vicinity did in those days apparently. Their friendly Overseer informant knows of just the man: George Bull. Once all that is done it is time to bring the cattle across the river.

The run is Scott's, as the licence he took out the following year shows, while the cattle, and the capital, are GM's. For William this is the nearest he has ever come to being in possession of his very own piece of land. This would be his moment of contemplative, pipe-smoking euphoria, before the troubles begin.

Chapter 25

1838-1845 Dispossession

In 1838-39 there was a drought, and the price of stock, sheep especially, took a dive, as did the value of land. Come 1841 the country hit its first depression, the land boom came to an abrupt halt, banks failed, the price of wool fell and sheep, the saviour of colonial Australia, lost so much value farmers began slaughtering them and sending them to be boiled for tallow. The only people to profit from the depression of the early 1840s were the owners of tallow factories.

As far as I can tell it was due to a combination of factors: the drought, a recession back in England, and the inevitable bust that follows every boom in history and which our capitalist system has never managed to control, or to predict, for reasons that are beyond most people, capitalists included. There were complaints from the new chums who had been encouraged to come to Australia to take up land that there was nothing to be taken up. The Nineteen Counties were spoken for. And for the inhabitants of the Gwydir and the Liverpool Plains there were the Kamilaroi.

It's said the Kamilaroi are a particularly clever people, taller than their coastal counterparts and, at least in the early part of the 19th century, more numerous than they were elsewhere in the settled districts. Moreover they did not take the invasion of their land by the likes of William and GM lying down.

Two years before GM and Scott arrived at the Gwydir two stockmen had been killed by Aborigines on Thomas and George Hall's property on the Liverpool Plains and they'd had to abandon their station. George Bowman had lost two of his men nearby at Terrie Hie Hie, though that was in retaliation for them trying to steal Aboriginal women. Stockmen, working all day in often open countryside, were particularly vulnerable, as were their stock. The Kamilaroi had invented a trick where they trained their dogs to chase a mob of cattle until they were exhausted and then the men moved in and picked them off at their leisure, the calves in particular. At the time of GM and William's arrival there had been several deaths reported in the area, on either side of the cultural boundary, and two months later one of the most violent and bloody massacres in Australia's colonial history took place a few miles away, at Myall Creek.

It happened while William Hobbs, the manager of the station belonging to Henry Dangar, was absent. There were around 50 Kamilaroi camped on the property, by invitation, and on 9 June while the male workers were out in the paddocks a group of men, mostly convicts, rode up to the hut, grabbed hold of the rest – mostly women, children and older men – roped them together, dragged them away and slaughtered them with knives and swords. Two days later they returned, dismembered the 28 bodies, and burned them.

There was no obvious motivation for the attack. When Hobbs returned and demanded to know what had happened he was told by one of his convict stockmen the Aborigines had been slaughtering cattle, but he could see no sign of it. Hobbs told a local squatter, who rode to Sydney to report the incident. Eleven men were sent to trial, and acquitted, but two weeks later the attorney general, an Irishman and a seeker after justice called John Hubert Plunkett, called a new trial and seven of the men were found guilty and hanged. It was a pre-meditated, cold-blooded murder of unarmed and innocent people, who with tragic irony had been invited onto the station in the first place for their protection. As the newly-arrived Governor Gipps declared, there were no extenuating circumstances.

There was outrage at the hanging. It was the first time white men had been hanged for crimes against the indigenous people and for some of the more red-necked among the squatters it was beyond the pale. There were other alleged massacres of the Kamilaroi at that time, some of them not reported until many years after they happened. It's also said that at one point the Liverpool Plains was abandoned altogether by squatters because it was too dangerous.

'There is no doubt that the aborigines could have made a clean sweep of the settlers in the north-west of this State, but the fact is that they did not,' said Mr R J Webb in *The Rising Sun*. D G Bowd said much the same thing about the Hawkesbury: 'It was well within the natives' power in the first decade to drive European settlers from the Hawkesbury completely.' So why didn't they?

Firstly, in the case of the Hawkesbury, the Darug were taken by surprise. By the time they realised what the Europeans were up to and that they were not just passing through, it was too late. Also while there were plenty of them the indigenous people did not form armies, or big enough groups of organised armed men to be able to defeat the whites, with their firearms.

The Kamilaroi did come close to driving squatters from their runs on the Liverpool Plains, for the time being at least. The ones who remained, and thrived, were those who managed to form friendly relationships with them, and the longer the intelligent and friendly squatter stayed and the more he was trusted the more he was left alone. According to *The Rising Sun* again, 'The price of safety was strict tact and everlasting vigilance.'

It would have been around 1841, just as the depression was beginning to bite, that William began to find the whole thing too much for him. He may have been on a visit to his run, which had acquired the name Bullerue – ironically, virtually all the properties purloined by white squatters in the Gwydir district had Aboriginal names – and had met up with his neighbour across the river, George Hall. George and his brother Thomas were in possession of several stations in the Gwydir district including the 44,000 acres across the river from William, called Weebollabolla. No one was having an easy time of it but William, even with the help and support of GM, felt himself more vulnerable and his circumstances more straitened than most. In a conversation he was to regret, and perhaps genuinely to forget, he admitted his problems to George. He'd been paying his licence fee faithfully since 1849 but the past two years had been tougher than he ever thought possible. Look at fellow squatter Bobby Pringle for instance, who'd 'sold' his station at nearby Gurley in exchange for a couple of horses, and when asked why said that it was all the property was worth, that he was 'tired of losing money' and had come to the conclusion that drought was the natural condition of the country.

Somehow during this conversation William promised his property at Bullerue to George. It was that or the debtors' court, he must have said, or words to that effect. Yet he continued to pay his licence fee each year, and gradually as the depression eased and things began to look up he forgot about his promise. That is until his neighbour Thomas Hall confronted him one day in the early part of 1845, when Scott was on his way to visit his property, to announce that as soon as his licence was up for the year he, Hall, was moving in.

'What makes you think you can do that?' William demanded.

'A promise is a promise,' said Thomas.

'That? That was nothing. You'll have to bring your army with you.' William shrugged, and tried to laugh.

'I will,' Thomas replied. 'Be assured I will.' He went to go and turned back to add, 'It's called the Supreme Court.' And he tipped his hat and continued on his way.

It was not long after that that William received a letter from the commissioner for the Liverpool Plains district, Francis Allman, summoning him to attend a meeting that very day at his office at the headquarters of the Border Police in Liverpool Plains.

Francis Allman was a decent man, perhaps too decent for the job he'd been given, which was to monitor the behaviour of the whites and blacks in the district and to make sure licences were paid for and manage any disputes that arose between squatters, of which there were almost as many as there were squatters. He was 65 years old now and ready for retirement.

William could tell the news was bad the moment he entered the room. Allman got to his feet to shake his hand and gestured him to a chair without looking at him properly once.

He'd been requested by Thomas S Hall to dispossess Mr Scott of his run at Bullerue on account of a promise delivered to Mr Hall's brother four years before, said Allman, to his desk.

There was a pause. Allman shifted uncomfortably in his seat and forced himself to look directly at the man opposite.

'So? What do you say?'

'What promise was that?' William was blistering.

'He said you made a promise, that's all he told me. Do you deny it?' Allman's eyebrows were twitching. This was the worst part of his job.

William paused. Of course he could deny it. There were no witnesses, there was nothing on paper.

'No I don't deny it. But it was made under threat.'

'What do you mean by threat?'

'He threatened to take me to the Supreme Court. Which I can't afford, of course, even if I did win the case, which I'm sure I would.'

'In that case, why don't you?'

William took a breath. 'What chance would I have against the likes of Thomas Hall? He owns half of New South Wales.'

'A slight exaggeration, I think,' murmured Allman.

'I don't have . . . ' William spread his hands and shrugged and slumped a bit in his chair. 'I can't take the risk,' he said finally. And then, pulling himself upright again and not to sound too defeatist. 'Which is not to say I would not win the case, as I'm sure I would. But all the same it's a risk.' He paused. 'And you know as well as I do whose side the law is on when it comes to this kind of thing.'

'I would like to think,' Allman offered mildly, 'it was on the side of justice.'

William snorted. 'There's justice for the rich and there's justice for the rest of us. And it's the rest of us who are not able to take the risk who get the second kind of justice. Second rate justice, you could call it.'

There was a long pause. Allman looked surreptitiously at the clock. He hated these disputes, not so much because they were unpleasant, although they were, but because they took up so much time and in the general run of things they were not important. Important to those involved in them, obviously, and as a decent man he could see William's point of view, he might even say he sympathised with it. As a failed farmer himself he understood only too well the hazards and the randomness of the whole business.

'I do sympathise with your point of view,' he began.

'It's not a point of view, it's a fact.' William raised a repentant hand, apologising for his aggression even as he spoke. 'Do you not agree?'

'Can you not sort this out between you, you and Mr Hall?'

William laughed. 'Don't think I haven't tried.'

It's true, he had tried, but his efforts were horribly hampered by the knowledge that he had, albeit without witnesses and not in writing, made a promise, in good faith at the time. At the time he meant it. But never in a thousand years did he expect the Hall brothers to call it in all these years later. Why would they bother?

'Unfortunately a promise is a promise Mr Scott, and I have already had to concede to Mr Hall . . .'

William shifted forwards in his chair and Allman imperceptibly leant away from him. 'I have the right of first occupancy on that land, I've paid the licence fee, every year since 1839. If that doesn't give me the right to stay there what does?' Scott waited for a response. Allman scratched his head. 'What is the purpose of a licence fee if it doesn't give a man the right to farm his own land?'

'It's not, strictly speaking, your own land.'

'You know what I'm talking about Mr Allman.'

'I do. I do.' Allman's hands fluttered and came to land on the desk in front of him.

'Mr Hall owns 44,000 acres of land, three times the size of mine, he has a river frontage of ten or twelve miles on the Gwydir, why would he want to be bothered with my pocket handkerchief in the first place?'

'That's not for me to say,' said the commissioner.

Allman may not have been much of a businessman but he was good at managing men, and he had a strong sense of right and wrong and a belief that men could and should treat one another like, well, gentlemen. Unfortunately there were not many of those around these days, so while his sympathies may well lie with the 'little man', in this case William Scott – even if he did have the backing of a slightly larger man, Mr George Matcham Pitt of Richmond – a promise was a promise. Of course if the protagonists were *reasonable* men it would all be over in an instant, leaving him to attend to all those other rather more important bits of business.

'Well?' William had taken to drumming his fingers on Allman's desk and when Allman looked up he stopped.

'I'm sorry, Mr Scott,' he said, with something approaching decisiveness. 'If you cannot sort the business out between you I can only suggest you appeal to the governor.'

William sat there for a long moment. Then he stood up, nodded briefly and left.

So Scott wrote to Governor Gipps, setting out his case in detail and asking for His Excellency's intervention in what he described as a case of great personal hardship. He enclosed a hand-drawn sketch of his property on the Gwydir. The lack of punctuation and handwriting suggests he had an attorney write the letter for him. He certainly misses nothing out. The governor, needless to say, was not inclined to intervene in the matter, so Scott asked to see a copy of Allman's report. He then wrote to the colonial secretary to say that 'Geo M Pitt of Richmond' having read it informed Scott that the report stated he had voluntarily surrendered his run, which William emphatically denied, reiterating his point about the legal threat.

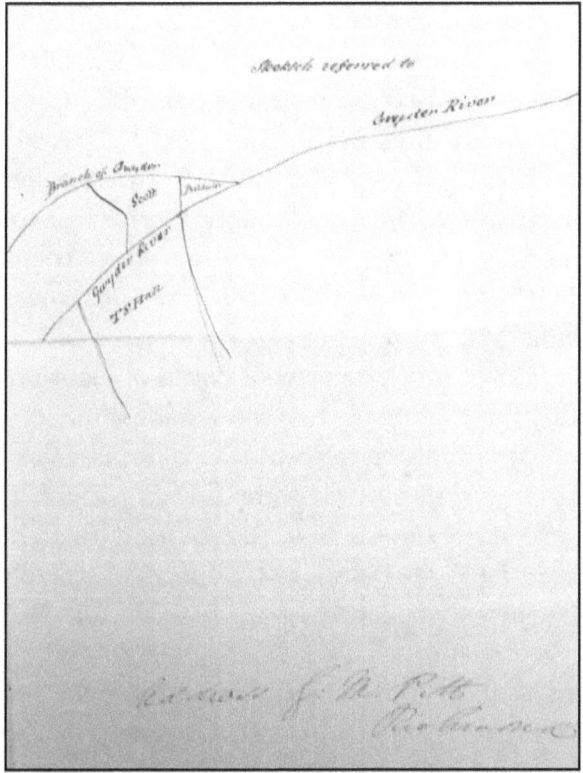

William Scott's sketch of his property on the Gwydir
(courtesy of State Archives, NSW)

The best part of a year went by during which, it appears, Hall moved onto Scott's property, Governor Gipps returned to England and Francis Allman was replaced by Roderick Mitchell, Sir Thomas's son. But still Scott kept on, and in response to his repeated appeal Mitchell wrote to him to say he was not inclined to evict Hall from the station called Bullerue as his possession of it had been authorised by the governor himself before he left the colony. As for Scott's request to have both that station and another station by the name of Courar transferred from their joint names into the sole name of Mr Pitt, Mitchell concurred with the latter but not the former.

The following year in July 1846 GM, taking advantage of the confusion, himself applied for and was granted the licence for 'Bullaroo' [sic]. He then wrote requesting once again the intervention of the governor (now Sir Charles Fitzroy) in order to prevent Commissioner Mitchell from acting in contravention of the licence that had been granted him for the station now occupied by Mr Thomas Hall. After a baffled pause he was told the licence had been issued to him in error – a fact he would have been aware of but presumably happy to exploit. It took several months for he and Scott to return the licence and receive their refund. And there, over two years since it began, the matter ended.

On the face of it it looks like a battle of David and Goliath: the wealthy landowner with the establishment behind him versus the smallholder. Except in this case the victor was Goliath. George Hall occupied 'three stations with a frontage of ten miles to each on the Big River' for which he had paid licence fees of £37, £47 and £48 respectively; while Scott and Pitt had paid two licences of £10 each for 'Bullaroo' and 'Coura'.

There was a fair amount of passing the buck on the part of pretty well everyone involved. Yet this was just one of thousands of land disputes, part and parcel of the early days of squatting.

Scott's landowning days would appear to be over for the time being; on the face of it it looks as if GM's attempts to bail him out had come too late.

But it was not the last time GM was to find himself in dispute over property.

Chapter 26

1840s: The price of capitalism

Squatters, particularly wealthy ones such as Gipps's *bête noir* William Wentworth, spent years running battles with various governors over their 'uncertainty of position'. They protested that 'The Authorities would not let, they would not sell; would give no tenure, would promise no compensation'. One squatter had had his station taken from him because of a misdemeanour committed by his stockman: 'a piece of justice equivalent to hanging a gentleman in England for a murder committed by his coachman,' Wentworth spluttered. In response Gipps commented that their protests only went to show the occupiers of these lands considered they had an automatic right to ownership of them in perpetuity, and that what they were really hoping for was for Her Majesty to divest herself of all her rights over her colonial Crown Lands.

The continuing arguments did nothing for Sir George Gipps's health and he left the colony in July 1846 a sick man, and an unpopular one: not just among the squatters but in the press as well, who accused him of siding with the Crown against the colonists. Like so many governors before him Sir George had arrived in the colony with the best of honest intentions, only to find it impossible to reconcile both the various factions within the colony and the pressures from Her

Majesty's government back home, who still held sway when it came to such things as land regulations. It wasn't until some time after he had departed the colony, and the world, that Gipps's achievements were properly recognised. (His online biographer, Samuel Clyde McCulloch, said of him years later, 'On Australia's roll of governors his name must rank high.')

In March 1847 at a meeting attended by Queen Victoria, her husband Albert, the Prime Minister Lord Palmerston, the Bishop of London and the Lord Chamberlain, the new governor of Australia Sir Charles Fitzroy was empowered to grant fourteen-year leases on grants of land to whoever he considered suitable; the rent to be proportionate to the number of sheep or cattle the run was capable of carrying. Each lot should be rectangular unless a river or creek rendered it impossible, and no single lot should have more than 440 yards of direct frontage onto a waterway. At the end of the lease the lessee had the option of buying the run for the value of its 'unimproved' (ie original) state. Applications for leases would be published, like wedding banns, in the government gazettes, so members of the public could object to any application if they thought they had grounds to do so.

So it was that GM finally took legal possession of 72 square miles of what we established to be completely flat and, in 2015, treeless country north of what is now the town of Moree. In 1848 his application appeared in the Government Gazette:

> 'Coorar - 72^2 miles. Estimated grazing capabilities: 1500 cattle. Bounded by Fitzgerald on the south 6 miles, Coorar Creek and Mr J Hoskinson N 12 miles; R Skulthorpe W 6 miles; SW* miles by waste lands.' [*From the map it looks as if this should read 'NW']

GM held Coorar for eight years before it was transferred to his neighbour John Hoskisson in 1854. At some point he also bought another run in the district along with Lewis Duncan Whittaker called Bangheet. It was sold in December 1857 and four years later it was the subject of a court case, about which more later.

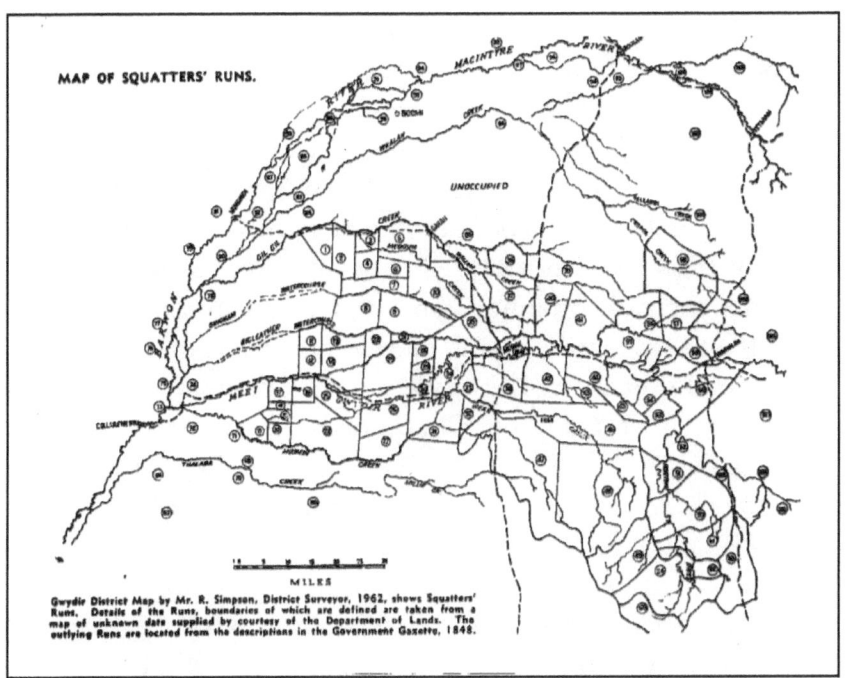

Early squatters' runs on the Gwydir (from *The Rising Sun*,
R J Webb, courtesy of Moree & District Historical Society Inc)
'Bullerue' is 38A (in Moree), 'Coorar' 5, 'Bangheet' 52

Many years after GM's death, on the occasion of his son RM's 83rd birthday in December 1932, the *Stock and Station Journal* told the story of how GM as 'a young fellow' left the Hawkesbury and drove a number of cows and calves on foot all the way to Moree.

> 'A few years later the calves, now grown into bullocks, were travelled to Sydney as fats and again Mr GM Pitt was on foot. Butchers met him out near Kurrajong, paid him £1 a head for the cattle and promised to give him 22/6 if he would bring another lot down. Mr Pitt brought them along. It was such stuff that the founders and builders of Australia were made.'

It's a romantic picture: the young GM tramping to and fro across the countryside with his cattle, and it's not true. If anyone was droving stock to and from his property near what was later Moree it would have been Jack Timmins, though it's more than possible GM did meet and negotiate with the butchers at Kurrajong.

By comparison with fellow squatters such as Wentworth, the Blaxlands, Benjamin Boyd, the Hall brothers and even his own neighbours Robert Fitzgerald and John Hoskisson, GM was very small fry. He continued to buy and sell leases on runs up until the 1860s, in the Wellington district particularly. But his main focus of attention remained on Richmond, home to himself and his family, and to most of his activities.

While William and he were still wrangling with the authorities over Bullaroo GM joined the committee of the Hawkesbury Agricultural Association and the Hawkesbury Benevolent Society (of which his father Thomas had been a founder), acted as steward at the Hawkesbury Races and was appointed trustee for the Windsor Branch of the Savings Bank of New South Wales. In 1847, he took out a loan of £500 against his property at Bronte – possibly to fund his activities further afield – which he paid back four years later. And he became the father of several children.

Chapter 27

1840s: The women

With all the talk of the drovers, the squatters, the stockmen and other Australian legendary characters including the swagman (an itinerant worker who travelled on foot looking for work with his 'swag' on his back) and the sundowner (an itinerant worker who travelled on foot and turned up at sundown, too late for a day's work but not too late for a meal and a bed), a person might wonder – what of the women?

I never did hear of any female drovers, stock- or swag-women, though there were women among the early landowners in the Moree area, and doubtless elsewhere. There were certainly female farmers in the earlier days of colonial Australia, most notably Elizabeth Macarthur, who was arguably more responsible for the success of her husband's Merino sheep farm than her largely absentee husband John, who was exiled twice to the old country for lengthy periods for misbehaviour of one sort or another. When William Cox, originally of the New South Wales Corps, was away for four years in England dealing with allegations concerning the misuse of army funds his wife Rebecca, along with their young sons, took great pains to preserve their carefully-bred strain of Merino sheep.

There was no shortage of notable women in 19th century

colonial Australia. Some, such as Anna King (wife of the governor) and Colonel Paterson's wife Susan set up an orphanage. Others like Mary Reibey ran successful businesses. Caroline Chisholm, who settled in Windsor, devoted her life to the welfare of destitute female immigrants. Catherine Helen Spence dedicated hers to teaching, writing novels, public speaking and campaigning – successfully – for women's suffrage. (South Australia introduced female suffrage in 1895, years ahead of the mother country and most of the rest of the world.) Not forgetting – while we're on this roll – writers Miles Franklin, Mary Gilmore and many others.

But it's true to say the typical 19th century Australian woman was more likely to be a wife or a mother or a daughter who helped out on the farm or whatever business her husband/son/father was concerned with, but whose main responsibility lay with the household and looking after the children. There were exceptions, Mary Johnson-Aull among them, who I surmise did more to keep the Governor Darling going than her husband. Some of these women, the drovers' wives especially, lived lives of extreme isolation like Henry Lawson's *Drover's Wife,* stuck out there on a property in the middle of nowhere, just her and the children, coping with venomous snakes, droughts, bushfires, dubious swagmen and who knows what other hazards of bush life, on her own for nine or ten months in a year. It wasn't easy being the wife of an early squatter either, again living miles from anywhere, often under canvas, or bark, far away from friends and society. It was those massive distances, and the lack of communication with the outside world. The harshness of the landscape and the unpredictability of the climate, the uncertain future. The loneliness, the tedium. The lack of good medical care.

There were women who had to put up with living under canvas while waiting not just for their house, but for the town their house was to be in to be built; like Mary Thomas, who arrived in what was not yet Adelaide in 1836 and spent her first year in a tent followed by a mud hut. The other prevailing occupation, for women of rank, was charity work.

But for the average wife and mother, domestic duties took up all their time. At Bronte there would have been prayers before breakfast every day, and then the children taken to school by horse and cart with GM, or Will, if they were around, or one of their workers when they were not. Those same children may have put in several hours' work in the morning before school, as their fathers had done. On Sundays there would be the obligatory pilgrimage to St Peter's Church in Richmond. Evenings would be spent around the fireside in winter or on the veranda in summer, the women sewing while the men read to them by the light of candles.

And then there were those standards to be maintained. Increased prosperity and status brought – along with the luxury of beeswax candles to replace the smelly and smoky tallow or the slush lamp (made from dripping from the family meal and a wick made of wood or rag) – increased work and responsibility, and therefore servants to do it all for you. Fine china had to be handled with exceptional care. Linen sheets were 'beetled', that's to say given a hammering to soften them and then stretched and folded in a particular way to avoid creasing. Woollen garments should be shaken and stretched after washing to avoid shrinkage - anyone could tell a poor or lazy household from the way the man of the house's flannels had turned to felt.

To make quite sure everyone knew their place, especially at formal events such as the local ball, a chalk line would be drawn on the floor or a rope rigged across it to separate the 'grandees' from the 'commonage', lest the guests be submitted to the horrifying spectacle of watching 'ordinary trades people dancing right in among the squatters and their wives and daughters', so said Mary Gilmore.

There was also fashion to keep an eye on. Despite the totally different climate and conditions Australians seemed to follow European fashion slavishly. Skirts were filling out, on their way to morphing into cumbersome crinolines. Hairstyles were becoming more and more elaborate, on formal occasions requiring extra hands to perfect the architecture.

In the politest households men and women understood their roles and did not criticise one another except in the politest terms, by enquiring, for instance, *sotto voce*, whether the vegetables had been picked and placed in the coolest part of the pantry to keep them fresh, or the burrs had been removed from the horses' tails. Thus, in this utopian world, men and women were happy in their skins and got along with one another perfectly.

Julia and GM's first surviving child, George Matcham junior, was born on 28 October 1837. He would have been around four months old when his father left on his trip to the far northwest. Australian women were used to producing and bringing up their children on their own, it was partly what made them so resourceful. Julia would have had some kind of domestic help, and there was always her mother Mary living nearby. Or was there?

I mentioned a few chapters ago a Eureka moment when I was hunting for news of Mary Aull-Johnson and came upon something quite unexpected. It was a notice, placed by Mary's husband Robert Aull in various newspapers in February 1839. It said:

> 'CAUTION
>
> THE Public are hereby cautioned against giving my Wife, MARY AULL, of Richmond, credit, she having left her home without any just cause, as I will not be answerable for any debts by her contracted from this date, and any person or persons found harbouring her hereafter, I have instructed my legal adviser to proceed against them for the same.
>
> ROBERT AULL.
>
> Richmond, February 5, 1839.'

The 'advertisement' appears three times in *The Colonist* and once in the *Sydney Morning Herald*.

So Mary walked out on Robert, and he did not like it. The

notice has all the hallmarks of an angry man, a man abandoned in his view 'without any just cause'. It is not unlike the many notices Robert placed over the years about his missing stock and threatening anyone who might be 'harbouring' them. It's as if he regarded Mary as chattel rather than wife.

What can one read into this? On the surface it seems clear: she left him for another man – hence the threat against 'anyone found harbouring her'. He is not so much concerned for her welfare as for his, or more specifically for his finances. Four times he placed the notice. *Four times.*

This where the novelist in me longs to invent some fantasy about the dashing young – or maybe that should be middle-aged – knight on the white charger who whisked Mary off to a life of delirium and derring-do. But the family historian reminds me that this was my three times great grandmother and my task is to search the records for the facts. And so I do.

The 1841 census throws up nothing: no Mary Johnsons, Johnstons or Aulls, which is not necessarily significant as the only person named was the (male) head of the household. Robert, as we already know, was living in Upper Richmond with a single woman who was neither his wife nor a servant.

GM is listed as living on Nelson Farm with four males, including himself, his son GM junior and two other males between 14 and 55, and three females: his wife Julia, their one-year-old daughter Jessie and a girl aged between 14 and 20 (who a family member tells me was Jane Bibben, who arrived at Nelson Farm from the orphanage in 1840 aged 16 and was working for the family as a domestic servant). So Mary was not living with them. I can find no sign of either of Mary's younger children John or Sarah, who would have been 21 and 19 respectively.

Then along comes another snippet of news, courtesy of another family member, and that is the birth of a James Aull on 26 March 1840, father Robert Aull, mother Mary Day, crossed out. Who Mary Day was is another unknown. In 1840 Mary Aull-Johnson would have been 50 years old, a bit long in the tooth to be producing children. James's mother may or may not have been the unnamed woman listed in the census as living with Robert. Since there is no sign of James on that census, or on any other records since, the assumption is he died an infant.

So Mary's story after she left Robert remains a mystery. Robert relinquished the lease of the Governor Darling soon after she absconded, and the only other mention of her was in 1842, when Robert sold his property in Richmond 'but preserved his wife's life interest in the land'. She died in Upper Richmond on 21 August 1867, aged 77, and was buried under the name of Mary Johnson. The death certificate, registered by John Johnson (presumably her son) only lists her first marriage, which is meaningful in itself.

One can only hope the last 30 odd years of her life brought some form of happiness to the woman who went from eighteen-year-old felon to shopkeeper, landowner, wife of two and mother of three (surviving) in the exotic and changeable world of early colonial Australia.

Meanwhile over the next twenty years Mary's daughter Julia produced twelve children, nine of whom survived into adulthood. She was 21 when her first child was born and 42 when she gave birth to her youngest, Eva Laura. She was coming near to fulfilling the expectation that, according to J C Fizgerald in *Those Were the Days*, 'Most people add one child to their family every year.'

Chapter 28

1842/3 The law and the Aborigines

In 1842 an Aboriginal man named 'Fryingpan' appeared at the Maitland Assize Court accused of spearing cattle on William Scott's property Bullerue, on the Gwydir. I was looking for details about the trial when I came upon what looked like an eye witness account of it written by none other than Charles Dickens.

To be precise, although Fryingpan did appear in the court along with his friend the Duke of Wellington (their monikers were probably bestowed on them by convicts), only Wellington was actually tried that day, possibly because the only witness to Fryingpan's alleged crime, Scott's overseer George Bull, was absent.

The detailed account of the trial appeared in a piece called *Going Circuit at the Antipodes,* one of many essays that appeared in Dickens's *Household Words,* published in 1852. The writer gave a vivid description of the accused: tall and gaunt, about 35 years of age, with 'large, flashing, expressive, deep-set eyes', a mop of 'coarse-matted black hair hung about his shoulders' and wearing nothing but a dirty blanket. It took some pushing and shoving to get him into the dock, but the moment he set eyes on the judge he broke into 'a violent grin', said the writer. Transfixed by the Chief Justice's wig and gown, Wellington's grin quickly developed into an outright laugh, but rather than attempting to suppress it he turned to the rest of the court and invited them to join in the joke; which, despite themselves, they did. Even the sour-faced Sheriff had to turn his back to laugh into his sleeve, and such was the air of general merriment the Chief Justice himself had difficulty keeping his face straight.

Notwithstanding, when the court eventually calmed down an interpreter was brought in and the indictment read and translated to the prisoner. There followed a brief, energetic conversation between prisoner and interpreter before the answer was delivered to the court: 'May it please your Honor, he only says it's all a pack of lies, and that he never speared the cattle at all; but he thinks he knows the blackfellow that did spear them, and he will bring him down to the court in a few days, if your Honor will allow him to go and look for him.'

Unfortunately for Wellington his plea was contradicted by several witnesses and he was found guilty and transported for ten years to Van Diemen's Land. He was led from the court still grinning, 'as if he had got to the end of a pleasant entertainment'.

Our onlooker, while enjoying the spectacle, was on reflection appalled and dismayed. What right do we have, he wrote, to submit 'this poor child of nature' to 'an English court of justice, mock his ignorance with a jargon of law forms, and conclude by tearing him from his hunting grounds, his wife, and little children, for ten years?' And yet, he went on to ask himself, how else might a colonist's property be protected? He had no answer to his own question.

I assumed the writer to have been Charles Dickens himself, but it wasn't until I tried to find out more about his trip to Australia that I discovered he never actually visited the country, even though it featured many times in his books, and that he was in America anyway in March 1842. *Household Words* was 'conducted' by him, which means compiled by him and edited by others, and the articles drawn from other writers, who remained anonymous by agreement – which was not unusual at the time. Further hunting revealed the writer was a 'London barrister' by the name of Archibald Michie, who'd arrived in Sydney a few years earlier and had been invited to attend the court by an Australian lawyer friend, who owned a property nearby.

The fact that the piece was written by someone else does not make it less noteworthy however, and notwithstanding the family historian's natural eagerness to find connections with famous people it is worth including here as an example of how colonial law dealt with Aboriginal wrongdoers. (In the early days of settlement it was believed an Aborigine could not appear in court at all as he or she could not swear an oath on the Bible. Governor Gipps tried to introduce an 'Aborigines' Evidence Bill' allowing Aboriginal people to testify in court if their evidence was corroborated, but the British Government vetoed it.)

Moreover the empathy and understanding the writer reveals for the plight of a man stripped of everything he has ever known – other Aborigines 'transported' away from their familiar lands invariably did not survive for long – sounds distinctly Dickensian. Dickens could well have written the article himself and most likely did, since it appears he often rewrote the stories that were sent to him.

Meanwhile Fryingpan's case did not come up in court until the following year, on 18 March 1843, and this time the recorder was a journalist from the *Sydney Morning Herald*.

The story went that one day back in August 1839 George Bull was out inspecting the property Bullerue with his employer William Scott when they came upon the cattle running around with their tongues hanging out, which Bull took to mean 'the blacks had been rushing them'. The two men gathered firearms and rode out to a waterhole where the cattle usually congregated, but found no one there. On his way back Bull, on his own by now, spotted a group of Aboriginal men cutting up a cow which had just been killed. They called out to him – 'coulou' – in a friendly manner, but when he began to approach they flung spears at him, at which he raised his gun and they scattered.

Why it took so long to bring the case to court was a mystery, to the judge and to everyone else, though it probably had to do with a lack of interpreter. (Both Fryingpan and Wellington had appeared in court before but their cases had been postponed until an interpreter could be found.)

Like Wellington, the defendant pleaded Not Guilty to spearing and killing the cow and again an interpreter was produced, though whether or not Fryingpan found the court proceedings as hilarious as his friend is not recorded. The only witness to the crime was George Bull, so it was the Aborigine's word against the white man's, and the white man's prevailed. Fryingpan, like Wellington before him, was sentenced to ten years' transportation to Van Diemen's Land. The reporter ended his account thus: 'It appeared that the prisoner was one of the most fierce and desperate of his tribe in the district, and at the time the cow was killed, he and others were armed evidently with the intention of committing depredations.'

Well, who knows, perhaps Fryingpan did have 'form', as we call it now. Nonetheless, as with his compatriot the Duke of Wellington it looks as if the odds were ludicrously stacked against a man who was not just regarded as inferior because of his race, but who had been submitted to a procedure completely beyond his comprehension and conducted by men in fancy dress. Worst of all, guilty or not, to tear such a man away from all he knew was a very harsh punishment indeed.

The fact that George Bull went to such lengths to bring Fryingpan to court over the killing of one cow at first glance might seem excessive. At the same time according to the *Maitland Mercury* 'Seven head of cattle and a horse had been killed that day by the blacks' – or so it was assumed rather than proven – and Fryingpan had already served a fourteen-month prison sentence (for crimes unspecified). I hunted to see what happened to him subsequently but, unsurprisingly, drew a blank.

In the course of my researches I came upon a scathing indictment in the *Colonial Observer* of Governor Gipps's attitude towards Aboriginal people on trial. Gipps had complained to the Legislative Council about the costs involved in providing counsel for men such as Fryingpan and Wellington. Hitherto the Reverend Threlkeld, who was a great champion of the Aboriginal people, had acted on their behalf in court cases, but since he had been 'dismissed' by the government (meaning he was no longer hired or paid by them) the chief justice had recommended that Aborigines should be represented by lawyers, who should receive moderate fees in the form of three guineas to the barrister and two guineas to the attorney. According to the governor however the two separate bills for representing Fryingpan and Wellington had soared to over £19 each, which suggested the lawyers were deliberately creating work for one another. It seems in the course of his complaints Sir George had called the judiciary names (not repeated in the article), thereby, in the view of the writer, bringing the whole profession into disrepute.

Moreover, 'The Governor's grudging the expense of defending the poor aborigines, Wellington and Fryingpan, and actually proposing the abolition of the office of standing counsel for the defence of such of that unfortunate race as may be arraigned on a criminal charge, furnish but a miserable comment on the generous sentiments to which he gave utterance only a week before,' said the man from the *Colonial Observer*. Sir George obviously preferred to see a black convicted and murdered than pay £19.15s for his defence, was the implication.

This is unfair on the governor. There is nothing in his remarks that says Gipps did not consider the Aborigines worthy of legal representation, he was merely complaining about the behaviour of the legal profession. After all Gipps was the same governor who had tried to pass a bill allowing Aborigines to become witnesses in criminal cases in court, and along with his attorney general John Plunkett made sure the perpetrators of the Myall Creek massacre were brought to justice and punished. In fact Gipps showed a good deal more patience and compassion toward the Aboriginal people than Governor Macquarie before him. Following the attack at the Broken River back in 1838 when seven men working for GM's cousins William and George Faithfull were killed by Aborigines, Gipps immediately and unilaterally (ie without consulting the Legislative Council) gave precise orders that there should be no random attacks of retaliation and that the incident would be thoroughly investigated by a police magistrate, using firearms in self defence only. He was attacked in the *Herald* (the forerunner to the *Sydney Morning Herald*) for being over-sympathetic to the Aborigines – whom that same organ called 'the most degraded barbarians known to exist on the face of the earth'. It appears the governor of New South Wales, whoever he was and however good his intentions, could do no right.

But even Gipps lost heart over the years. It was his determination in the early days of his tenure to uphold the rights of the Aboriginal people that made him so unpopular with some squatters and members of the press. But he must have felt he was fighting a losing battle. By the time he came to leave he'd closed down all government support for missions and dismissed the Reverend Threlkeld, who'd worked alongside the Aboriginal people all his adult life, without explanation or thanks. He left the colony, like so many governors before him, defeated and disliked by landowners, the press and the Legislative Council; everyone, in fact, except the ordinary people and his loyal colonial secretary Sir Edward Deas Thomson.

Chapter 29

1843: Self government

Australia has rarely been the major focus of British attention, partly because in their eyes nothing much of interest happens there, or ever did. There were not the major wars or organised frontier disputes between colonists and indigenous people as there were in South Africa, or even New Zealand. Local skirmishes aside New South Wales was pretty peaceful by 19th century global standards, yet it took until the 1840s before the British government even began to think about proper self government for their still fledgling outpost.

In the late 1830s the Mother country started to reassess her policy of transportation. It was regarded as an 'archaic' form of punishment, and migrants were still understandably reluctant to make their home in a colony peopled by convicts. 'To dwell in Sydney,' pronounced Sir William Molesworth, MP, who'd never been there, 'would be much the same as inhabiting the lowest purlieus of St Giles's.' There was also pressure to abolish transportation within Australia from those who resented this scurrilous perception of their country. The only people who directly opposed abolition were the landowners, led by William Wentworth, who wanted to continue to benefit from the free labour.

Transportation to New South Wales ended in 1840 (it was

briefly and temporarily resumed in 1849, to great public outcry), and in its place the British colonial office introduced a 'bounty system', whereby able-bodied people were offered money to emigrate, and single men could be sponsored by settlers. The last convict ship to set sail arrived in Sydney in November 1840.

Immigration meanwhile rose from 407 in 1831 to more than 20,000 in 1841, and the population as a whole increased in that time by 70 percent to over 130,000. Of them less than a third were still-serving convicts or ex-convicts, many of whom had become wealthy pillars of society. At last, 'Australia . . . had ceased to be a joke in Britain', according to historian Frank Welsh.

The Legislative Council (that later became and still is the Upper House) was conceived back in the 1820s under Sir Thomas Brisbane in the form of a five- and later a ten- and fifteen-member advisory council to the governor. It was introduced by the Motherland as a way of curtailing the authority of the governor following what they considered to be the presumption of Governor Macquarie – who tended to do what he wanted and only later inform the British government, by which time it was too late to undo anything. In 1843 the Constitution Act expanded the membership of the Council to 36, some of them elected by wealthier landowners, and some appointed by the governor himself.

The first New South Wales election in 1843 was accompanied by riots in Sydney, Melbourne, Windsor and other regional centres, the causes of which differed according to which account you happen to read. The franchise was confined to adult males owning property worth at least £200, which excluded two-thirds of the male population (and one hundred percent of the female). In Sydney the main target of mob rioting was William Wentworth and his fellow party member Dr Bland, who despite having their polling booths wrecked and their 'colours' destroyed were duly elected.

The election in GM's local constituency of Cumberland

Boroughs – which comprised Windsor, Richmond, Campbelltown and Liverpool – was also accompanied by fanfare and rioting. The contenders were William Bowman of Richmond and Robert Fitzgerald of Windsor, both of whom held public meetings in their respective towns in the run-up to the election to drum up support. GM joined the General Committee in support of Bowman, along with what looks like most of the other male residents of Richmond.

Come the day of the election itself each candidate provided their own uniformed band and colours – blue flags for Bowman and green for Fitzgerald – playing in turn and congregating at the Windsor Courthouse. On his arrival in his carriage Bowman was hit by stones thrown by members of the crowd and his flagpole seized and broken in two, at which point general rioting broke out that lasted throughout the day and well into the evening, despite the presence of mounted troopers. Another account claims the trigger for the riots was an unprovoked attack by Bowman's people on a Fitzgerald supporter, to which the latter retaliated with interest, as they say.

Amidst the melee the votes were counted, and while initially it seemed Fitgerald had prevailed in Windsor and Richmond, when results arrived from Campbelltown later that evening they appeared to be for Bowman, by one vote. The final count was a majority of three votes in favour of Bowman.

It's not clear why Australia's first ever elections spawned riots. It may have been general discontent on the part of the majority of the un-enfranchised, or in the case of Wentworth something more personal, or because of the general helplessness brought about by the depression. The landowners, led by William Wentworth, blamed Governor Gipps. The governor blamed the banks for handing out insecure loans. The people blamed everything and everybody.

Chapter 30

1848-1860: Local matters

In July 1848, the Pitt and Scott household increased by one when Betsey, William's eldest daughter, gave birth to a baby called William. The father was Jack Timmins, the drover, and it's said by a family descendant (Gene Makim) that he was away at the time of the baby's arrival, probably at the Gwydir with GM. The happy couple legitimised baby William a couple of months later when they married in the Presbyterian Church in Kurrajong in September that year.

Despite having named her first-born after her father Betsey fell out with him at some point, as she was the only one of his offspring who was not mentioned in his will. Ms Makim claims this was because William, whom she describes as a 'dour Scot', took against Betsey's marriage to Timmins because he was 'a Paddy', though she offers no evidence for this. My theory, and it's only a theory, is that the breach had more to do with Timmins' association with the Hall brothers, who'd 'stolen' William's property on the Gwydir.

Thomas Hall was known for not just owning over a million acres of good New South Wales farming land but for breeding dogs. They were a cross between his own border collies and wild dingoes and he called them 'Hall's Heelers'. At some point in the late 1840s Timmins went to work for Thomas Hall as a contract drover in the Upper Hunter region and was given a pair of Hall's Heelers, from which he bred his own brand of dog that came to be known as 'Timmins' Biters' (for obvious reasons).

My theory goes that Timmins and Thomas Hall made one another's acquaintance while Jack was at the Gwydir with Scott and GM. A skilled drover like Timmins would have been much sought-after, and I'm speculating Scott may have witnessed his future son-in-law doing the deal with his arch-enemy. True or not, I prefer this theory to Ms Makim's assertion that Scott was bigoted towards 'the Paddys and Micks' and was jealous of his son in law's horsemanship.

There are signs Timmins continued to work on and off for GM – droving his stock to and from his properties at the Gwydir and elsewhere – and some years later he received a silver pocket watch from him in recognition of faithful services rendered. GM also helped Timmins to acquire a block of land in 1871 called Rocky Holes, adjoining Gunyerwarildi station north of Warialda (east of Moree), where he and Betsey lived for fifteen years. Jack and Betsey's son James, born in 1850, later married GM's niece – his sister Mary Matcham Laycock's daughter – also confusingly called Mary Matcham Laycock (who made a brief appearance earlier in the Wollumbi Museum).

Meanwhile back in Richmond GM was appointed onto the committee of the Richmond branch of the Hawkesbury & Nepean Church of England Lay Association of NSW, along with his by now ageing uncle William Faithfull; joined a citizens' group campaigning for a road from Windsor and Richmond to Bathurst; collaborated with others to acquire the deeds to Richmond Common; was appointed a trustee for the Windsor branch of the Savings Bank of NSW and became a commissioner for the Richmond Road Trust. His role as a founder member of the Hawkesbury Agricultural Association included acting as judge of the various ploughing competitions at the local show (categories included the best son of a farmer and best youth under eighteen, and a medal was also awarded to the servant 'who has been longest in the hired service of one master').

GM also completed some profitable property deals in the Highlands south of Sydney, on a 32-acre farm at Yarramundi and further afield in the Wellington district.

In 1855 there was a rumour GM was intending to stand as candidate for the Legislative Council for the counties of Cook and Westmoreland, though nothing appeared to come of it. The following year his cousin James Robert Wilshire presented a petition on GM's behalf to the newly-formed Legislative Assembly protesting against the incorporation of the Richmond Bridge Company.

It might seem odd that Richmond and Windsor residents had managed for so long without a proper bridge across the Hawkesbury. Traffic across the river was heavy and the only form of conveyance for people, carriages, horses and sheep (but not cattle) was by a large punt, which caused huge queues and tailbacks and delays lasting up to a week. The year before a few 'enterprising men' had formed a company to build a bridge over the Nepean, upriver from Richmond. It spanned 70 feet from bank to bank and cost a fair whack. A year after it was completed, to great fanfare and celebration, a flood destroyed four of the bridge's spans. This – the Hawkesbury-Nepean's tendency to flood – presumably explains why it took so long to find a way to build bridges across it.

Undeterred Robert Fitzgerald (he who lost out in the election by one vote) proposed to form another company named 'The Richmond Pitt Bridge Company' in order to build a bridge over the Hawkesbury at Richmond. George Matcham Pitt, seemingly unimpressed at the suggested use of his name, objected on the grounds that he had taken out a five-year lease on the punt, and while he was in theory in favour of the bridge – although he felt it should be made of stone rather than wood, to withstand the inevitable floods – he felt it only fair he should be compensated for loss of revenue. It was for this that he asked his cousin to petition on his behalf in the Assembly, a petition that did not impress the Speaker, who dismissed his demands out of hand.

And so work began the following year to construct a massive nineteen-span bridge connecting Richmond to the Kurrajong Hills. Made of ironbark, it was 850 feet long and cost upwards of £1,000. It was completed in 1860. The punt continued operating however, transporting sheep and people and charging, by agreement and presumably in competition, the same toll as the bridge.

It was in operation on 20 August 1857, when the Hawkesbury flooded yet again, and 'old Mr George Pitt rode down on his horse' to check on Alfred Smith, who operated the punt, and who later described his employer as 'a grand old man and always solicitous for those in his employ'. ('Old' George Pitt was 43 years old in 1857.)

In 1860 GM joined the Freemasons and became a Volunteer.

The Volunteers were a body of laymen who were formed to defend their country from what they saw as possible invasion, especially by the French, bearing in mind the threat of war hovering over the Motherland. They swore allegiance to Her Majesty Queen Victoria and promised to defend her against all her 'opposers'. A meeting was held in September 1860 at Windsor to explain the duties and purpose of the Volunteers and GM was one of many to put himself forward.

According to 'Cooramill', aka local resident Sam Boughton, back in 1851 (probably a mistake, as the Volunteers weren't formed until 1860) a Captain Egerton promised some of the Richmondites, including GM, that if they could muster ten or twelve men he would send his drill-instructor Sergeant Mawson to put them through their paces. 'Twelve good men and true' were duly recruited and taken to a quiet spot near Hobartville where they learned the 'goose step', away from the public eye. 'After they had got over their nervousness, and knew the right foot from the left without the proverbial piece of hay and straw attached,' Boughton wrote, 'the drill was carried out in the pound paddock.' Observing them, Boughton recorded the 'veteran Mr Pitt' (he'd have been 37 in 1851 and 46 in 1860) was as active and more enthusiastic than any of the younger men. He was a crack shot with the rifle too. 'There was no rifle match without him being one of the selected to take part.'

~

By the end of 1857 GM and Julia's family was complete. Their lastborn, Eva Laura, joined eight surviving siblings – GM junior, Jessie, Julia, Edwin, Harry Austin, Robert (RM), Colin and Charles Bryan – each of them born roughly two years apart. Three died in infancy.

There was not a lot in the way of midwifery in those days. Some of the older generation – Elizabeth and her sisters in law Susanna, Lucy, Hester and Jemima – had been cared for by the convict Margaret Catchpole, self-made nurse, general help, all-round legend and subject of 'Catchpoleiana'. But Margaret had departed the scene years earlier. In pre-anaesthetic days the go-to painkiller for birthing mothers was opium, which was apparently freely available, in Steedman's Teething Powders among other tinctures.

Doctors, midwives, medicine men and healers in general were in short supply in the early colony, and in cases of need priority was inevitably given to the head of the family, the breadwinner, who was very rarely a woman. The gentler sex had to be tougher than their other halves in many ways, and you could say they still are.

Chapter 31

1850s: Australia and how to find it

The 1850s was an eventful decade in Australia, and not just because of the discovery of gold.

It was a man by the name of Edward Hargraves, an Australian who had worked the goldmines in California, who first discovered gold near Bathurst, west of Sydney, early in 1851. Minerals found on Crown Land were naturally declared to be the property of the Crown so the quick-thinking governor, Sir Charles Fitzroy, immediately introduced licenses costing 30 shillings a month for anyone who wanted to chance their arm as a prospector, in the hope of avoiding a rush.

The Bathurst find was nothing compared to what turned up further south, near the towns of Bendigo and Ballarat in particular. The result was an explosion in the population as migrants from all over the world – Britain, Europe, America and China – flooded into the newly-formed colony of Victoria. Pamphlets were hurriedly produced to help them on their way, including one called *The Australian Colonies: Where They Are and How to Get to Them*. In 1852 alone 100,000 people arrived in Australia. In the ten years from 1850 to 1860 Victoria's population went from 97,000 to 540,000, and in the country as a whole from around 405,000 to over one million. Ships' crews deserted and the salaries of government officials were doubled to deter them from abandoning their positions. In the outer reaches there was an acute shortage of labour as swathes of farm workers downed tools and raced to try their luck in the goldfields. Central Melbourne became a ghost town, with only two policemen left on duty. Society ladies, finding themselves suddenly servantless, were forced to abandon 'all thoughts of appearance' and even had to open their own front doors to visitors.

Meanwhile the colony was beginning to split into what 50 years later would become identified as separate states. Port Phillip had been renamed Melbourne (there was a glorious moment when it was very nearly called Batmania, after its earliest white settler John Batman), and in 1851 the colony of Victoria came into existence. South Australia and its capital town of Adelaide had been planned, named and established in 1836 before there was anything there, and the land was advertised and sold to free settlers 'off the plan' before any of them had set foot in the country. Mary Thomas was just one of around 4,000 new migrants living under canvas in 1838 while they waited for their house to be built in a city that did not yet exist. The Colony of Queensland was officially established in 1859, and in Western Australia the Swan River Colony renamed itself Perth and elected Sir James Stirling as its first governor. Meanwhile Van Diemen's Land was granted responsible self government in 1856 and changed its name to Tasmania.

The 1850 Australian Colonies Government Act authorised Legislative Councils for Victoria, South Australia and Van Diemen's Land, with two-thirds of the members elected by a restricted franchise, as in New South Wales. The colonies were also allowed to amend their own constitutions and create their own form of government, with one or two chambers, and electoral districts and a voting system of their choosing.

So by the end of the 1850s New South Wales was just one of five colonies or provinces within Australia, with no overall federal jurisdiction. Britain was gently loosening her apron strings.

Far from applauding this huge step towards autonomy however the New South Wales Legislative Council metaphorically threw up its hands in dismay. The one thing they wanted above all else, which was control of the distribution of what were called 'Waste [ie unclaimed] Lands' and of the income generated thereby, stayed in the hands of the Colonial Office of the British government. The wealthy landowners who largely controlled the Council were not remotely interested in spreading the franchise to include *ordinary people*, perish the thought. They fought a rearguard action against democracy, dragging their heels in the shuffle towards self government. At that stage, the 1850s, there were no discernible political parties – voters tended to vote for the individual they liked most. In the 1851 New South Wales Legislative Council only eleven of the 54 members represented urban constituencies even though 40 percent of the population were now living in towns.

In 1856 an elected Legislative Assembly – or Lower House – was created, the franchise initially restricted to wealthier landowners over the age of 21, and then extended two years later to include all males who'd lived in the colony for three years, whether or not they owned property, including emancipists but excluding women and Aboriginal people.

Australia was now well and truly on the global map. In the decade of the goldrush Australia's immigrant population more than doubled, and a third of them were living in Victoria. Melbourne's population was now nearly one and a half times that of Sydney. New South Wales was rapidly losing status as the capital province of Australia.

~

The goldrush was not regarded as a Good Thing by everyone, needless to say.

In September 1860 GM presided over a grand dinner at the Fitzroy Hotel in Windsor in honour of Mr Darvall and Mr Piddington, Members of the Legislative Assembly for the

Hawkesbury.

The honourable members both spoke at length, as did the Chairman. GM opened proceedings with a series of toasts to the Queen, the Prince Consort, the Royal Family, the Governor General, the Army and the Navy and finally, 'our respected representatives and guests, Messrs. John Bayley Darvall, and W. R. Piddington, Members of Parliament for the Hawkesbury'.

Darvall rose amid loud cheering to say he had nothing of importance to relate to the assembled company as parliament had achieved little in its short life due to internal squabbling. This, he asserted, was the direct result of universal (male) suffrage, which meant the vote had been extended to include 'the idle and worthless'.

He particularly regretted the discovery of gold, which had made Australians wealthier yet less contented. 'It was an historical fact,' he pronounced, 'that no gold producing country in the world ever became prosperous or happy', because increased wages made the men lazy. They could make enough money working two days a week and the rest of their time they squandered, while the roads and buildings crumbled around them. Why, Australia couldn't even make its own boots or brew its own beer!

He was followed by Mr Piddington, who appeared to agree with Darvall in every detail. The two lengthy speeches were followed by another from Mr Walker, the local representative in the Legislative Council. The evening was finally rounded up by further toasts proposed by the Chairman, to the Parliament of New South Wales and 'to the land we live in'; following which GM could not resist quoting the 'noble sentiment of the poet Scott':

'Breathes there the man, with soul so dead,
Who never to himself has said,
This is my own, my native land!'

'The spot where a man was born on' was a subject on which he could enlarge for an hour or more, said GM, given the chance. Toasts were then drunk to the Ladies, the Chair, the Vice Chair, MPs, their electors, the Volunteer movement and, finally, their gracious hosts.

It is a wonder the guests found the time to enjoy their food and drink amid the plethora of speeches and toasts. But it was clearly a convivial evening, chaired with his usual passion and patriotic fervour by the 46-year old GM: farmer, landowner, father, master of rhetoric and all-round pillar of the local community.

Chapter 32

The romance of the bush

The bush, which comprises most of the continent but holds around ten percent of its population, is not a place many visitors to Australia spend much time in. I certainly didn't when I was living there in my youth – why forsake Sydney's golden beaches for swathes of nothingness?

It is nothingness of course only if you don't know it. The bush is something that changes before your eyes, like to a short-sighted person when he or she puts on his/her glasses: the more you focus, the more you understand it, the more you see. In my youth a gum tree was a gum tree, with greyish leaves and bark that was either peeling or peeled. I realise now there are hundreds of species of eucalypt, all with quite different characteristics if you look closely enough. I can even now identify different forms of 'scarring', some of them created by galahs and some of them by Aboriginal people over the millennia where they carved into the bark of a tree to make canoes.

The bush in the 19th century was a very different thing to what it is now. To begin with the majority of the population still lived in rural areas in the 1850s, and agricultural issues held sway in parliament. It was the inspiration for a wealth of bush poetry and yarns, from the likes of Banjo Paterson and

Henry Lawson, and more recently Les Murray and Roger McKnight. To writers such as Russel Ward and Don Watson it was where 'the real Australians' lived, and in Watson's view it was from the bush that 'Our literature, our language, our politics and our prejudices' sprang.

It was also the butt of jokes. For every eulogiser there was a detractor. In an article for *The Bulletin* in the 1890s the satirist 'Ah Chee' took aim at the 'fatuous writers' who 'warbled' about the pleasures of country life. 'The miserable wretch who is condemned by hard fate to live in the city', with its regular postal deliveries, shops and transport, is made the butt of public sympathy, he wrote; while the 'lucky individual' who lives in the backwoods, 'about 387 miles from nowhere in particular' in a humpy made of bark with rocks to keep the roof in place, is supposedly the envy of all. He went on:

> 'If a ton or two of these miscreants were . . . dumped down in judiciously chosen spots in the back-blocks where they would have to chop wood, and cook damper, and boil junk, and 'graft' hard all day, and walk to the township for provisions, and do without society and clean shirts and socks, the amount of imbecilic verse on the glorious lot of the bush dweller would be reduced by several cubic yards.'

Banjo Paterson, the most famous of them all, chronicler of *Clancy of the Overflow* – 'For the drover's life has pleasures that the townsfolk never know' – and *The Man from Snowy River* among many others, champion of the bushman and the pioneer, loved to take the mickey out of everything and everyone, especially the stupidity of merino sheep. The animal on which the prosperity of the entire country depended was in Paterson's words 'a monomaniac', whose sole aim was to ruin its owner by inventing newer and better ways of committing suicide – by following its mate into fires and floods or oceans, or by deliberately avoiding waterholes so it could die of thirst. 'For pure, sodden stupidity there is no animal like the merino sheep.'

Even now, or maybe especially now, the Australian bush and the Australian city are two quite different countries. You begin to sense it barely two hours' drive out of Sydney: you are entering a totally different environment with different weather and different people. The air is sharper and dryer, even the pace is different. A joke in my brother's home (country) town goes that if you get stuck behind a slow driver, he's a farmer. He moves at a slower pace, he speaks at a slower tempo, and I wouldn't mind betting his pulse beats at a slower rate. His life is governed by the cycles of nature and his animals, he has time to listen to the grass grow, so what's the point in hurrying?

It was the bush that spawned the legend of the swagman, the jolly yet suicidal version of which was immortalised in Banjo Paterson's *Waltzing Matilda*. He was a labourer who wandered the land ('went on the wallaby') with his home ('swag', 'humpy' or 'Matilda') on his back in search of work; and then having found it, was known to sweat his guts out for a couple of weeks and then hit the bottle for a couple of weeks, earning himself the moniker of 'gabelrunzie' (Scots for 'beggar', according to Graham Seal's *Larrikins, Bush Tales & Other Great Australian Stories*).

The bush is also the origin of the famous Australian phenomenon known as 'mateship'. It's said to have sprung from early settler and convict days when the men depended on one another for survival, and it continued on through the goldrush and the forming of trade unions and on to the battlefields of Gallipoli. It was what held the farmworkers 'beyond the black stump' together, the one and only unbreakable law: all good Australians stand by their mate, no matter what.

The bush also has its own special kind of magic. It may be the clarity of the air and the absence of noise pollution that magnifies sounds and sights like nowhere else I've been. I've never known silence like the silence in the bush. I've never been so aware of the ear-splitting racket of the cockatoos, especially at dusk, as they make their way to their dormitories in the trees and then, as the sun sets and as if matron had turned a switch, snap into silence. Nowhere else have I seen the moon on a clear night flood the surrounding countryside as if it was daylight; or been so transfixed by a sky covered from horizon to horizon with a dazzling canopy of stars, so bright and so near you feel you could touch them. I've never known darkness like the blackness of a moonless night in the bush. It takes your breath away. It makes you stop, and look. I can well believe people who live there truly can hear the grass grow.

But imagine what the early settlers thought as they first set eyes on it: endless scrub and trees from horizon to horizon, brown as dust and dry as paper. No wonder nothing would grow in it. The Aboriginal people were no help, they managed to exist without any need to domesticate the land. The settlers were left to find their own way of surviving the merciless sun, the blinding heat, devastating droughts followed by apocalyptic rain. Nothing is by halves in Australia.

And so the bush took on an almost mystical life of its own and bush people developed their own superstitions and methods for predicting the weather. Black cockatoos and kookaburras calling signified rain; ants building nests meant rain in a week; flying ants rain in six hours; a yellow sunset forecast wind the next day; 'a mackerel sky, never long wet, never long dry'; 'rain before seven, clear by eleven' and so on.

For the cattle farmer, like GM, life was both simple and complex. Before the days of refrigeration the only market for beef was a local one, so when they were ready to sell they would walk the cattle to the nearest saleyards and take their chance. But it was the market, and the buyers, who dictated the price, and this could fluctuate unpredictably if there was an over-supply, or a drought, or if the wholesaler buyers had formed a cartel and decided between themselves not to bid over a certain amount that day.

Imagine the frustration of the farmer at the mercy not just of the elements, or political decisions made in cities hundreds of miles away, but of local conditions over which he had no control. Nowadays a farmer can check the going price of stock online before venturing to the saleyards to buy or to sell, and if he doesn't make a deal on the day he can just pile his stock into his trailer and come back another time. Back then it could be several days' drove to get the cattle to the nearest market and if the price wasn't right he either took what he could get or it was several days' hard droving back home again.

He was also relatively helpless when it came to raising money. Banks were reluctant to lend to pastoralists who didn't own the freehold of their land so they had to look for other sources, such as stock agents or brokers.

One way or another, farming was a mug's business. True, some people made money out of it – fortunes even – but for the average man of the land it was a ridiculous game and even the cleverest of them could go under any day. The fact that GM was not living on his remote properties meant he was even more removed from the seat of control.

And there was always the possibility of litigation.

Chapter 33

1840s-60s: The law and the Europeans

The law would have been a good profession for a young man in 19th century New South Wales. There was never a shortage of work. Land disputes in particular were highly profitable.

Between 1848 and 1861 GM continued to acquire and dispose of pieces of land in the Gwydir and at Wellington districts. (The full list is in the Chapter Notes.) These latter runs would have been second- or even third- or fourth-hand properties, developed by others and passed on from hand to hand. There is never any indication GM lived on any of his runs and no way of knowing if or how often he visited them. In 1866 the population of Wellington was 70 and the number of runs was 450. So GM was not the only absentee landlord.

Some of these transactions he shared with others, such as Thomas Sullivan, with whom GM was to go into partnership later for a brief time. Dr Whittaker, co-owner of Bangheet, was a surgeon. Presumably GM made money out of his buying and selling, which makes him more of a property speculator than a pioneer farmer; although some of the transactions – in the case of Coorar for example, which he hung onto for six years – were transfers of leases rather than sales.

In those days of sporadic communication, before the mail-coach and certainly before the telegraph, GM would have left most of the management of his land to his overseers. There were too many properties scattered over too large an area for even the most energetic and assiduous pastoralist to have kept a close eye on all of them. Not to mention all the local activities he was involving himself in at the time.

Then in 1861 GM came up against a problem.

Four years after he and Dr Whittaker had sold Bangheet, in the Gwydir district, the buyer, Francis Rusden, MLA, sued them for 'false and fraudulent misrepresentation'.

GM and Whittaker had sold Rusden their station in 1857, along with cattle branded 'Scot' [sic] and some stock horses, for £10,000 – half in cash and the remainder over five years at seven percent interest. The animals had not been mustered and GM estimated their total to be in the region of 3,000. Since Rusden and GM had agreed between them the property itself was worth around £3,000 the remainder of the value lay in the stock, which worked out at £2.6s a head, Rusden estimated. Rusden agreed to the conditions, the deed was signed and he took possession.

Some time after the sale a muster was taken of the stock and the total turned out to be closer to 2,000 head. This, claimed Rusden, cost him trouble and money, so in February 1859 he wrote to GM asking for remission of part of the purchase money 'and suggesting arbitration' – a suggestion GM presumably rejected.

Dr Whittaker, who was in England at the time of the trial, had never been to the station, and GM had visited it only once. They had bought Bangheet in 1853 for £6,000 from a Dr Mitchell, with unmustered cattle in the region of 2,100. In the intervening four years GM said he'd added some heifers and 'sold around 600 or 800'. In order to find the defendants guilty, the defending counsel explained, the jury needed to be convinced GM and Whittaker had deliberately made false representations.

The trial lasted a day, and 'The jury, after retiring a few

minutes, returned a verdict for the defendants.'

Now I would not venture to say the law is an ass, and since there was no evidence of deliberate fraud on GM and Whittaker's part there could have been no other verdict. But it does seem Rusden got a bit of a raw deal here. If the value of stock made up two-thirds of the value of a property it seems extraordinary that any sale could take place without a muster. Moreover GM and Whittaker had themselves bought the property without a muster and seemingly had not held one during the four years they owned it.

GM was a tough customer. Another man may have agreed to arbitrate, but not him. Perhaps he was too busy elsewhere; as it was round about the time he sold Bangheet that his life changed direction.

Chapter 34

1850s: Birth of a salesman

'If you're passing by the "Yards",
Call and give my kind regards
To the fellow with his coat off in the pen.
For the fat stock auctioneer
As a salesman has no peer,
And he's also pretty cute at handling men.

And his tongue at rapid-fire
Never seems to halt or tire,
Sounds a cross between a rifle and a hen.
With a score of pens to sell,
He has got to "go like Hell",
Or be blown off when he's only finished ten.

When he's auctioneering flocks
He is seldom "on the rocks",
Though he may have had a narrow shave or two;
Never look him in the eye
If you don't intend to buy,
Or you'll find he's knocked a pen-full down to you.

He's a don at selling "crackers"
To the meat pie men and packers,

Though his "bulls" would find it hard to make the grade.
But his captivating smile
Is quite innocent of guile,
When he's passing on "stale pastry" to the trade.

When he's fixing up the "drawing",
With imagination soaring,
There are mythical consignments on the slate.
If they're missing at the yards
It is quite upon the cards,
He'll suggest some country trains are running late.

He's alert and self reliant,
Does his best for ev'ry client,
And succeeds in pleasing some, it would appear.
For, amid the noise and rattle,
Near three hundred thousand cattle,
And four million sheep are handled in a year.'
('The Fat Stock Salesman', by 'R.J.W.', from *The Remarkable Record of Pitt, Son & Badgery Ltd*.)

~

On Tuesday 6 October 1857 the *Sydney Morning Herald* announced that George M Pitt had received instructions to sell 130 prime fat cattle at 'Mr John Fullagar's Star Inn' on the Western Road on behalf of Sloper Cox Esq of Richmond.

Now, GM may have been buying and selling stock on his own behalf for most of his life, but to be asked to sell on behalf of someone else was another thing entirely. To begin with it was illegal for anyone to sell anything by auction without a license. The first list of licensed auctioneers that I could lay my hands on was dated 1859, and GM's name is one of seven in the district of Windsor. (Which is not to suggest – God forbid – that he was operating in 1857 without a licence, simply that lists of authorised auctioneers before 1859 are not available; and it's possible they were not being issued then.)

The profession of auctioneer is as old as the hills, and his qualities – and invariably in those days it was a 'he' – have remained unchanged through the centuries. He works for the seller and it is his job to generate the highest bid possible by means of jokes, or coercion, or by whatever means possible. He must be able to think on his feet and 'feel the pulse of the auction', and if the bidding is slow it's up to him to coax reluctant buyers out of their corners, if necessary by focusing his attention on a novice buyer in the hope he will be encouraged to set the ball rolling (according to J H ('Alf') McGeoch in *The Role and Art of Auctioneer*). He must know the market and the needs of both his employers and the buyers. He should be a good mixer, honest, canny, have a razor-sharp memory and be able to hold a huge amount of information in his head. He is a mix of showman and hard-headed businessman. He is the Master of Ceremonies and the conductor of the orchestra.

This all sounds hugely entertaining, but in reality time is a crucial factor in any auction and no auctioneer has enough of it these days to stand on a podium and crack jokes, as was evident at my recent visit to the Wagga Wagga saleyards. With single animals fetching over a thousand Australian dollars (unprecedented, according to Chris McCarthy), it boggles the mind to think how much money these buyers, many of whom look way beyond the normal age of retirement, are forking out. Be not misled by their grubby moleskins and well-worn hats, many if not all of these craggy, roughshod, leather-faced players must be millionaires.

~

The Sloper Cox sale was presumably a success, as was GM's auction of cattle belonging to John Hoskisson later that same year. Because the year after, in 1858, GM bought 67 acres near Fullagher's saleyards in order to provide grazing for stock awaiting sale. And while he continued to buy and sell pieces of land here and there one can almost hear his mind ticking over: if it's that easy to sell stock on someone else's behalf then . . .

It did not require a huge leap of faith on GM's part to realise he could take his talents onto another level. He could become a stock agent. He had the knowledge and the experience, and he was fast building a reputation as a salesman. It was a natural course of action, an extension of what he was already doing, and at considerably less risk to himself.

As one beleaguered farmer called Tom Harvey said a hundred years later, after drought had wiped out all but 500 of his entire flock of 2,700 sheep: 'The last ones to go in a drought are the emus and stock and station agents.'

A stock agent, as the term suggests, makes his money from commission on sales of the stock he sells. In return he is expected to be at the 24/7 beck and call of the client, ready to drop everything and present himself wherever he or she happens to live, no matter how remote, to attend to whatever business she or he has in hand, no matter how trivial. He will smile and doff his hat and spend a good part of the day saying 'No worries, mate', even if he is secretly exhausted and/or exasperated and ready to wring his client's neck. He cannot always rely on a client's loyalty, although in most cases if the match works the marriage should last a lifetime and beyond, down the generations.

He will spend much of his time travelling – these days in a car or truck of course, before that on horseback. He will carry with him a gentle aroma of cowshit which no amount of laundering will completely erase; even though, as all country people do, he invariably removes his boots before entering a house.

He is an auctioneer plus. Along with the head for business, the super-sharp memory and the latest knowledge of stock prices he is a counsellor: an adviser on all things from when and what stock to sell to arranging the farmer's daughter's wedding. (I made that last one up, but it's not beyond the bounds of possibility – agents and auctioneers are frequently asked to act as Master of Ceremonies at weddings apparently as they know how to get a crowd going.) Along with his team he is responsible for arranging the sale, booking a place in the saleyard and getting the stock there, organising the paperwork and making sure payments are made on time. It's his job to cheer the struggling pastoralist in hard times and keep him on the rails when things are looking up. He is your uncle, your mate, your mechanic and your saviour, he will offer you his coat or his boots, find you a new sheepdog pup, help you out in a bushfire, book you into a pub or motel and ferry you from hither to yon when your wife gets sick of waiting for you and pushes off with the car. He will change nappies, make your tea or pull you out of a ravine. Perhaps most important of all, he can – or in the old days certainly he could – offer you financial credit when the banks won't touch you. He has the advantage of knowing what's going on elsewhere, on other properties all around the colony, and an overall knowledge of what's happening in the stock business that no single farmer can ever hope to acquire.

In 1861 GM was 47, young enough still to have the energy to travel yet old enough to have acquired a good grasp of business. His journeys throughout New South Wales would have made him plenty of friends, grist to the mill for the new stock agent. Like all people who make a living on the land he was a 'can do' man, who could turn his hand to anything even if he's never done it before, to whom a problem is a challenge, a setback is simply par for the course. A man who'd sit next to you on a train and immediately start talking to you in a booming voice that'd have fellow commuters tutting, and in the time it took to get from Euston to Milton Keynes he'd have given you his whole life story, with the odd coruscating comments on the state of the nation thrown in along with a joke or two – not all of which you'd have got but you'd have laughed anyway because his enthusiasm demanded it – and solicited yours in return, to which he would listen with total concentration. His parting shot would be a pithy quote from Burns or Byron; and when you next make that journey you'll find yourself looking around for him and feeling a pang of disappointment when he doesn't appear.

Pitt and his friend Thomas Sullivan began selling – on behalf of other people, including GM's brother in law Thomas WEB Laycock – at Fullagher's until 1862, when they switched to Homebush.

Homebush is best known to Sydneysiders these days as a shopping centre, home of the Olympic Park of 2000 and of the Royal Easter Show – an annual event which I have never had the pleasure of attending but which appears to be a mixture of children's funfair, showground and 'on-trend fine food and beverage destination' (to quote the website); where participants can take part in all manner of competitions from cutest puppy to plumpest pumpkin. On the more serious side, it is a place for farmers, agents, brokers and agricultural people in general to get together and network, and for the more ambitiously-minded among them to enter their prize cows, sheep, horses, alpacas and who knows what else to win Cow/Sheep/Dog/Horse of the Year.

Back in the 1860s the lessee of the Homebush Estate, a Thomas Dawson, was proud to advertise the excellent facilities of his 2000-acre property with its fenced paddocks and first-class saleyards – 'a stone's throw' from Homebush station and half an hour by train from Sydney.

For the Pitt family however Homebush has another, and rather more significant, connection. The original 795-acre plot of land was granted back in 1803 to GM's grandfather Thomas Laycock, Quartermaster with the New South Wales Corps, who named it Home Bush. (The land was subsequently sold, or according to one apocryphal account won over a game of cards, to D'Arcy Wentworth.) Whether or not my g-g-grandfather was aware of the family connection, through his mother Elizabeth, it is a nice symmetry.

In 1862 GM and Sullivan, 'at the request of a large number of supporters', officially set themselves up as stock and station agents, with offices at 341 George Street, next door to the Commercial Bank.

The existence of an office, I have recently discovered, is significant. To the stock agent a base was a sign of respectability and set him apart and above the 'pocket book' agent, who operated informally, if not illegally, and might just be hard to track down if a transaction goes wrong. (Although a bad reputation for any stock agent meant a short career.) An office in the heart of the city symbolised Accountability, and Stability.

Meanwhile Pitt and Sullivan were still leasing runs together in the Wellington district. And as if all that wasn't enough to keep a man busy, GM also decided in 1864 to contest the parliamentary seat of Windsor.

Chapter 35

1864: Politics

It seems to have been a relatively last-minute decision, and not necessarily GM's own idea to stand for the electoral seat of Windsor in 1864. His rival was William Walker, the current incumbent, who'd been in office for five years. The local electors, around 150 of them, gathered at the Windsor courthouse on Wednesday 23 November to listen to the two speakers put their points of view. The meeting was reported in detail in the *Sydney Morning Herald*.

In nominating Mr Pitt a Mr Moses explained it was his intention to remove the Martin ministry from power as they were totally incapable of governing the country. The Cowper administration on the other hand had introduced both manhood suffrage and free selection before survey, measures to which Mr Walker 'and the party whom he blindly supported were opposed'.

At this point I had to pause for a moment to figure out what Moses meant by 'free selection before survey', and free trade – another measure which, Moses alleged, Mr Walker also opposed. Not to mention who Cowper and Martin might have been.

Windsor had one representative in the Legislative Assembly (or lower house), elected by the residents of Windsor and

Richmond. There was also now a Premier of New South Wales, who was appointed by the governor and represented a party elected by this same (male) populace. The premiership had been passed to and fro over the past eight years between Sir Charles Cowper (third son of the aforementioned Reverend William Cowper) and others, ending up in 1864 with James Martin. The parties did not yet seem to have names, or anything else that identified their political leanings, though Cowper supporters regarded themselves as 'liberals'.

Manhood suffrage, introduced in 1858 under the Cowper administration, meant 'every beggar in the street with a bludgeon at his back' was entitled to vote on equal terms, grumbled a former premier, Stuart Donaldson. However since voters had to pay to register the majority of them were still probably the better-off, particularly since voting had to be done in person on the day, which pretty well ruled out rural labourers.

As for free selection before survey: this is something most Aussies know all about but which I confess, while I've heard it talked about many times, I've never quite managed to get my head around.

It seems to have arisen out of a concern that too much of the land was owned by too few people. Around 44 million acres of New South Wales was divided into just over 1000 properties, in other words a good proportion of the colony was in private hands and out of bounds for the majority of the population. Moreover electoral districts were so distributed that a relatively small number of rural voters had the same voting influence as what was now a larger urban population. There was a strong move, particularly from town dwellers, to 'unlock the land'.

So in 1861 John Robertson, who'd served with Cowper and was by then premier himself, introduced a Crown Lands Act aimed at solving this problem by allowing anyone to choose their own plot of land of between 40 and 320 acres, for a small fee, on condition they lived there, farmed it and improved it. After three years they could claim freehold tenure on the land in return for a small annual interest payment.

In theory this meant anyone could fetch up on a squatter's run, pitch his tent and stake out his own 320 acres and there was nothing the squatter could (legitimately) do about it. In practice the squatters wasted no time in creating their own blocking techniques, which included creating 'phantom' selectors who laid claim to the only parts of the run with access to water. The plan, well-meaning though it was, didn't work overall for a number of reasons, not the least of which was many of the selectors' inexperience of the business of farming and the squatters' attempts to do everything they could to obstruct them.

Meanwhile back in Windsor courthouse: William Walker rose to speak, to loud cheering. It was the third time he'd appeared before the electors to contest the seat at Windsor, and until a few days ago he had expected to 'walk over the course'. He devoted a good deal of his speech to refuting the "claptrap" (a favourite word) put about by his opponents, to wit his opposition to free trade and manhood suffrage. He was at pains not to point the finger at Mr Pitt himself, who was a friend and would remain so no matter what the outcome of the vote, but some disreputable 'friends' of his. Mr Pitt had been one of the first to sign a petition against manhood suffrage, and as a squatter himself could hardly claim to be a supporter of free selection. Walker went on to complain that he'd been the subject of misrepresentation through word of mouth and in handbills stating a vote for him was a vote for 'a shilling on a pair of English boots'. His support of tariffs on imported goods was, he insisted, to reduce the deficit left behind by the Cowper administration. He regretted that his opponents had been forced to 'fall back upon Mr Pitt' in their attempts to find someone to stand against him.

GM then rose and was similarly 'greeted with loud marks of approbation'. He began by apologising for his presumption in opposing such a tried and trusted 'servant' as Mr Walker, and for his ignorance of political matters, explaining the only time he had attended the Assembly Chamber it was so crowded he could not hear a thing. (Pause for laughter.)

He went on to say what he lacked in political experience he hoped he made up for as a man of honour. He opposed the Martin ministry because of their introduction of tariffs, which was completely at odds in a country that believed in freedom. 'It is self evident the Almighty never intended this country for the produce of cereals sufficient for a large population', he said. 'Should we have starved to death rather than import it from abroad? Would we still have had such jolly faces?' The Martin ministry was taking them back to the bad old days of protectionism. They were 'harping upon one string, and music must be cleverly played to produce sweet tunes out of one string. Few musicians have done it; the Martin ministry could not do it.'

He talked about crime, which was rampant, yet the government's response was to remove the funds from 'those who are instructing our young men in the art and science of self-defence' – in other words, the Volunteers.

> 'You may remember some part of Asia where the people became so luxurious they taught their horses to dance. And while they were busy entertaining themselves a neighbouring race came down upon them and slew them and drove them into slavery. We need to give all the encouragement we can to every young man who wishes to stand in defence of his country. They need nurturing, their rough natures polished; like the diamond on Golconda's shore, found in a rude state, the more it was polished the more it showed the gem. Stick to your volunteers!'

On other topics, such as education, he was in agreement with Mr Walker: 'Let education be like the genial dew of heaven - let it fall upon all alike,' he pronounced. 'It is through education that we might raise young men who the rods of empire might sway, or wake to ecstasy the living lyre.' He had sent his own children 'among all classes and creeds, and affections and friendships have been gained that will never die – friendships that could not exist without knowledge, for knowledge is power'.

He concluded by saying if elected he would hope at the end of a year to return to them 'with something I had done that would be of honour to myself and credit to you; and you would then say in the language of Scripture: "Well done, thou good and faithful servant"'.

The speech ended amid huge cheers, and a show of hands being taken it was declared to be in favour of Mr Pitt 'by a large majority'. Walker demanded a poll to take place the following day, though as reported in the *Maitland Mercury*, '[Mr Pitt's] return is considered certain.'

~

GM's speech, which needless to say was considerably longer than recorded here, is an insight not just into the man himself and his political beliefs, but his astonishing powers of rhetoric. Where he got his classical references from and his use of metaphor is a mystery. Pastoralists are not usually known for their eloquence – not that kind of eloquence at least – nor, I imagine, would rhetoric have been taught at school. It must simply have been part and parcel of his passion for the words of classical poets and his determination to find every opportunity to quote from them.

Nowadays, with television and social media, it's fair to say we choose our politicians as much for their appearance and general manner as for their policies, or their integrity. The ancient art of winning over the people through rhetoric is reproduced in the television debate. The meeting that took place that November day in 1864 was the 19th century version of both the ancient and the modern: by popular vote it was eloquence that won the day, hands down. On virtually all subjects except free trade GM and Walker were in total agreement so far as I can see. No matter GM was a stranger to politics and Walker a known entity, if the vote had been decided on that show of hands GM's life would have taken a very different turn.

The vote proper took place the following day and the results were announced late in the afternoon in front of the courthouse. The total votes from the electors of Windsor and Richmond were 228 for William Walker and 220 for George Matcham Pitt. Walker had won by 8 votes.

Walker stepped forward, among cheers, to thank the electors and to once again denounce the scandalous behaviour of his opponents, claiming that had it not been for several voting papers having been spoiled the real majority would have been 32. He also railed against a certain newspaper – 'a lying, poverty-stricken rag' (he doesn't say which one) – that had also been used against him. He felt sorry for Mr Pitt, whom he respected as a friend but who had allowed himself to be 'strung along'.

GM also came forward amid cheers, to again thank the electors for rejecting him (laughter), and to say he was satisfied with the result. He said nothing about being patronised by his opponent.

One might wonder how serious GM was about becoming a politician. With all his other commitments it's hard to imagine how he'd have found the time to take his seat in the Assembly. He never contested a parliamentary seat again.

Chapter 36

1864 Railroads and rivalry

Days after the election, on 29 November 1864, the railway finally arrived at the Hawkesbury.

The idea was first mooted back in 1846 – before any railways had been built in the colony – but not deemed viable by the Legislative Council for another ten years. Construction on a branch line linking Blacktown to Windsor and Richmond had begun a year earlier but was delayed when floods in July – the worst in 45 years – swept away part of the riverbank.

The opening was attended by the full rank of New South Wales officialdom, including His Excellency the Governor Sir John Young, with his wife and entourage, and important aides such as Sir Edward Deas Thomson, the Hon. Charles Cowper (Pitt's man went on to win the election even if Pitt himself had not), the commissioner for railways and various aldermen and other gentlemen.

The party began their journey in Sydney just before 10am and arrived at Blacktown 40 minutes later, where the train was divided into two for some reason, and both parts proceeded 'at a tolerably rapid pace' along the new stretch of line to Windsor. They passed through forests, swamp, chains of ponds and rolling countryside – startling the cattle and causing the local farmers and their families to come running from their farms to gawp at the 'iron horse' – until they reached the viaduct approaching the town of Windsor. Here the whole town had turned out in welcome but, to the surprise of all including the reporter from the *Sydney Morning Herald* the train did not stop but 'rushed on with unabated speed to Richmond' (fourteen miles an hour in fact, the maximum speed allowed at that time), where it wheezed to a halt at 11.30am.

His Excellency and cohorts were again greeted with pomp and ceremony and a lot of speeches, before they proceeded via a brief tour of the town to the goods shed – tarted up for the occasion with flags and foliage – to enjoy a slap-up breakfast in the company of '50 or 60 local gentlemen'. Among them of course was GM, who proposed a toast to the success of the railways and responded to another to 'the ladies of the colony'.

The train shuttled to and from Richmond and Windsor for the rest of the day, offering free rides for all. Come the evening there was further celebration at Windsor, where a roasted ox drew a crowd in front of St Matthew's Church and a greasy pole with a hat perched on top invited the more adventurous to climb it and claim a prize. The gentlemen of Windsor then gave an address to Sir Charles Cowper. Describing themselves as 'the undersigned Liberals of the town and district of Windsor' they congratulated him on his success at the recent election and thanked him for their new railway. Cowper had no hesitation in claiming the credit for a cause he had championed for fourteen years, despite general ridicule.

For GM and others it was a lifeline: the five-hour journey from Richmond to Sydney by road had been reduced to an hour and a half by train.

~

Early railways in Australia were beset with problems. The private company that built the first public line between Sydney and Parramatta in the 1850s went bust and had to be bailed out by the government. There was a shortage of labour thanks to the goldrush, and then there were the different gauges.

I remember my Australian mother telling me how

passengers travelling by train interstate back in the day, which was not that long ago, had to disembark at the border and reboard another train on a different track.

The first railways in New South Wales were initially intended to be built to the English gauge (4ft 8½ ins); but their chief engineer of the time, who was an Irishman, persuaded the government to change its mind in favour of the Irish gauge (5ft 3ins). This became the official gauge when the colonies of Victoria and South Australia were first formed back in the 1850s. But when the NSW chief engineer was replaced by a Scotsman he persuaded the government to revert to the original gauge – too late for Victoria and South Australia, which had already ordered rolling stock to fit the Irish gauge. Further complications arose when South Australia started constructing feeder lines at the smaller gauge of 3ft 6ins, a gauge that was adopted later throughout Queensland and Western Australia. With three quite different gauges the poor passenger passing through South Australia to Victoria and/or New South Wales faced the not-so-merry business of having to change trains several times. The various parties refused to budge, and it wasn't until the 1960s that Victoria and New South Wales agreed to adopt the standard (as in the original) gauge and the happy traveller faced the unusual luxury of being able to stay in her seat all the way from Sydney to Melbourne.

I have had mixed experiences on Australian railways. In Britain it is the standard, if expensive, way to travel. In Australia the car and the plane dominate and travelling by railway is often a second-class, not to say unpredictable alternative. I've been on that Sydney-Melbourne train many times over the years visiting my brother in Wagga Wagga, which is approximately halfway between the two cities. It was not unusual for the train to leave Sydney late – for reasons unspecified – and crawl at what seemed like walking pace, taking unscheduled breaks so the driver could exit his cabin to inspect the track; or to stop dead and wait for a considerable time at a spot where the train travelling in the opposite direction could pass – most of the line being single-track – arriving in Wagga two hours later than scheduled. And no one seemed to turn a hair. (When I told my Wagga friends that in the UK passengers are entitled to compensation if a train is half an hour late, they said if that rule applied there New South Wales Railways would be out of business in a day.)

On the other hand I have taken an extremely spacious and comfortable train from Perth to Kalgoorlie – a journey of around 7½ hours – where they actually show *movies*. Eat your heart out, Southern Rail.

~

Meanwhile, inter-colonial rivalry reached its apex – or nadir – in the latter part of the 19th century. It wasn't only the railway gauge the colonies could not agree on. The great Murray river flows along the border between New South Wales and Victoria to exit into the Southern Ocean at Adelaide in South Australia; but come what may the three colonies could not come to any kind of agreement on its management, and attempts from all sides to impose tariffs ended in near-fisticuffs. The Victorian and New South Wales governments even argued over who should pay for the bridge across the Murray at the border town of Albury (NSW)–Wodonga (Vic). As recently as the 1970s a man was shot dead and discovered with his feet in the river – technically New South Wales – and his head on dry land in what was considered Victoria. Nobody could figure out which state should prosecute the alleged perpetrator. He was first tried in Victoria and found guilty, but when his lawyers appealed on the grounds the victim's body was not in Victoria the case went to the High Court, where it was eventually decided the New South Wales border covered the river as far as the upper part of the bank on the Victorian side, which meant the victim died in New South Wales. So the (alleged) murderer was tried again in New South Wales. And found guilty yet again.

It seems everything the Victorian government tried to do,

particularly concerning tariffs and free trade, the New South Wales government opposed, and vice versa, often for the sake of it. The miracle is the six colonies managed to stay together as one nation at all. The original colonial city of Sydney had long been surpassed by Melbourne population-wise, thanks to the goldrush. But the two capitals still vied with one another to be the seat of government, which seems to have remained in Sydney until Federation and the creation of a brand new purpose-built capital called Canberra. But none of that was to happen in GM's lifetime.

Chapter 37

1860s: Weddings & inundations

Meanwhile GM and Julia's offspring were growing up, as offspring do.

Their eldest, George Matcham junior, qualified as a surveyor in 1859 under Charles Whittaker, the government surveyor, and the following year he married a local girl, Elizabeth Town, and took her to live across the river in North Richmond in a house named Sunnyside. In 1865 a GM Pitt was made a magistrate in Richmond and I am assuming it was Pitt junior (the ancient habit of naming sons after fathers does not make the family historian's job easy).

The younger GM Pitts were great socialisers evidently, renowned for their 'generous table' and 'open door', through which in times to come would step luminaries such as the artists Arthur Streeton, Tom Roberts and Albert Henry Fullwood. Streeton painted 'A Surveyor's Camp' while accompanying GM junior on one of his surveying expeditions apparently.

In the latter part of the 1860s the Bronte nest was beginning to empty. In 1868 eldest daughter Jessie married William Garling at St Peter's Church in Richmond. Garling, described as a 'sketcher, station manager and auctioneer', was the son of the famous artist Frederick Garling and earned his living at the time managing properties belonging to GM's friend Sloper Cox. Among those properties was the Cox family's Hobartville, across the road from Bronte, where I imagine William and Jessie met and went to live after their marriage. Hobartville was also home at a later date to Andrew Town, who was Elizabeth's younger half cousin (thanks to a spot of illegitimacy).

The following year, in 1869, second daughter Julia married Henry Septimus Badgery, grandson of James Badgery: an early settler after whom Badgerys Creek is named. Henry had been brought up on his father's property near Goulburn and was a farmer and an auctioneer, like his father in law, selling stock at Homebush, like his father in law. Since Badgery was not a local man I am speculating it was GM who one way or another brought his daughter together with the man who was to become his future business partner. Henry and GM were both members of the Hawkesbury Agricultural Association and it's possible that it was GM who encouraged Henry to become a stock and station agent in the first place. Soon after their marriage Henry and Julia moved to Maitland, 100 miles or so north of Richmond, where he became a partner in the stock agency firm of Brunker & Wolfe.

~

Before the departure of the two elder Pitt girls to lives of married bliss the Hawkesbury area suffered the worst flood on record.

Hawkesbury floods are legendary. From the earliest days of European settlement – and for eons before that, as the Aboriginal people had experienced – the river has been prone to flood. Described (by the NSW State Emergency Service) as 'a bathtub, with five main taps (tributaries) but only one plug hole to let the floodwater out', the Hawkesbury has a catchment area of 27,000 square miles, and when heavy rain falls the bathtub simply fills up and overflows.

For some reason known only to nature the river had remained uncharacteristically calm between the years of 1819 and 1857, so GM and his siblings grew up without ever having to worry about the sudden inundation of their land and the destruction of stock and grain. (Unlike their parents Thomas and Elizabeth and their grandmother Mary, who experienced several disastrous floods in their lifetimes.)

The 1860s however were bad years. In 1864 the river rose to over 49 feet (15.05 metres), the second highest flood since European settlement. Miraculously no one was drowned, although over 1,000 people lost their livestock or their houses, and their livelihoods.

Three years later came the catastrophe.

On Monday 17 June 1867 the rain began to fall, accompanied by a piercing westerly wind. The ground, already saturated, could not absorb the water. Come the Wednesday as the rains and the gales continued boats were commandeered, locally and by train from Sydney, to take vulnerable people to safety. By Thursday the district was one large sheet of water. People scrambled onto their roofs for safety and the lucky ones were rescued by boatmen – many of them railway employees – who 'plied their oars with almost superhuman energy' without a break from Thursday evening until Saturday. On reaching safety at Windsor the boatmen were besieged by people urging them to go to 'such a place for such a person'. They kept their calm apparently as they deftly manoeuvred their craft around chimneys, over fences, telegraph lines, orangeries and vineyards, in the freezing cold (June being antipodean midwinter) and often in the pitch dark, through a raging wind and battling billowing waves, rescuing people from rooftops and trees and through the doors and windows of their houses.

Late on Friday the Eather family – Thomas and his brother William with their wives and ten children – took to the roof of their brother George's house at Cornwallis (on the southern bank of the river east of Richmond). A wave washed the men and one of the boys off the roof, leaving the women and children still hanging on. In an awful irony the men grabbed hold of trees and were rescued while the women and children

– twelve of them in all – were drowned.

By Saturday the water was continuing to rise at a rate of seven inches an hour, until only the odd chimney or roof of a higher house in Windsor was visible above it. From Pitt Town to Kurrajong on the northern bank and Riverstone on the southern to the Blue Mountains was a vast 'inland sea', twenty miles across, dotted here and there with odd islands made up of the higher parts of Richmond, Windsor and Pitt Town. Cats and chickens perched terrified on rooftops, cattle and horses swam for their lives and were mostly drowned. Furniture, household goods and bales of straw drifted aimlessly in the churning water. The river continued to rise throughout the night until 5am on the Sunday, when at last it halted. Three hours later, at 8am, it had begun to recede, and it continued to fall throughout the Sunday.

At its peak it had reached 64½ feet (19.68 metres) above normal level.

The aftermath was almost as bad as the flood itself. Three quarters of the houses in Windsor had been destroyed. The inhabitants of Richmond were cut off and starving. Survivors crowded public buildings in Windsor such as the School of Arts, the Courthouse and whatever churches remained. The ground, once the water had receded properly, was in places fifteen feet deep in silt and sand. The *Sydney Morning* Herald reported the beaches along the east coast from Barrenjoey to Long Beach were strewn with door frames, dead pigs, broken bedsteads, hay, wheat, pumpkins and melons 'and other debris, that scarcely any portion of the beaches can be seen'. In all 21 people died, twelve on the Hawkesbury and the others elsewhere, as far as Bathurst in the west. It's surprising the death toll wasn't higher. And with no such thing as insurance untold numbers of local residents lost everything and were forced to start again from scratch, or to give up and go elsewhere.

In all the copious and detailed reports of this terrible tragedy there is no mention of any of the Pitts, either among the rescued or the rescuers. Bronte being set back from the Hawkesbury with another property between it and the river means it was not on the front line of flooding. However the lower part of the property has flooded several times over the years (the latest as recently as 1991 according to the current owner Margaret Betts), destroying crops and stock, and no doubt it did so in 1867. The various homesteads, built on the top of the slope, would probably have survived even the 1867 inundation. GM, had he been there at the time, would no doubt have been one of the first to have grabbed a boat and set off in rescue. The family would without question have taken in their less lucky neighbours. One could invent a scene of dramatic rescue and outstanding heroism, were one inclined to do so.

It is enough to record that, as in most disasters then and now, scenes of devastation and terror and loss of life inspired acts of astonishing resilience and selfless bravery. This, after all, is Australia.

~

Two months after the flood, in August 1867, Julia's mother Mary died. She was buried at St Peter's Richmond under her first married name of Mary Johnson. What had become of this brave ex convict woman, shopkeeper, mother of five and wife twice over since she absconded from the family home in 1839, remains a tantalising mystery.

Whether Mary's death or the prospect of further floods had anything to do with GM and Julia's decision to leave Richmond forever is not known. What is known is that at some point in 1869 they left their elder sons Edwin and Harry Austin, 25 and 22 years old respectively, to look after Bronte, while the younger siblings RM (20), Colin (18), Charles Bryan (15) and Eva Laura (12) accompanied their parents and went to live in Manly.

Chapter 38

1860s/70s Manly Beach

It must have been quite a wrench. To say goodbye to the Hawkesbury, and to Bronte: the two 100-acre original grants given to Mary Pitt and her son Thomas, home to, farmed and transformed by three generations of Pitts.

GM never cut his ties with Bronte completely. He left his sons to care for the property and continued to own it until his death. It was Edwin who built 'the fine modern cottage' (according to the reminiscences of local character Alfred Smith) back in the 1870s, after GM and Julia had left, and thought to be the beautifully-restored house that stands there now in 2018.

He left behind quite a legacy. He was remembered, and chronicled in times to come, by several local people, one of whom (J C Fitzgerald in *Those Were the Days*) described him as 'a grand old man, full of mental and bodily vigour'. Sam Boughton, aka 'Cooramill', portrayed him as a man with 'a big heart, and a kindly nature ... [and] good business tact', fond of quoting Shakespeare, Byron or Robbie Burns 'till further orders'; and who, on being asked to deliver grace at some banquet and realising he was flanked by a doctor on one side and a lawyer on the other, quoted 'an eminent statesman in England' thus:

'From doctors' pills

And lawyers' bills
Good Lord deliver us!'

So the move to Manly Beach (as it was then known) seems like an odd choice. If you don't know the place, Manly is a suburb of Sydney situated on a narrow strip of land adjoining North Head (a promontory that juts out into the mouth of Sydney harbour on the northern side, then a quarantine station for passengers arriving on ships with sickness and death on board), nine miles from Sydney city as the crow flies. It fronts onto the harbour on one side and the ocean on the other, and nowadays it is a mecca for surfers and tourists. But in the early days of colonisation it was more or less ignored – other than to be given its name, by Governor Phillip, because of the 'manly' appearance of the Aboriginal men he saw there – as the land was not arable.

At the time GM and Julia took up residence in Manly there were fewer than a thousand people living on the North Shore, and around half of those lived in Manly Beach – thanks mostly to the regular ferry service linking it to the city. Nonetheless it is not obviously convenient for a man who spent part of his time in his office in the city and part of it in saleyards way to the west of Sydney.

The Pitts rented a magnificent house called Fairlight from Henry Gilbert Smith. The imposing two-storey structure, built on land stretching from the harbour on one side to the ocean beach on the other, was described in the *Sydney Morning Herald* as 'commanding a magnificent view of the heads and harbour, and containing about eleven rooms (four of which are large) besides kitchen, pantry, and servants' bedrooms. The main portion of the building is of stone, with slated roof. The grounds, extending over 35 acres (more or less), comprise good-sized garden and a large well-grassed paddock, and a never failing stream of the purest water running through them'.

Smith had begun buying and leasing land in Manly back in the 1850s. He recognised its potential as a seaside resort along the lines of Brighton in England, despite the fact that sea bathing was prohibited in Manly in daylight hours, for reasons of decency.

(Talking of which, a slight digression:

We think of Sydney as a golden city surrounded by water – harbour on one side, the ocean on the other – where lucky Sydneysiders can indulge in water sports to suit all kinds, from the gentle bather to the bravura surfie. So it came as a surprise (to the writer) to discover that until the early 1900s swimming, in the ocean at least, was banned, for reasons aforesaid.

Manly employed an Inspector of Nuisances, whose task was to remove dead animals from the streets and to monitor the beaches to check for illicit swimming after 7am. There was a story that one hot day in September 1902 a group of young lads who'd arrived at Manly on a yacht plunged merrily into the sea and were promptly arrested for breaking the local by-law. When word reached the editor and proprietor of the local newspaper, a man named Henry Gocher, he announced in his paper that he was going to bathe in the sea the following day in full daylight in protest against the law, expecting to be arrested. In the event there were very few people about other than a passer-by who idly enquired who was the lunatic bathing in the sea. He tried again and was again ignored, but on the third attempt he was at last arrested and politely questioned by the police and released without charge. It wasn't until November of 1903, following copious letters from Mr Gocher, that the by-law was rescinded and another passed allowing daylight bathing on condition that adults over the age of eight wore neck-to-knee costumes. (Part of the problem was clothing, or the lack of; bearing in mind Victorian women did not expose so much as a bare ankle.) Years later, in 1907, Gocher received a watch from supporters inscribed 'Presented with a purse of fifty sovereigns. W H Gocher Esq. Pioneer of all day surf bathing, by his Manly friends, Feb 11 1907. Entered the water 2 October 1902.')

Henry Gilbert Smith provided land for the building of

several private and public buildings, including a hotel, a school and a wharf. He also helped initiate the ferry service which ran daily trips to and from the city (weather permitting) as early as 1858. He was known, unsurprisingly, as the Father of Manly.

Fairlight, designed by the architect Edmund Blacket, was completed in 1860, but Smith and his family only lived there for four years. When his wife died in 1867 Henry returned to England, leaving his various properties, including Fairlight and two hotels, in the hands of agents to sell. GM leased the building, as did his predecessor (and his successor).

Photos of Fairlight show an imposing, symmetrical building (including a tower added later), with a wide veranda and a set of steps leading up to a grand portico at the front, and another at the side leading onto a garden with a driveway flanked by a pair of stone lions on plinths. The inside is filled with pattern: flowered wallpaper, with frieze, jostles with patterned floor-tiles and decorated tablecloths. In the hallway a patterned rug is laid atop more patterned tiles and the archways are swagged with heavy, patterned fabric. Ornate mirrors and pictures hung from rails cover the walls, and a pair of miniatures – presumably of the original owner and his wife – are set into the panels of the living room door. There's not much bare space. There's very little bareness altogether. With wealth came opulence and with opulence came, presumably, clutter.

In those days Manly Beach was a quiet spot. The Ocean Beach was just sand dunes and scrub: the famous Norfolk pines (planted by GM's son RM among others) were yet to come. Gilbert Smith's Steyne Hotel sat on a large piece of fenced land with stables at the back where horses ran. Further along there was a small dairy owned by Smith, and next to it was a creek surrounded by 'lilli-pilli trees' with clinging vines on which children used to swing. The Corso, named by Smith, was a sandy lane; and while there were hotels, shops, houses, a school, two churches (Anglican and Catholic), a police station (with one constable who was responsible for policing as far as Palm Beach) and a post office, not to mention a *camera obscura*, there was no hospital, chemist or doctor.

Life at Manly Beach sounded simple, and pure, not to say healthy, and children and their parents would play games in their leisure hours such as rounders or cricket in Ivanhoe Park; or go on fishing expeditions or swim among the rocks on the harbour (which was allowed presumably) or take long walks in the surrounding hills and collect rare wild flowers with innocent abandon. There was a Pavilion in Ivanhoe Park where concerts were held, and the Port Jackson Steamship Company, who ran the Manly ferry, organised 'greasy pole' recreational events at the ferry and in the park.

GM and Julia immediately immersed themselves in local activities. Julia joined the committee of the parochial association of St Matthew's Church. GM was appointed to the board of the Manly Public School, chaired a meeting concerning the state of the roads, became a trustee of the Wharf Reserve and helped to sell tickets for a 'Grand Amateur Concert' at the Pavilion in aid of the local cricket club.

For GM the commute into work would have been a rather pleasant one: a short stroll to the wharf, hop onto the ferry, a leisurely 40 minutes or so to Circular Quay and another short walk to his office in George Street. He was a familiar figure on the ferry evidently, described by a resident of the time, George Aurrousseau, as a 'portly' old man who 'used to wear a straw boater hat, and sat on the deck of the Manly steamers full of fun and cracking jokes to other passengers'. In March 1874 he and other 'lovers of piscatorial sports' spent an enjoyable weekend fishing off the coast at Pittwater and Broken Bay on board *Mystery*, a wooden paddle steamer owned by a Captain Heselton. The (entirely male) expedition was for whatever reason reported in some detail in the *Sydney Morning Herald*.

It's a wonder that GM found time amid his leisure and community activities to pay much attention to his business, but he did. In 1867 the partnership with Sullivan had ended and GM was operating as GM Pitt, stock and station agent, with offices at 325 George Street. Then in 1871 he took on a new partner.

Robert Matcham (RM) Pitt, GM's second son and my great grandfather, was 22 years old when he joined his father's company. Up until then he had been working for the Railway Commissioners as an engineer. What made him change course isn't known, but from that time on the family firm traded under the name GM Pitt & Son.

In later life RM claimed that as a lad he 'cut his teeth on a corn cob . . . No one had any money in those days. We were all poor, and lived on what we grew on the home farm'. This is relative of course. RM never experienced the hardship of his grandparents, arriving in a strange country and eking an existence from hitherto uncultivated land; not to mention his own father, who grew up fatherless. RM's comment is more of an illustration of the family's astonishing rise in fortune in the 19th century, you could say.

In this, the Pitts epitomised the kind of families who arrived in the colony with nothing (other than, in their case, important connections), and through hard work and determination managed to make good lives for themselves. It was three generations and 70 years on from the day Mary Pitt set her first tentative foot upon Australian soil and by now all branches of her family were, in their own way, thriving.

Fairlight, rented though it was, was several steps up in terms of comfort and affluence for the Pitt family. With its abundance of rooms and its magnificent views and beautifully landscaped gardens, and – since there were servants' quarters – presumably servants, GM's business was obviously flourishing.

Moreover the Pitts' new home brought them marginally closer to the city and to its culture, which was growing in popularity – and respectability – to match the aspirations of the colony's increasingly middle class population. Theatre was no longer considered a corrupting influence, with audience members fighting among themselves or throwing missiles at the actors. 'Legitimate' (ie improving) theatre was available to all, as was serious opera. Furthermore, whereas previous visitors to Australia, while marvelling at its beauty and the other-worldliness of its wildlife had been less impressed by the squalor of the streets and the coarseness of its population, visiting chroniclers were now starting to talk about Sydney as rivalling the best that Europe had to offer.

The most notable of these was the writer Anthony Trollope, who like Dickens before him had sent a son to Australia, but who unlike Dickens actually spent a year touring the colony in 1871. He was delighted by Sydney in every way: he pronounced its hansom cabs and its public gardens the best in the world. 'Sydney is one of those places which, when a man leaves it knowing that he will never return, he cannot leave without a pang and a tear. Such is its loveliness,' he declared. He loved the chaotic layout of the city streets, and he was particularly impressed by the country's standards of education, especially in rural areas.

So Australia was at last becoming a nation at ease with itself, with an infrastructure, a parliament, railways and the beginnings of a telegraph service. For many people there was some way to go yet: less well-to-do inhabitants of Manly had to manage without any kind of water or sewage service and resorted to buying rainwater in which to wash their clothes. But times were changing rapidly: the population of Manly nearly trebled in the ten years from 1871 to 1881 and doubled again the decade after. This was fortuitous, in particular for young Robert Matcham Pitt, who was to play such an important public role in the development of Manly in years to come.

~

At the age of 24, two years after he'd joined the family firm, my great grandfather RM decided to get married.

She was described in an article written 100 years later as 'a very pretty little woman, of French descent'. She was the daughter of Julien Charles Blanchard, who had emigrated to Australia in 1836 from his home in Mauritius. Her name was

Marie Emilie Eugenie Blanchard.

I confess that all I know of Mauritius, other than as a fabulous tourist destination for the seriously moneyed (and as I recently discovered, a tax haven), is that the explorer Matthew Flinders was once held captive there for several years by the French during the Napoleonic Wars, in the days when it was known as the Isle de France. Further research shows me it is a tiny island in the middle of the Indian Ocean, the nearest landmass being Madagascar, and that it has been colonised over the centuries by several European countries including the Dutch (who called it Mauritius), the French (Isle de France), and the British (Mauritius), before it gained its independence in 1968.

I learn that at the time of Julien Charles's emigration the island had been under British control for 26 years and that slavery had been abolished the year before, in 1835. Under French rule – which lasted a hundred years from 1710 to 1810 – the country's economy was largely based on sugar plantations worked by slave labour, so the impact on daily life following abolition would have been acute. The majority of the population in the late 18th and early 19th centuries had been slaves, from various African countries. Now labourers had to be shipped in from other countries such as India and China.

So in my attempt to figure out why my other great great grandfather decided to emigrate several possibilities emerge: he was a plantation owner who saw his future prospects declining without the use of slave labour (despite the fact that plantation owners were very generously compensated); he did not fancy the prospect of living in a country full of immigrants from India; other members of his family had already migrated to Australia; or maybe he just fancied a change of scene.

So here, in the gap between two chapters, is a pause of a week or more, while the family historian sets out on yet another path, this time to investigate the seeds of the Mauritian connection.

Chapter 39

The Mauritian connection

With the help of other family members such as my cousin Libby, whom I know well, and a well-informed and helpful distant relative named Marg Kaan, whom I have never met but discovered on the internet, plus hours browsing in the British Library and on Ancestry, an image of this generation of my ancestors is coming ever so slowly into focus.

In the centre of the picture is my g-g-grandfather Julien Charles Blanchard. Born in Mauritius in 1809 to a French father Julien Yves, a sea captain, and mother Francoise Royer, from Rennes, in Brittany, Julien Charles (henceforth JC) arrived at Port Jackson on 20 January 1836 aboard the appropriately-named *Exporter*, along with four other people whose surnames I cannot immediately decipher. One of them appears to be a 'Madame Francis [sic] Royer', who I surmise was Julien's mother Francoise. Also listed are 'Two [unnamed] native Servants and their children' travelling steerage.

The indecipherable surname, so Marg Kaan informs me, is 'Masse'. It appears JC's mother Francoise married a second time, to Alexis Antoine Masse, by whom she had the three children who were the three other passengers mentioned on the list: her son Monsieur Anthony and two daughters, Mesdemoiselles Eugenie and Eulalie.

Of Monsieur Masse senior there is no sign, other than in an item Marg Kaan discovered some years ago in the Mauritian Archives, viz: '1831. Charles Blanchard to open the tomb of Antoine Masse to place therein the remaining of C Amanda. Sum paid 1.10.0.' It's a slightly macabre, not to say obscure reference, but who- or whatever C Amanda was Antoine Masse was presumably Francoise's second, now late, husband.

(Which means, you'd suppose, husband number one, Julien Yves, had died. Yet it turns out he too had married again, in 1813, two years after the birth of his youngest daughter. Since there could have been no divorce on Mauritius it seems the authorities either condoned bigamy or, as Marg suggests, they didn't care one way or another.)

Another character, dimly lit, joins JC in the picture. She is Marie Emilie Blanchard, who emigrated to Sydney from Mauritius in 1829 along with a man named Frederick Manton and a servant called Uranie. It transpires she was JC's younger sister. She was only seventeen years old at the time and Uranie, a family slave, was just thirteen. You would wonder why two teenagers might be let loose in a foreign country and you might suppose, rightly, that Emilie and Frederick had met before they travelled. The two lovers married soon after they arrived and went to live in Yass, where Frederick had been granted land and where he built a stone house called Mon Reduit. It was at that property that young Uranie met and married a shepherd called Richard Manton Jeffrey, with whom she went on to have nine children. (Mon Reduit was also briefly the home of Miles Franklin at a later time.)

The picture sharpens, and it now holds three people centre-frame: JC, his younger sister Emilie and her hubby Frederick Manton, twelve years her senior, who hailed from England originally, despite his French-sounding name. These three are closely bonded it turns out: JC worked for Frederick on occasion, and looked after Mon Reduit when the Mantons left on a trip to England.

So my faint hopes of discovering I have African slave

ancestry are dashed. The Blanchards were obviously a well-to-do family, with servants. They probably owned land in Mauritius and even, God save us, slaves. For the entire family to have migrated *en masse* (I could not resist) there must have been either strongly favourable reports of her adopted country wafting back from young Emilie, or maybe the abolition of slavery did have something to do with it.

Class and race differences were very specific in Mauritius at that time. The populace was divided into 'Whites' and 'Coloureds' and there was an official colour bar that, for example, forbade Coloureds from acquiring property from Whites or from holding high office in the militia. JC described himself as a 'gentleman' (a title forbidden to Coloureds), and comments made about him later by his future son in law indicated he was a bit of a 'prig'. So I can't help wondering what an affluent and effete young man, of French origin, would have made of the rough-and-ready, comparatively egalitarian colony of 1830s Australia.

In December 1838 in response to an advertisement JC bought an allotment in the town of Yass, for which he paid 'Eighteen pounds of lawful British money in hand well and truly paid'. There were conditions attached: that within two years he built himself a permanent dwelling worth at least £70, with proper drains; and the authorities held the right to take everything off him if necessary for the 'improvement' of the town, with three months' notice and with full compensation.

Then in July 1839 he bought a year's licence for a property called Hoombango, not far from Mon Reduit in the district of the Murrumbidgee, near current-day Tarcutta. How big this property was or what he did with it I have no idea.

So within months of one another both my great great grandfathers were acquiring land, one in the northwest corner of New South Wales, the other in what was to be called the Riverina. Within three years of arriving in his newly adopted country my Mauritian g-g-grandfather was doing all right for himself. It was time he found himself a wife.

Chapter 40

1839: Anna Sparrow

On 27 May 1839 a cargo ship called *Tropic* weighed anchor at Port Jackson, from London via Hobart. It brought, along with its cargo of wine, boots, printer's ink, rams, vinegar, several pianofortes and a plethora of other merchandise, a handful of 'unassisted passengers'. Among them were three members of the Sparrow family, from Ireland, and two branches of the Manton family with their nine children and a servant.

Anna Sparrow, aged sixteen, was travelling to Sydney from her home in Dublin along with her surgeon brother Thomas and his wife. She was not what you'd call a conventional beauty – a portrait of her later in her life shows her with a distinctly aquiline nose and a severe hairdo. But she had the sweetest nature and a transforming smile, and that long five-month journey from London gave her plenty of time to become acquainted with the Manton tribe, and in particular – I like to think – with their children.

Frederick and Emilie Manton were on their way back to Sydney after a two-year stint in England. In company with them and their six boys was Frederick's brother Charles and his wife and three children. Five months is a long time for young things to be cooped up on board a not particularly comfortable cargo ship with not a lot to do. So is it too fanciful to suppose Anna was able to get her hands on one of those pianofortes, tucked away in the hold of the ship, covered and trussed and no doubt out of tune, but just about playable? And that she was able to entertain the youngsters with some old Irish songs such as the Kerry Jig and Captain Playfair's Hornpipe, and the adults with snatches of Schubert and Chopin?

Music was Anna's life. She had plans to become a piano teacher in the new colony, even perhaps to open a music school one day. She was young and unworldly enough to assume everything to be possible. It was fortuitous for Anna and her brother and sister in law that the Mantons, fellow immigrants from ten years earlier, were travelling back to Australia on the same ship and able to tell them everything they needed to know about their new home.

Emilie took to Anna immediately. Not only had she endeared herself to her sons and kept them amused on the journey, she reminded Emilie of herself, arriving at Sydney for the first time ten years ago at much the same age and with similar rose-tinted expectations. Of course it helped that Emilie had had a husband-to-be in tow, and while there were things about the new country she might not have wanted to divulge to her new young friend – the lack of culture for instance, especially when compared with England, not to mention a unique form of egalitarianism she still struggled to get used to – there was a plan hatching in Emilie's mind that, if successful, would bind the two young women together in times to come.

She discussed her plan in private with Frederick, and with his endorsement, when *Tropic* docked at Hobart en route to its final destination she sent a message to Julien Charles to please be there to meet them on their arrival at Port Jackson.

There are no portraits of Julien Charles, but I have conjured an image of him as a dapper, precise young man, upright, snappily dressed – perhaps with a cane – and a touch of the dandy. Anna had never met a Frenchman before, certainly not one with such impeccable Gallic manners and delectable vowels. He was as gracious as you like with the lively Irish girl, disarmed even, despite her age. Anna had no intentions of marrying so young, not yet, there was far too much to be done before she embarked on the long journey into multiple motherhood. But what she may not have realised, in this strange, self-invented community, was that a married woman was perfectly able – if not, in Anna's case, expected – to continue to work for as long as she had the energy and the time.

I've no idea why the Sparrows chose to come to Australia in the first place. It would have been an expensive voyage for the three of them since they were travelling 'unassisted'. Nor do I know why they decided to pay for their own passage rather than take advantage of the assisted migration scheme. One can only assume it was because they did not meet the required occupational criteria: they were not labourers or domestic servants or followers of 'useful', or specifically, 'required' trades. Thomas Sparrow was merely a surgeon.

The Sparrows made their home somewhere in Sydney. In July Thomas Sparrow announced himself in the press as a qualified medical witness at coroners' inquests. Then a couple of months later he wrote to the *Sydney Monitor* to complain about the misreporting of a recent suicide attempt, at which the credit for saving the man's life from drowning was wrongly accredited to a Dr Bell. On the contrary, the writer insisted, '*I* and not Dr Bell, administered what was necessary ... the case was strictly mine, and I beg you will have the kindness (in justice to me) to contradict your statement'. The letter is signed 'Thomas W Sparrow, LRCSI AB HD &c.' 'LRCSI' means 'Licentiate Royal College of Surgeons of Ireland' according to Google, which identifies him as our Thomas. Why Thomas should spend time over something relatively trivial (except for those directly involved of course) is a puzzle. Maybe he was just trying to establish himself, a roundabout way of advertising.

Meanwhile Julien Charles continued to pay court to young

Anna, and on the 10th September 1840, 16 months after her arrival in the Great South Land, they married, first at St Mary's (Catholic) Church and then at St James's (Anglican) Church in Sydney, by special licence. The announcement in the newspaper describes Anna as the 'only daughter of the late Thomas Sparrow, Esq'.

There is no sign the newly-weds went to live at either of JC's properties in Yass or Tarcutta. They seemed to have spent their married life in Sydney, first in Elizabeth Street in the city centre and then in William Street in Woollomoolo. Later on they fetched up at different addresses in nearby Forbes Street, where against Anna's name appears 'Ladies School'. The dream I had bestowed upon Anna had come true.

Anna and Julien's first child, Marie Francoise (known as Mimi), was born in 1841, followed by Julien Thomas in 1844 and ten years later, Julien Charles. Marie Emilie Eugenie was born in 1857 and their last child, Marie Adele Emilie (known as Mae) in 1861. A 'Marie P A' was born and died in 1860. So it appears my great grandmother Marie Emilie Eugenie had no fewer than two sisters called Marie and two brothers called Julien, which, I belatedly discover after a great deal of hair-tearing confusion, is due to the fact that Mauritians are traditionally known by their second name (or in Eugenie's case, the third). So Marie Emilie Eugenie was known as Eugenie throughout her life, and occasionally 'Ginny', but never Marie.

It's fair to assume Anna Blanchard's school focused on music, and that Eugenie and her sisters were educated there. There was a rumour handed down that Julien Charles was a 'kept man', and not popular among members of the Pitt family. So it was the Ladies School that kept the family going.

It was there that Eugenie and her sisters would learn to read and write in English and perhaps, thanks to papa, in French. They would have lessons in needlework, music, deportment, elocution, books and the rudiments of cooking and domestic management, with especial emphasis on music: proficiency on the piano was essential for a young lady wishing to make a good marriage in mid 19th century Sydney society.

Ladies' Schools held concerts from time to time, at which their protégées performed solos and duets at the piano and sang Irish and Scottish airs. So let's suppose it was at one such event that the tall and handsome Robert first set eyes on the sweet-looking Eugenie at her mother's academy in Forbes Street, having been dragged there by a friend whose sister was a pupil at the school. It may have been the music that first caught RM's attention, or it may have been the early evening light that settled on Eugenie's chestnut-coloured hair and appeared to dance upon it as she moved her head in time to the music. She played the piano like a dream, Robert said later, accompanying her fellow pupils' songs with great delicacy and self-effacement.

When questioned on her appearance RM simply said she was 'perfect': perfectly proportioned, with eyes, nose, mouth and ears exactly the right size and in exactly the right place, and all of it precisely symmetrical. He may as well have been describing a building, but that's the way of men. As for her hair, it was neatly parted in the middle and drawn back over her ears to end in a loose bun at the back. She wore a voluminous dress with baggy sleeves and a large collar that made her appear smaller than she was. She looked very young, yet very assured.

She was cool with RM to begin with, as she was with everyone. It took several visits to the Ladies School before he could get her to acknowledge him. So instead he turned his focus on the mother, who was altogether more forthcoming and so obviously proud of her daughter and always happy to talk of her musical accomplishments. It was through Anna – whom RM described later as 'an angel' – that RM became first a friend of the family and then a very special friend of the middle daughter. Eugenie's reserve, and a certain snobbery, was inherited from her father, to whom RM never did quite take (hence his description of him later as 'a French prig'). She was choosy about her friends, although as time went on and as RM was to discover, once she felt comfortable with a person she was the warmest and sweetest person you could ever hope to meet.

On 15 August 1874, the 17-year-old Marie Emilie Eugenie, spinster, of Sydney, (aged 20 according to the marriage certificate), married 24-year-old Robert Matcham Pitt, bachelor and auctioneer, of Richmond, at St Peter's Church in Woollomooloo. The witnesses were RM's brother Charles Bryan Pitt and a Blanchard – the signature is hard to decipher.

The couple then went to live at Hill-Side Cottage on the Esplanade (now West Esplanade) overlooking the harbour at Manly. It was a simple, attractive place with a deep veranda, built on three-quarters of an acre and large enough to contain a drawing room, dining room and three bedrooms on the ground floor and a large attic room and two small servants' room above; plus a good kitchen, washhouse and laundry 'with water laid on' and a 'bathroom with patent watercloset'. It was here that Eugenie gave birth to Lionel, Adele and Arthur while RM constructed a much grander dwelling next door. This was Leona, a two-storey stone structure with bay windows on both floors, built 'with every modern convenience' including rooms with high ceilings and a bespoke billiard room. During 1878 and 1879 RM advertised first Hill-Side Cottage and then Leona to let or, in the case of the latter, to buy. One theory goes RM overreached himself, but one way or another matters resolved themselves and it was at Leona that my grandmother Muriel was born in 1880, followed at regular two-year intervals by her younger siblings Robert, Effie and Clive.

RM served as an alderman on the recently-formed Manly Council for thirteen years, from 1878 until 1891. Like his father he attended fortnightly meetings to discuss such pressing matters as drains, rates, drinking water and straying animals. (Drains and sewage seem to have been a perennial problem on the North Shore.) His hobby – which he was able to indulge later in his life at Wentworth Falls – was horticulture, and he was responsible, with others, for the planting of Manly's magnificent pine trees.

At this point however it is time to gently remove this happy branch of the family into the background of the picture as we focus once again on the main subject of the book.

Chapter 41

1870s/80s: Kirribilli

In 1875, six years after they moved to Manly, GM and Julia left Fairlight and went to live in Kirribilli.

Kirribilli – again for the non Sydneysider – is also on the north side of the harbour, opposite the city and a lot closer to it than Manly. Today it is one of the most highly desirable (and expensive) places to live in all of Sydney. Whether the same applied in the 1870s is another matter.

The Pitts rented a house called Holbrook. It had been advertised to let, and then for sale, by its owner Marshall Bayley, who described it as 'newly built of stone, containing 12 rooms, bathroom, pantry, etc. The grounds comprise about three acres, with extensive water frontage, bathing and boathouse, coachhouse and stabling'.

Like Fairlight it was a two-storey building, L-shaped, with a veranda. The entrance was in Carabella Street – where Holbrook Avenue is now – north of Kirribilli Point, Wotonga (now Admiralty) House and Kirribilli House, homes now to the governor-general and the prime minister respectively, but then in private ownership. A long driveway led to the house and beyond that to the garden and the harbour.

For GM and Julia, used to their 100 acres in Richmond and 35 in Manly, three acres sounds like a pocket handkerchief. But as handkerchiefs go it was as it were made of the finest silk. There was simply nothing to compare with that stretch of magnificent harbour frontage, and I can just see GM's eyes lighting up at the prospect of the fishing opportunities. Not to mention being able to hop onto a ferry from his own garden and be in the centre of the city within minutes.

In September they advertised for a cook, laundress and housemaid. In January the following year they decided to buy Holbrook, for £3,200.

GM soon became such a familiar figure sitting in front of his house and fishing that 'instructions were given to the ferry skippers that should he be seen at his favourite sport the steamers were to give the point a wide berth' (according to LF Mann in the JRAHS). The ferry collected him from a rock at the end of his garden and he 'would come aboard with a cheery 'Good morning!' to all, the passengers in the meanwhile trimming the ship to receive the weighty old gentleman'.

'Trimming ship' of course meant the passengers shifted themselves to balance the boat in order to avoid capsizing. Another account of GM's journeys across the harbour says the ferryman brought with him two 56lb weights to act as counterweights. All of which is not just an indication of my g-g-grandfather's huge bulk, but the fact that both fellow passengers and ferrymen were prepared to accommodate him without objection.

It was not all rosy on the North Shore in the 1870s however. The city may have been a matter of minutes away by steam ferry, but looking at newspaper reports of the time the north and south sides of the harbour may as well have been different countries. The 'hardy suburban pioneers' of the North Shore had the advantage of living amid open spaces of native bush containing beautiful wild flowers and birds, but when it came to the necessities of modern living it was the poor relation of its neighbour across the water. The ferry service to Circular Quay was infrequent, and there were complaints about preference being given to, for example, the building of a railway line in the Eastern Suburbs rather than on the North Shore. There was no hospital, the streets were in appalling condition and the sewerage, or lack of, was disgraceful. Some years later a reporter from *Freeman's Journal* described St Leonards (now North Sydney) as 'a Lazarus at the gate of the Government'. While southern suburbs enjoyed tramways and other privileges the North Shore was staunchly ignored by the powers that be. Part of the problem, according to the same report, was the squabbling, disagreement and general corruption amongst the representatives of the three local councils – St Leonards, East St Leonards and Victoria.

This was not a state of affairs a man like GM could ignore. Three years after going to live in Kirribilli he put himself forward for mayor of East St Leonards.

Meanwhile he continued to attend public functions. In January 1876 he co-vice chaired a banquet at the Masonic Hall in Sydney in honour of Mr J S Farnell MP. RM attended also. Ten days later GM was again vice chair at a banquet to celebrate the arrival of telegraphic communication in Manly, and a month after that he convened a meeting of the Sydney and Suburban Water Supply at his offices in George and King Street.

Then in January 1877 GM and RM, aka Pitt & Son, announced they had sold, 'on behalf of Mr Hoskisson, Coorar and Carar stations, in the Gwydir district, with about 8000 cattle'. Thus had events come full circle, as the very first property GM had acquired on his own behalf in 1848 and passed on to his neighbour John Hoskisson six years later, he had now sold on behalf of Hoskisson's son and under the auspices of GM Pitt & Son.

~

It's a balmy April day and I am on a crowded bus going north over Sydney Harbour Bridge, there being engineering works on the railway lines, just like back at home. I'm aware travelling in this direction of the mountain of glass and steel that is North Sydney. You wouldn't think there was a building here more than fifty years old or less than twenty storeys high. Once in the quiet streets beneath the bridge, in Kirribilli especially, it is very different. On this occasion as I wander across the grassy stretch towards the harbour all I can hear is the soulful sound of a saxophone, played by a lone figure sitting on the grass and leaning against the supports of the bridge.

It still is a beautiful sight, the harbour, despite what's happened in Circular Quay. There's the iconic Sirius building, public housing, perched right by the side of the bridge as you approach the city from the north, with its 'Jesus Saves' sign. It's the quirkiest example of brutalist architecture I've ever seen, but it's under threat of demolition – or it was when I was there last – like so much of old Sydney. Money talks loudly here it seems.

Anyway I am on my circuitous way to the Stanton library in North Sydney to investigate my g-g-grandfather's history as mayor of East St Leonards. At this stage I am blissfully ignorant of the comments made about the state of the streets on the North Shore, and the alleged corruption of local aldermen who were said to favour the roads surrounding their properties above all others.

The library is quiet this Saturday afternoon. There's just one other person in the family history section, and a very helpful assistant who guides me to the various indexes and drawers stuffed with random manila files containing random sheets of paper with snippets of news and gossip on old North Sydney.

Then, to my excitement, I discover the complete Minute Books of the Borough of East St Leonards 1879-1885, on computer. Here, I think, I will find the essence of my grand old ancestor, who was elected mayor on 6 February 1879 and held the office unopposed for five years. He must have been quite something to have commanded so much respect and authority.

To say it's all a bit of an anti-climax is not to say my findings are useless, far from it. They reveal a side to GM I'd hitherto been unaware of. To put it briefly, the role of mayor of East

Leonards was neither glamorous nor exciting. GM presided over monthly meetings, held at the Council Chambers, which often did not take place because he was the only one to turn up. When they did take place they were concerned with stuff like rates, petitions for road improvements, extra street lamps (gas), better drainage and requests for a resident policeman (rejected). I keep scrolling through the archives until closing time, hoping, hoping to find something truly memorable, even heroic. But it's all admin and bureaucracy.

Well now, I think to myself as I wander down Miller Street wondering where the bus stops are, my findings may not make front page news but they do show an interesting side to a man like GM. He was not just a man of enterprise, he was a man of detail. A man prepared to give of his time (unpaid) to conduct dull meetings about mundane everyday things. His office stood for something, of course. But how much more heroic it is for a man with GM's charisma and personality to cosset himself in some dim room in a municipal building attending to the minutiae and everyday needs of everyday people, away from the limelight and the public eye. GM, I say to myself as I arrive back in the heart of the concrete and glass: I salute you.

Chapter 42

The North Shore Lazarus

Throughout the 1870s and 1880s there were calls for the three municipal councils of St Leonards, East St Leonards and Victoria to merge. Looking at old maps it appears East St Leonards covered an area from Milsons Point in the west to Mosman Bay in the east, including Kirribilli; Victoria covered the Blues Point peninsula and Lavender Bay, and the largest of the them, St Leonards, made up the rest: north and east of the other two and reaching as far as Middle Harbour in the north and including Mosman. It's said the two larger councils were in favour of merging but Victoria was holding out: the minnow resisting being swallowed by the whale, you could say.

So I am trawling through Trove for evidence of squabbling between councils, and of the claim from the man from *Freeman's Journal* that the North Shore was a 'Lazarus'. The first item I come upon is a letter written by 'A Correspondent from East St Leonards' demanding to know why no one was organising a banquet for the Mayor and aldermen of East St Leonards to thank them for the miles of 'cleanly' streets, the 'paternal solicitude' they displayed for the safety of pedestrians by enclosing many of the said streets within private, and 'aldermanic' grounds, and in particular for a 400-yard length of drain piping, part of a sewage scheme between 'where and where', of which the council were apparently so proud they decided to display it to the citizens after it was laid, so they dug it up, before burying it again at a different depth.

It took me a while to twig the writer was being ironic, in a particularly Aussie way. So this adds weight to the claim in the *Freeman's Journal* that the council members were looking after themselves. Moreover in an election meeting held in 1883 a Mr Glacken, a candidate 'for municipal honours', objected as a ratepayer to 'being ruled from Kirribilli Point . . . Messrs Pitt, Lord, and Wilson had for a long time faithfully represented Kirribilli' he declared, at the expense of poorer ratepayers. Of course he was making political points, but again, it's looking like game and first set to the man from *Freeman's Journal*.

Reading on however, and I see that for as many complaints as were raised in the press there were meetings and petitions between the three mayors and various members of the government to do with water, tramways, railways and a proper sewage scheme. At that time it appears raw sewage was running down a creek and emptying into Careening Cove, leaving residue lodged on its banks. In response the Works Department said they would look into it, but warned that anything they might do to assist this borough would cause jealousy on the part of all the boroughs.

The following year 'Nomad', reporting again in the *Freeman's Journal*, vented his spleen on the councils for the poor state of the streets, and the government and its broken promises to provide the inhabitants of the North Shore with tramways, not to mention a bridge – a petition and designs for which had been submitted years ago. The only reason the local residents put up with this state of affairs, he ranted on, was because most of them spent their days working in Sydney and were too tired when they got home to care.

However I can find no reported evidence of disagreements among the three councils. In public at least they seem to present a united front in their efforts to 'de-Lazarus-ise' the North Shore. The fact that gaslight did not arrive there until

1877, 36 years after Sydney town, and the first cable tramway appeared in 1886, seven years after steam trams had been established in the city, definitely adds to the Lazarus claim; as does the fact that the latter event, which was accompanied by the usual pomp and ceremony and holiday atmosphere, marked the first official appearance on northern soil of the governor, Lord Carrington. (He'd been in the colony six months.)

Amid all the fire and fury, while a number of names crop up as targets for general vitriol, GM's is not among them, despite the fact that he was part of what you might call the 'Kirribilli elite' (my term). As far back as 1876, long before he became mayor and very soon after he went to live in Kirribilli, he had called a meeting in his office to discuss the business of water supply. He had personally donated £20 towards the improvement of drainage, and it's also said in a book called *The Municipality of North Sydney* (GVF Mann) that he had 'set aside a piece of vacant land near the foot of Mount Street where an inexhaustible spring existed. Residents were permitted to obtain supplies from the spring. It was known as 'Pitt Spring'.' There is no reference supplied and I can't find any other evidence for this elsewhere, but the implication is the spring was on land that belonged to GM, even though it was some distance from Holbrook.

Up until 1885 the only water available to the Lazaruses on the North Shore, in Manly and elsewhere, was rainwater. In dry seasons they had to buy it, at some cost, and from time to time shipments of water arrived from across the harbour, or from Lane Cove. There'd been outbreaks of cholera and typhoid as a result. Early in 1885 the government announced they had plans to sink a pipe across the harbour from Dawes Point to Milsons Point as soon as they could find divers. Come May this had been done, ready for the grand public opening in July, which was attended by Mr Moriarty, Engineer for Harbour and Rivers, the serving mayors of the three North Shore municipalities, 'ex-Mayor G M Pitt' and other VIPs from both sides of the harbour. The success of the venture was celebrated with champagne, needless to say.

Progress had its own minor irritations however. In 1891 'Burglary and blasting' hit the residents of Kirribilli and Lavender Bay during the building of a tunnel for a train linking the latter to Blues Bay. The lives and dwellings of several local residents were threatened by fragments of stone landing on their roofs 'with all the force of aerolites' [meteorites], the stables of several gentlemen at Kirribilli were relieved of saddles and harnesses, and 'Mr G M Pitt's premises having been twice visited, that gentleman has good-naturedly invited the thieves to complete their work by taking his coach and horses,' said the man from *Freeman's Journal*.

I know he was my great great granddad but it seems GM's name rarely crops up in public without the words 'genial', 'generous' or 'good-natured' attached to it. Whether or not he could have done more for the people of the North Shore it's worth remembering the job of mayor was not just unpaid and under-appreciated but subject to the whims of government. There was only so much a mayor could do.

In 1890 the three boroughs of St Leonards, East St Leonards and Victoria were finally amalgamated under the name of North Sydney; at which point the *Freeman's Journal* man exclaimed, 'Hurra! Huzza! North Sydney for ever! Twelve years it took to bring it about.'

~

Among the reports on the angst and complaints and endless meetings I came upon the following comment in the *Evening News* in June 1883, when GM was still mayor of East St Leonards:

> 'A wonderful fact! Mr G M Pitt, Mayor of East St Leonards, made a long speech before the Minister of Works today and did not quote poetry.'

Chapter 43

1879 & 2017: Captain Cook, then and now

In February 1879, two weeks after he became mayor, GM was invited onto the committee for the unveiling of a new statue to Captain Cook in Hyde Park.

It was the biggest public event the colony had ever witnessed and the *Sydney Morning Herald* devoted seven columns to the reporting of it. A public holiday was declared, and proceedings kicked off in the afternoon of Tuesday 25 February with a grand procession of 'public bodies', including the Mounted Police, Oddfellows, Friendly Societies, volunteer Fire Brigades, Druids, representatives of the Churches and of the Army and Navy and two military bands.

The various groups assembled in the Domain, accompanied by around 12,000 people and 30 brass bands. From there the procession progressed past the statue of Governor Bourke in Macquarie Street, along Bridge Street to George and Park Streets, pausing at the Town Hall so the mayor of Sydney and aldermen could join the parade. They marched on past buildings festooned with bunting, flags and extravagant floral arrangements to Hyde Park itself. It was estimated between 70,000 and 100,000 people turned up to watch the goings-on, all of whom had 'cheerfully submitted' to the loss of a day's pay: 'a pretty conclusive indication', according to a current newspaper report, 'of the estimation in which they hold the name of Captain Cook'.

Such was the air of celebration and good humour even the rival societies cheered one another as each individual group entered the park. It was believed the Holy Catholic Guild of St Mary and St Joseph presented the most attractive appearance (different newspapers had different views according to their various allegiances), though the Sydney Marine Benefit Society carried the most flags and 'the novel costume of the Ancient Order of Druids caused much amusement to the uninitiated'. It took half an hour for the whole procession to arrive and there were so many of them some were forced to stand outside the fenced area surrounding the statue.

At 4.15pm the governor, His Excellency Sir Hercules Robinson, arrived along with a number of dignitaries and took his place on a dais 'elegantly draped and upholstered by Messrs. David Jones and Co'. In front of him sat the members of the committee and behind them, 200 schoolgirls clutching bouquets and dressed in white frocks with blue sashes, and a male choir 50 strong. Every stand, every tree, lamp post, pillar and building roof was smothered in humanity. Among the crowd could be seen a small number of 'gentlemen of colour' and the 'sombre visages' of 'a few Australian aborigines'.

Proceedings began with a rendition from the choir of 'Rule Britannia', including one verse written especially for the occasion, following which the governor rose to his feet to deliver his speech. He began by acknowledging that since only the people immediately surrounding him could hear what he was saying and the majority of the crowd were standing he would keep his narrative as brief as possible. He then launched into a detailed biography of the 'great navigator', with special emphasis on his humble beginnings and education, his 'courage, fortitude, patience, self-denial and resource', his dedication and 'plodding, persevering industry' and respect for the rights of others; a hero and role model for the rising generation to admire and imitate. He marvelled at the transformation that had taken place since 'the discoverer of this land' sailed through Sydney Heads barely a century earlier. 'Cook found this land a desolate waste,' he said, 'inhabited only by a few naked and hostile savages, and what is the prospect which meets the eye to-day? A country covered with flocks and herds - dotted over with cornfields and vineyards - with busy cities and peaceful hamlets with churches and schools . . . the happy home of over two millions of our own race, who are in the enjoyment of civil and religious liberty to as full an extent of any people upon the face of the earth.' He looked forward to the day of federation of the Australian provinces, and of 'closer political association with the mother country . . . while still remaining an integral part of the Empire of which it is now their pride and privilege to form a part.' His 'brief' oration, which at a guess lasted a good two hours, was then followed by the unveiling of the statue, accompanied by the merry peal of the bells of St Mary's Cathedral and three cheers for the Queen, the governor, the Royal Navy, the governor's wife and the mayoress and the ladies of the colony. Proceedings ended with an interestingly modulated version of the National Anthem sung by the choir, after which the governor and his entourage began to disperse. By the time the last people had vacated the park night was falling, at which point the entire city was illuminated by lights atop the Post Office, and George Street and surrounds were 'made as bright as day'. The whole event, it was concluded, had gone off without a hitch or a hint of discord or 'larrikinism'.

One can imagine the excitement, the joy and sense of celebratory euphoria on the part of everyone who was there. In just over 100 years their country had gone from 'nothing' to a thriving community of free-spirited individualists. What was there not to celebrate?

GM's name is not mentioned in the newspaper report, but as the mayor of East St Leonards and a member of the organising committee he would have been up there on the dais along with the governor and his retinue, and I have no doubt he would have been cheering louder than anyone in praise of the Great Navigator and 'Discoverer' of the proud country called Australia.

I was wondering to myself what the crowd reaction might have been had a similar event taken place a hundred years later when I was reminded by an Australian friend of the James Cook Bicentenary 'celebrations' of 29 April 1970. I was in Australia at the time and while I was aware of various events happening around the state I confess I didn't then take a lot of interest.

29 April was the day Captain Cook and his crew first landed at Botany Bay in 1770. Two hundred years later the event was commemorated in the presence of Queen Elizabeth in the form of an ambitious re-enactment of Cook's landing, with a tall ship masquerading as *Endeavour*, a number of actors portraying Cook, Joseph Banks and the ship's crew and a handful of Aboriginal actors representing unidentified 'warriors'. It was attended by around 50,000 spectators, among whom were several Aboriginal protesters, who threw wreathes into the water as 'Captain Cook' and his men stepped ashore to purloin their country.

Times had changed over the two hundred years it seems, but not that much.

As I explained in my previous book I was aware, in the brief three years I spent in Australia as a Pommie migrant in the early 1970s of a distinct change of attitude towards the mother country. I was an actress then, and revered for my British background. I found it relatively easy to find work, as did my fellow Brits. As time went on and a local film industry was beginning to emerge with the likes of 'Sunday Too Far Away' and 'Picnic at Hanging Rock', the mood was changing. Australian culture was beginning to be taken seriously.

Moving on 50 years or so and the mood has sharpened. In August 2017 the indigenous journalist Stan Grant, responding to the tearing down of Confederate statues in America, started asking questions about Australians' attitude to their own history, drawing particular attention to the inscription on the statue of Captain Cook in Hyde Park. '"DISCOVERED THIS TERRITORY IN 1770" maintains a damaging myth', he wrote, 'a belief in the superiority of white Christendom that devastated Indigenous peoples everywhere . . . The idea of terra nullius was the law of whiteness.' This in turn led to the statue – and others of Governor Macquarie and Queen Victoria – being vandalised and daubed with 'No Pride in Genocide' and 'Change the Date' (this referring to Australia Day – the annual commemoration of the arrival of the First Fleet on 26 January 1788); which in its turn drew outrage from the Prime Minister and others, including Stan Grant himself, who explained it was the word 'discovered' he was objecting to and gently suggesting the inscription might be amended to reflect modern views on Australia's past.

Here and now is not the time for an in-depth debate on Australia's 'forgotten' history, or the official attitude to its indigenous people, then or now. But these commemorations do point up Australia's changing perceptions of its past. It is easy and tempting to condemn those pillars of 19th century establishment such as GM as imperialists, glorifiers of what we might now call white supremacy, and of a country (Britain) he had never been to and never would. But in the context of the times he was a patriot, unashamedly proud of his nation's achievements, along with what sounds like the majority of Australia's white population.

What might have been going through the minds of those few sombre-faced 'Australian aborigines' among the crowd that day back in February 1879 is another matter.

Chapter 44

Julia

Meanwhile, what of Julia? GM's world – whether it was his stock and station business, his mayoral commitments or his social engagements – was almost entirely male oriented. There is hardly ever a mention of women being present. So how did the likes of Julia Pitt fill their time?

She was 60 years old when she moved to Kirribilli, and it would have been just her, GM and 23-year-old daughter Eva; plus a number of servants. It was what you might call a luxury lifestyle, with no young children to care for, few if any household chores and a husband who was frequently out attending to business, banquets or fishing expeditions. So what did Julia *do*?

Was she lonely? Did she even feel a bit spare perhaps?

I am picturing her sitting on the very spot where GM liked to fish. She is looking out over the harbour, as I did 150 years later from a point close by. On the far side of the water she sees a sizeable town with several substantial buildings: the Customs House at Circular Quay and behind it, the Town Hall and the Museum and, just visible perhaps, the spire of St James's Church. Many-masted vessels of all sizes line up against the sides of the quay next to the ferry terminal. There is no bridge of course, and a multi-storey warehouse where the Opera House is now. Steam ferries chug past, churning the water and throwing up spray into Julia's face; and the odd passenger waves to her from one of them and she waves shyly back. The sun is comfortably warm this early in the day, though later it will be stifling. The fashion for the ample crinoline of recent years has been modified somewhat and replaced by what we know as a bustle (what Mary Gilmore described as 'a bolster case with a gusset'): the skirt draped over a complicated form of scaffolding to keep it in place and provide extra fullness behind. But oh those layers, so many of them, from neck right down to ankle. Not forgetting of course the obligatory hat, boots and gloves. The whole outfit suited to the temperate English climate maybe but punishing in the Australian heat. It's a wonder the ladies did not continually faint.

Time stretches ahead of her.

Time. There was never enough of it when Julia was young. Back in the Brickfields of Sydney, the eldest child of a single mother – a single working mother, who not only ran a shop but after the death of her husband had four children under the age of ten to care for. Life for Julia had always been work, as it was for everyone she knew, whether it was looking after the younger siblings or helping her mother in the shop, and then later, when they moved to Upper Richmond, in the pub. It was a day-to-day existence, a lot of it was drudgery, but life had a purpose, even if it was simply getting through the day and making sure there was a way of surviving the next.

Marrying GM changed everything. At the age of twenty, an age when many young people in the 21st century are still studying and planning what to do with their lives, Julia Johnson, daughter and stepdaughter of convicts, married a gentleman. Son of a free settler, owner of valuable property on the Hawkesbury. Overnight she became a lady. She wore fine clothes, and had a housekeeper to do all the chores she was used to doing herself. All that was expected of her was to run the household and produce babies. Which she did, relentlessly, over a period of 21 years.

I feel there was a bit of Julia she regretted leaving behind. The struggle for survival, and respectability, was a constant challenge in those early days, but there was satisfaction too. There was the look on her mother's face at the end of a busy and fruitful day's work in the shop, totting up the takings, knowing there was enough extra to put towards 'the grand outing to a glorious place' she was always going on about, that may or may not have existed and certainly never materialised. The move to Upper Richmond was a wrench in many ways, and there were times when Julia noticed her mother's restlessness. Thank goodness she had a pub to run, otherwise what would Mary have done with her time?

But while GM would never have been one to dwell on – or to deny – Julia's background she was aware of a change, a shift in sensibilities in the colony. There were no longer convicts in Australia in the 1880s. Everyone was respectable now. Nobody spoke of the old days when the country was an open prison. Few people had experienced it, a whole generation was growing up knowing nothing about it. It was simply never mentioned. And that, Julia thought, was a shame. She felt at times invisible, as if her childhood, her parents, had never existed.

This is all guesswork of course. I have absolutely no idea what was going in Julia's mind. Of all the Pitt women she is the one I know least about. She did not produce children out of wedlock and she did not abscond from the family home. No scandal attached itself to her and she never rated a mention in anyone's memoirs, or in the press. Unlike many of her descendants she continued to live with her husband up to the end. But just because she is invisible does not mean she should be ignored.

Was Julia happy? Let's hope so.

Chapter 45

1879: Pitt, Son & Badgery

Henry Septimus Badgery entered the orbit of the Pitt family back in the 1860s.

He was younger than GM by 26 years but he came from a similar background: born in Sutton Forest (in the country near Moss Vale, south west of Sydney) and brought up on his father's farm, he had already acquired his auctioneer's license and was selling stock when he and GM met – as I suppose – at a meeting of the Agricultural Association. I imagine the two, who were similar in nature it appears, got along rather well. And since GM was already by then an established stock and station agent he was happy to take the younger man under his wing and act as what we would call his mentor.

How Henry came to meet GM's daughter Julia is not on record. So let's imagine she was attending a social function in Richmond following the local agricultural show at which Henry and GM had acted as judges. She was introduced to the dashing young man by her father and was immediately taken by his commanding stature – he was a tall man, almost as tall as her father – and his resemblance to the recently deceased President of America, Abraham Lincoln (though she may not have made that connection). So she did not in the least mind being placed next to him at dinner; at which he spent the evening regaling her in detail with the weird and wonderful goings-on behind the scenes at the show: the rivalry, the small but deadly acts of sabotage, the feuds that had their roots in arguments about the precise shape and colour of the perfect pumpkin, and lasted a lifetime. And whereas she would as a rule have found such garrulousness resistible her companion had such a gift for making potentially dull activities sound interesting, even at times hilarious, the time passed by very quickly. When he paused to apologise for talking too much, with a self deprecation young Julia did not find entirely convincing, and to confess his nickname was 'Yabber Joe', she was charmed all the more. And finally, when he ended the evening by confessing he wrote poetry under that very same name, the wedding bouquet was all but complete.

GM would have been delighted. The marriage between his friend and protégé and his beloved daughter took place at St Peter's Church in Richmond on 13 November 1869. It was a marriage of both love and business convenience.

For the next eight years or so the Badgerys lived in Maitland, where Henry worked for the stock agents Brunker & Wolfe and involved himself in local affairs, while Julia did the wifely thing of producing children and disappearing from the records. He became mayor of Maitland in 1876 and two years later was elected member for East Maitland in the Legislative Assembly, where according to his biographer Bobbie Hardy he became known as 'one of the few genuinely independent members of the Assembly' and focused his attention mostly on rural affairs. He stayed in parliament, first representing Maitland and then Monaro, south of Sydney, for seven years. Oddly he never seemed to live in the electorate he represented, as by late 1877 he and his family had moved to Sydney, shortly before GM Pitt invited him to become a partner in his firm. In 1879 Henry was living in Roslyn Terrace in Darlinghurst, although according again to Bobbie Hardy he sent Julia and the children to live at Bronte, for the sake of their health and to save money, where 'he joined them once or twice a week'.

Thus it was announced by Henry Badgery on the 3 February 1879 that the partnership of Brunker, Wolfe & Badgery had 'expired by effluxion of time on 31st January last' and that he had joined the firm of G M Pitt & Son, which would hitherto be known as Pitt, Son & Badgery.

For his part GM welcomed his son in law to the company and announced that Mr Badgery would 'personally attend to the receiving, classifying and disposal of all fat cattle, lambs, calves, and horses, and our Mr R Pitt to the receiving and disposal of fat sheep'.

The word 'effluxion' had me baffled for a moment, but since it appears to mean the expiration of a contract the switch from one company to the other was presumably an amicable one on all sides.

Photos of Henry Badgery taken around the time he joined his father in law's business show him to be a still striking figure, broad-shouldered and more portly than a few years previously, his hair receding slightly and his beard gone but more than compensated for by an imposingly waxed moustache. A man of distinction, one might say.

Taking on an extra partner meant GM could ease off a bit from the day-to-day running of the company. Not that he ever gives the impression of someone who was inclined to ease off on anything, not even when he was approaching 70 years old. Nonetheless having another experienced auctioneer and stock agent on board would have enabled him to spend less time at the saleyards knee-deep in cowpats and more time wooing new clients.

In GM's lifetime the selling of stock had gone from seemingly casual (if pre-arranged) meetings by the roadside between seller and buyer to purpose-built saleyards set up by private individuals such as William Fullagar, in whose yards on the Western Highway GM had cut his selling teeth. In the 1860s Homebush had become the go-to centre for stock trading, but ten years later that was looking pretty rundown: in wet weather the animals were often belly-deep in mud and had to be physically pulled out of it, and newspapers were full of complaints from butchers and stock owners about everything from conditions to location.

So in 1882 the City Corporation finally opened spanking new saleyards, again at Homebush. It was the result of years of campaigning in parliament by GM and others for the government to take over the whole business of creating, running and maintaining proper yards to replace the current ones, since according to GM stock owners and agents were unable to reach a consensus between them. 'We would have had yards long ago if all could have agreed to sell at one place,' he told the committee.

GM's appearance before the special committee of the Legislative Assembly reveals the pragmatic farmer in him. He held strong views on the hardiness of stock, which did not need shelter in saleyards in his view, so long as 'the bottom [of the yards] was made sound . . . I do not believes in luxuries,' he was reported as saying; the bedraggled appearance of a rain-drenched ewe would not affect its value and besides, buyers were 'getting more sensible now; they begin to handle their ribs to see if they are fat'. As for the coating of mud on the cattle that was at times so thick you could not tell what colour they were, this had even worked to his advantage on occasion when a buyer mistook the layer of mud for a layer of fat that wasn't there.

Slaughtering animals a long way from the saleyards was 'monstrous', in his opinion; they suffered not at all from being driven long distances by an experienced drover. As for the idea of importing dead meat from elsewhere: 'If we ever live to see the day when meat is brought from Melbourne here,' GM expostulated, 'it will only be when we are starved out.'

For the new yards, he estimated they needed 25 acres of land, at a cost of around £10-£12,000. With stock owners and agents paying 6d a head for cattle and 1d for sheep for the use of the yards the government would receive 'a tremendous income . . . the best paying thing under the Crown'.

Three years later on 5 June 1881 work began on the new saleyards and in November the following year they were officially opened by the mayor of Sydney, along with the customary pomp and ceremony and accompanied by sundry aldermen, butchers and stock agents, among them GM and Henry Badgery.

The yards comprised 40½ acres, of which 20 were ready for immediate use and able to accommodate 1,200 cattle and 12,000 sheep, in well-drained pens. There were covered platforms for the auctioneers and buyers and a reservoir capable of holding twelve months' supply of water. The yards were connected to the main route to Parramatta via especially-built roads, and to the railway by means of new sidings provided by the Railway Department. The total cost, including the purchase of the land, was £60,000.

The honour of conducting the inaugural auction fell to Henry, following which the party adjourned for a 'first-class' luncheon and the customary toasts. They drank to 'Success to the new sale-yards at Homebush', the Associated Stock Auctioneers, the Master Butchers, the Contractors, the Press, the Mayor and Aldermen of the City of Sydney and, proposed by GM, 'the pastoral interest' and finally, of course, 'the ladies'. The party then returned by train to town.

The City Corporation had excelled itself, it seems, albeit at roughly five times the estimated costs according to GM. Needless to say this did not stop Henry Badgery, twelve years later, complaining in the press about conditions at Homebush, and pointing out that despite the yards having paid for themselves within a few years of their inception the Council ignored all pleas for improvements or changes. The only solution to this problem being, in his view, a repeal of the Act under which the Council owned and controlled the ground so 'we can have a new form of management'. Back to the old days of private ownership, in other words.

~

That same year, 1882, GM was granted 40 acres of land in

Wentworth Falls, a result of an application he had made three years earlier. Why Wentworth Falls, and why he should be granted land at that point are joint mysteries. The first, which being some way into the Blue Mountains west of Sydney was way outside any of his catchment areas, may have had something to do with his son GM junior, who according to one account had visited the area in his post as surveyor in the Surveyor General's office and 'was so charmed by the country that in 1879 he applied for a grant of 50 acres'.

The answer to the second, according to the same source, appears to lie in the Volunteer Force Regulation Act of 1867, which – if I interpret the jargon correctly – allowed for anyone who had acted as a Volunteer for seven years or more a grant of land.

GM never built on the 40 acres, but in 1889 his second son RM began building a house there – closely watched by the *Katoomba Times*, who published regular updates on his progress – and the following year GM himself 'launched' the house and called it 'Coorah', after the first land grant he had received back in 1848 on the Gwydir. RM and Eugenie began living at Coorah full-time from around 1915 onwards (from GM's death until then they were living at least partly at GM's house Holbrook in Kirribilli), and over the years they transformed it into a horticultural paradise. They hosted celebrities such as the opera singer Dame Nellie Melba and the property magnate Lord Vestey. (RM was a patron of grand opera apparently, though his granddaughter Barbara claims he was pretty tone-deaf and that it was Eugenie who was the music-lover in the family.) The house played a crucial role in the lives of subsequent Pitt generations but was eventually bequeathed to the Country Woman's Association, and thereafter became the Blue Mountains Grammar School, which it still is to this day.

(Some years back I queried the fact that the house was given away because, it was said, 'no one in the family wanted it'. Bearing in mind it held such fond memories for RM's grandchildren, including my mother, this seemed odd, to say the least. When my cousin Libby and I fetched up at Coorah in 2008 for a family reunion we told the people behind the desk we'd come to reclaim the house. For a glorious split second their faces told us they believed us.)

Meanwhile business at Pitt, Son & Badgery's was burgeoning. According to the *Illustrated Sydney News* in 1882 the company was averaging annual sales of 250,000 fat sheep and 40,000 fat cattle, and over a million of each of store animals. (Store animals being animals that are kept until they became fat enough to sell as fat animals, or so I understand it.) Their premises had moved from George Street to King Street and back to George Street again, this time on the middle floor of a magnificent three-storey building called Pastoral Chambers, next to the Joint Stock Bank. 'No more central position could have been selected, or one in which the healthy throb of the great heart of the colony is more marked in its beat,' marvelled the *Illustrated Sydney News*. The building had an atrium and a glazed roof, providing 'a perfect flood of light and complete ventilation'. The three partners of P, S & B each had his own office, and there were spacious lavatories and 'the special luxury of a bathroom – a novel but very necessary feature in the internal fittings of a large establishment in a city like Sydney,' said the writer.

(The building is still there, and appropriately or otherwise the ground floor was, in 2017, a McDonalds.)

These premises obviously reflected the expansion in the business of Pitt Sons, as they came to be known, to include what you might call the pastoral needs of their clients and their families. (That's 'pastoral' in the sense of 'caring for'.) In years to come they would provide accommodation for clients visiting Sydney from their country properties. They'd even offer to escort their clients' children across town, to school, or to catch a train. The stock and station agent may have begun as simple auctioneer, salesman, financier and general advisor on all things from stock prices to breeding; he was now fast becoming hotelier, nanny, secretary, entertainer and host to anyone who was or was likely to become a client, plus their extended families. A combination you could say of agent, mentor, therapist, landlord and life coach rolled into one.

In 1888 Pitt Sons became a registered company under the name Pitt, Son & Badgery Ltd.

According to their 50th anniversary booklet by the time of its registration the company was regarded as 'the leading stock and station business in the State of New South Wales'. Its 'authorised capital was £100,000, and £50,000 was issued in 100,000 shares paid to 10/- each'. Partners in the 'old' company were issued with a certain amount of shares each, part for assets and part for goodwill, and further shares were issued for property adjoining what were now known as the Flemington saleyards at Homebush.

The company paid out dividends of ten percent up until the early 1890s, when the country hit a depression, after which no dividends were paid at all between the latter part of 1893 and 1904. This is an indication of the state of the economy rather than the efficiency or otherwise of Pitt, Son & Badgery Ltd. From 1909 dividends of between ten and twelve percent were paid out annually. In these days of rock-bottom interest rates that sounds like a fortune.

Chapter 46

1885: The world without a sun

On 22 September 1885 GM and Julia celebrated their fiftieth wedding anniversary. There is no record of how – or indeed whether – they actually did this, so once again it is left to us imagine the happy event.

I have gathered together the entire Pitt clan at Holbrook on this balmy spring evening. It is warm enough for the guests to congregate on the lawn outside the house to be plied with champagne. Julia moves among them, smiling, kissing cheeks, occasionally breaking into a gentle laugh. She is 70 years old now and frail, and she leans on the arm of her youngest daughter Eva. She is dressed plainly, as is her wont, in green silk, unadorned but for a pearl on each cuff and a touch of lace at the neck.

Of the older generation there is only Robert, GM's younger brother, now 68 years old, and his wife Sarah, both still living in Trafalgar at Kurrajong. Of the younger, there is George Matcham junior, the surveyor, with his wife Elizabeth, of Sunnyside in North Richmond; Jessie and her husband William Garling, one-time mayor of Richmond, of Hobartville; Julia and Henry Badgery and RM and his wife Eugenie, all living in Manly, where RM is now an alderman; Edwin, also one-time mayor of Richmond, with his wife Julia Johnson (at some point

Edwin left Bronte at Richmond to live at Bronte in Artarmon, and became a banker) and his younger brother Harry Austin, also living at the Richmond Bronte, who is unmarried. Charles Bryan lives in St Leonards with his wife Ada Perry and has a solicitor's practice in town; Colin works for the family firm and lives around the corner from Charles with his wife Madeleine; and finally Eva.

Among them are solicitors and surveyors, bankers, stock and station agents and several mayors, but no farmers (except perhaps for Harry Austin). And they are all still grouped in Richmond, Manly and the North Shore.

At 8 o'clock the guests retire to the dining room which is laid with two long tables decked with solid silver cutlery, glass candlesticks, woven bamboo place mats and bowls of wild flowers. GM deposits himself at the end of one of the tables and places his wife Julia at the end of the other.

As the party take their seats for dinner the volume of conversation increases as the Richmond branch of the family – GM junior, Jessie, Edwin and Harry Austin – exchanges gossip with the North Sydney branch of RM, Charles Bryan, Colin, Julia and Eva. Julia looks on with fond if detached amusement as they tuck into a dinner of beef paté and roast duck with plum sauce with the uninhibited greed and total abandonment of manners peculiar only to family groups.

Her family, Julia muses, represents what many would consider the best the colony has to offer. They are the new Australians: prosperous, hard-working, community-spirited and proud. None of them looks back to the past, to the old country they never knew or the old ways of the colony they never experienced. They are unencumbered by doubt about their position in the world or guilt about anything that may have happened in the past. On the surface at least their lives seem blessed. Unlike their ancestors not a whiff of scandal attaches itself to any of them. Like the continent they inhabit, they have become respectable. They are, Julia ponders with a wry smile, pillars of the community, every one of them.

And the origin of all this, the stoutest pillar of them all, is standing right there at the head of the next table and doing what he loves to do most: delivering a speech. It was the moment Julia was half dreading and so she bows her head and closes her eyes and shuts out the world. Truth be told she is a little deaf now, so much of what is being said doesn't reach her, despite the booming voice. She is aware of a reference to a castle called Marriage and a cage called Love, of captives and captors and a lifetime spent bending to an iron will. 'And while outwardly it would appear it is the captor who steers the ship do not be fooled! It is she, this meek, humble, unassuming soul you see before you, who powers the engine, who calls the shots, who rules the roost.'

What nonsense, thinks Julia, I was just a wife and a mother, that is all I ended up being. But I did them both well, and if that is all I am remembered for, so be it. My job is done now.

'As I said before, many times, it is my belief that a man finds his own luck,' the voice thunders on. '*Virum solum amatores digni*. But just occasionally, luck will find you. As it did fifty-one years ago when I walked into a pub and saw Aphrodite standing behind the bar serving alcoholic drinks.'

Yes, because in those days a woman worked, Julia's thoughts meander on, and never thought more of it. If my own daughters had experienced what I experienced of my own mother – if they had seen me working from dawn to dusk, building a business . . . But it's an unavoidable fact that children only remember their parents in old age, and in my case, as the one who stayed at home and kept the fires burning while the father of the house . . .

'Ladies and gentlemen, if I can just about call you that,' says the great man, 'I invite you to raise your glasses to the strength behind the throne: to my saviour and my muse; my rock, my sage, my Golconda diamond. Without whom there would be no light in my world and no joy in my heart. Girls and boys, I give you your mother, Julia Pitt!'

And now the guests are rising as one to drink her health,

and Julia's husband bursts into a version of *Old Lang Syne*, in its original Scottish brogue, and Julia doesn't know whether to laugh or cry so does both. The room cheers and stamps and behaves in an altogether riotous manner while her husband of fifty years goes to her and bends to kiss her on both cheeks. And the celebrations continue on and throughout the night, while the main actors retire quietly to their quarters.

~

Well, whether or not such an event took place it would be good to think the long marriage of GM and Julia was celebrated in some way, as the following year Julia was dead.

She died on the 2 August 1886, of 'natural decay', aged 71. Her funeral took place the following day in Richmond, to which her body was conveyed by train from Redfern to St Peter's churchyard – just as GM's was to be ten years later.

~

In the various speeches GM delivered throughout the years he invariably proposed a toast to 'the ladies' – 'without whom' he said on one occasion, it would be 'a world without a sun'.

The loss of his companion and lover of fifty years must have cut a swathe through George's heart. There is no sign of his slowing down at the end of his life, though there are signs of an irascibility that was not obvious before. This may have had to do with old age, or as I like to think, the loss of the woman who had acted as a moderating influence on a man who never liked to do anything by halves.

GM outlived all his younger siblings except Robert. Sister Mary, who married her cousin Thomas Laycock, died suddenly of a heart attack in 1878 when her husband was away prospecting (so suddenly apparently the coroner was called, from some distance away and to his considerable annoyance, to diagnose the cause of her death). Youngest sister Eliza, who also married her cousin Austin Forrest Wilshire, had died back in 1861 in childbirth, aged 40. He also outlived two of his daughters, Jessie Garling and Julia Badgery, who died in 1887 and 1894 respectively.

Chapter 47

1880s/90s: Battling on

GM remained active throughout the final decade of his life, and not just in the business of Pitt, Son & Badgery. He was elected president of the North Shore Working Men's Rowing Club and joined the committee of the City Railway Extension. He attended a Highland Sports day held at the Association Cricket Ground, a garden party at the Observatory to meet members of the Australian Association for the Advancement of Science, and celebrations at the US Consulate in honour of the 'Glorious Fourth'.

He also took to firing off letters to the press, mostly complaining about the appalling state of parliament and the execrable behaviour of its members, who did nothing but sit around all day talking and spending money freely without parliamentary sanction – 'Like the Premier's sow,' he proclaimed, 'they all want a suck' – rather than concentrating on vital matters such as the prevention of Chinese immigration, the importance of a Local Government Bill and the necessity to reduce the number of MPs to one-third of their number. All of which skulduggery GM put down to manhood suffrage, which he dubbed 'the greatest curse that ever befell this country'.

He also sounded off about the North Shore Ferry Company's decision to replace season tickets with single penny fares paid in 'copper coin', which he considered not only inconvenient but an insult to loyal and regular customers such as himself. The company's shares had risen from 6s.6d to 41s, he was at pains to point out. But 'Not satisfied with doing so well, they call on their best friends to give up taking tickets . . . because they are unable to prevent dishonest persons from passing over free.' All of which he deemed nothing short of dictatorial and he hoped that should they agree the shareholders would call on their directors to resign.

GM's letter inspired a response from a 'Salus Populi' (roughly translated as the welfare of the nation), who not only took the Mickey out of his own 'dictatorial' attitude but heartily endorsed the ferry company's decision, with the added hope they would provide a speedier service than the current one averaging 22 minutes 'from Quay to Bay'.

Then I came upon a reference in the *Evening News* in October 1888 to an opinion GM apparently expressed regarding the Newcastle miners' strike.

The strike was over pay, and the requisitioning of non-union miners to take the place of the strikers. There were riots, and the police and the military were sent in. Seven of the rioters, three of whom were aldermen, were tried at Maitland Circuit Court and, to the disgust of the judge – who in his lengthy summing-up expressed his opinion that the police should have fired into the crowd rather than over their heads, on the grounds that 'sacrificing a few lives [could] . . . save a greater number' – the defendants were acquitted.

The strike, which lasted three months, evidently had the support of the local community and the press, including the *Evening News*. On 11 October 1888 it published a short piece under the heading 'Mr G M Pitt's Opinion', which is worth quoting virtually in full:

'Mr. G. M. Pitt does not like the attitude of the Evening News over the miners' strike. He thinks it is like the Bridgenorth election — all one sided. On the subject of strikes in general, Mr. Pitt observes that the laborers who built the

Great Pyramid of Egypt did not strike for wages. Probably not, but Mr. Pitt, from the depths of his historical researches, does not say why. The reason was that these laborers were in effect slaves who labored without pay, and lived on something like an onion and a pint of grain a day . . . The only striking they knew of was the lash that fell on their shoulders.'

Five days later, under the heading 'Masters and Men', the *Evening News* appeared to quote GM verbatim on the same topic:

'Mr. G. M. Pitt writes apropos of the miners' troubles at Newcastle: "At one time a working man was considered to be part and parcel of an estate. The masters gave the orders, and men obeyed them. The man was paid off by a joint agreement, and he was satisfied. Nowadays the working man is not satisfied with his lot, and he would fain be dictator, and bring his employers to the same level as himself. He forgets that every man is not born with the same amount of brains. Some are born to rule, and some are born to work. This has been the case from the beginning, and it will be the case to the end of time."'

If this is a true representation of GM's words then to the 21st century person it is no less than shocking. It smacks more of medieval feudalism than of 19th century egalitarian, opportunistic Australia, where ex-convicts could be landowners and working men became parliamentarians and premiers. He'd married the daughter of convicts for goodness' sake!

GM had obviously enjoyed running battles in print with the *Evening News* over the years. Why they reported these two letters indirectly I've no idea, but I can only assume they were a true representation of his words as there's no doubt GM would have taken issue with them if they weren't.

Taking these and his other comments (to do with the scourge of manhood suffrage in particular) at face value, it shows a whole new side to my genial great great grandfather – a rather less genial side, you could say. Despite the difference in time and prevailing attitudes there is no doubt he was of the far right in his views, vigorously outspoken and opinionated, almost an oligarch in his views on the inequality of mankind.

It's an occupational hazard for the family historian of course, to discover an ancestor with unpalatable views. Yet that's not take away from the generous, gregarious man that GM obviously was. The *Evening News* seemed to view my g-g-grandfather with some affection, and his opinions as those perhaps of an elderly eccentric from another era.

In possible mitigation of GM and his opinions, I came across something called the 'Servants and Labourers Act' of 1828. Known colloquially as the Masters and Men Act it set down in distinct clauses exactly what might occur should a servant decide for whatever reason to disobey his or her master or mistress, and what the ramifications might be: viz imprisonment, with or without hard labour, and/or loss of wages. There were rules also as to how a master or mistress should treat his or her servants, but obviously such an Act was more likely to favour the well-connected masters than the rather more vulnerable servants. So clearly defined divisions did exist, and not just in GM's sensibility, between master and servant generally.

Besides, a person is important for his deeds rather than his words, is he not?

Chapter 48

1890s Conclusion

In the 1890s Australia suffered its second depression of the century, and in the life of GM. There were the usual causes – an economic boom leading to excessive lending and borrowing and inflated prices – plus the explosion in immigration. Banks collapsed, the market plummeted and many companies went bust.

Pitt Sons soldiered on. Their sales even increased in the 1890s, though they paid no dividend to shareholders. And GM continued on as chairman, presiding over every AGM until 1895.

He would not have enjoyed the 1890s. It was a decade of strikes, of which the Newcastle miners' strike was just one. The maritime dispute of 1890 spread not just to seamen and wharfmen but to coal miners, who refused to dig coal for ships operated by non-union members. The seamen reciprocated by refusing to handle coal dug by blacklegs. At one point there were 28,500 workers on strike. (They lost.) The following year there was a shearers' strike, which again was lost when the striking men ran out of food and were forced to capitulate. In 1892 miners in Broken Hill went on a sixteen-week strike against the use of non-union labour, mostly imported Chinese. They also lost. Despite the growth and popularity of the union movement (it's said some girls refused to dance with blacklegs at country balls) the Masters, so-called, did not seem to have much difficulty recruiting non-union labour, and for the most part they had the Government on their side.

Fortunately perhaps, for his sake, GM did not live to see an Australian Labour (now Labor) government, though the first Labour parties were beginning to form in his lifetime and for a while they held the balance of power between the Free Trade and the Protectionist parties in the 1890s. Nor did he witness the Act of Federation – the bringing together of all six Australian colonies under one Commonwealth government (though not yet their railway gauges) – even though that too had been on the cards for several years.

What he did live to see, unfortunately, was the death of his daughter Julia Badgery. She died on 29 July 1894 at her home Oyama – built for her by her husband Henry in Manly – from influenza, brought on by an attack of asthma. Once again her remains were conveyed to Richmond by train and buried in the family vault in St Peter's churchyard.

It's said GM took an active part in the running of Pitt Sons even in his eighties. But come 1896, when he reached 82, the man who'd never had a day's illness began to feel distinctly under par. Listless, lacking energy and appetite, he was compelled for the first time in his life to call the doctor.

Dr Clarke diagnosed 'Bright's Disease', a form of kidney disease sometimes connected to diabetes. The big man, who enjoyed nothing better than a hearty meal and a drink or two, was ordered to rest and stay in bed as much as possible. And when that didn't work (or rather GM did not comply), he was placed on a regime of warm baths, blood-letting, opium, diuretics and laxatives, and a diet that excluded alcohol, cheese and red meat.

'What?' I can hear the old man bellowing – his voice could still thunder when he needed it to – 'You're denying me everything that makes life worth living!'

He'd have been a terrible patient. He'd have worn the

endurance of poor Dr Clarke down to the bare bones. Rest was anathema to the man who was used to fifteen-hour working days, attending meetings, presiding over conferences, often travelling the back roads of New South Wales for days at a time; and when he wasn't working, living it up at banquets and luncheons and other festive events; why, if he took a sip of wine with every toast he proposed he'd have downed an entire bottle before the evening got going!

In August of 1896 the *Stock and Station Journal* announced with regret that GM had been 'ailing and confined to his house' for some weeks past; although on enquiry it seemed he was slightly better and they trusted the 'Veteran Stock Salesman' would soon be restored to full health.

But he wasn't. On 12 October the great man breathed his last. He died in his bed at Holbrook. The following day his body was placed in a coffin and transported to Richmond, via Redfern, and to his final resting place alongside his wife in the family vault at St Peter's Church.

~

GM's death spawned a dozen full obituaries and death notices in the press as far afield as Launceston in Tasmania, Coolgardie in Western Australia and Brisbane & Toowoomba in Queensland. They referred to him as 'venerable', 'respected', 'energetic', 'popular', 'widely-known' and 'a grand old man'; a hardy pioneer and an old warrior, 'one of the type of men who made this colony what it is today'. They spoke of his generosity, not as someone who appeared on the official list of charitable donors so much as a man who gave freely and spontaneously 'to those who had not been so fortunate in the struggle of life'. They recalled his thunderous voice, his cheery manner and his remarkable memory, 'never at a loss for an apt quotation' from his favourite writers, Burns and Shakespeare. They described his early beginnings on the Hawkesbury and his adventures further afield on the Gwydir and elsewhere – not always with total accuracy – and his reincarnation as a stock and station agent and founder of Pitt, Son & Badgery:

'one of the best known firms In pastoral and financial circles In Australia'. They paid tribute to his years as mayor of East St Leonards and the vital part he played in obtaining 'a proper and permanent water supply' for Sydney (the 'North' is missing here). 'Were honors evenly distributed, his name would now figure In the City Council-chamber as one who had devoted the most years of his life to the welfare of the citizens', said the *Daily Telegraph*. The *Evening News* fondly recalled the letters that appeared in their columns, 'often coming down with sledge-hammers blows upon public men', and the curious fact that in all his long life he never ventured beyond the borders of New South Wales.

Some newspapers, the *Stock and Station Journal* in particular, told the story of GM's grandmother Mary Pitt, the family's true pioneer, of her arrival in the colony in its very early days and the family connection with Admiral Nelson. This same newspaper devoted two full columns to his funeral, which they described in great and even emotional detail. The body was placed in a lead coffin 'encased in a polished cedar shell, mounted with silver bearings', taken from his home in Kirribilli across the harbour to Redfern and placed upon a car attached to a train and transported to Richmond, the town of his birth, where:

> 'As the procession moved through the streets of the sleepy old town, every place of business was closed and not a soul was visible, apart from the long procession. As a hot wind swept across the flats, and the church bell tolled its deadly message, it seemed as though the whole place were in mourning for the man who had been born beside the river long ago.
>
> ' . . . he was the link between the fat stock men of to-day and the ante-saleyards days of an almost forgotten time. He was a grand old landmark, and in losing him we lose one of the noblest of the fast-perishing pioneer race . . . we ne'er shall look upon his like again.'

Among the 150 or so men present at the funeral (women did

not attend such events then I believe), were GM's six surviving sons and two sons in law (Antonio Tornaghi and Henry Badgery, now remarried), four grandsons, representatives from Pitt, Son & Badgery and many others from Richmond and elsewhere. The ladies sent wreathes.

~

For us in the second decade of the 21st century the rush to keep up with the latest technological innovations in mobile phones, home computers, video games, virtual reality machines and other trinkets often seems overwhelming. But it is nothing compared with the enormous changes that occurred during the lifetimes of GM and his 19th century contemporaries.

From the sailing ship to steam transport; from rough wood fencing to barbed wire; from a time when three days' travel on foot or horseback could take a white man outside the official limits of location, where he could pitch his tent, mark out his land and hope for the best, to an established country with six colonies. From days when the Aboriginal community was visible everywhere to its almost total sublimation and near-annihilation.

In GM's lifetime the colonial population of Australia had spread from its original confines of Van Diemen's Land and the Nineteen Counties surrounding Sydney Town to the outer fringes of the continent; from the Pacific in the east to the Indian Ocean in the west and what was now called Tasmania, and the new cities of Melbourne, Adelaide, Perth, Brisbane and Darwin. The country's interior had been surveyed or explored by intrepid Europeans such as Ludwig Leichardt, John McDouall Stuart, Allan Cunningham, Thomas Mitchell, John Oxley, Charles Sturt and John Eyre, with the aid of Aboriginal guides. The continent had been crossed and mapped from south to north through the famous Red Centre and its iconic rock formations which they named Ayres Rock (Uluru) and the Olgas (Kata Tjuta), and the myth of the inland sea had been scotched. GM had lived through the reigns of fourteen governors, witnessed the birth of a two-house parliamentary system and – through gritted teeth – manhood suffrage; a Supreme Court, trial by jury, the end of transportation, the creation of Australian Rules football and the discovery of precious minerals including gold, silver, lead, copper, zinc and iron ore, as well as the ubiquitous coal.

Most importantly GM had seen the country of his birth go from a land of tentative promise – if not then quite the 'worst country in the world' – to a nation of progress and celebration by all Australians 'young and free'; though perhaps not so much by its Aboriginal people.

Personally speaking, despite his eccentric views on the Master-Servant relationship there's no question my great great grandfather was a man of enterprise, energy and generosity and a passionate patriot; that the community and the people around him were enriched by his presence and by everything he did for them, and that Australia was a slightly better place because of the 82 years he lived in it. You cannot say fairer than that.

So farewell George Matcham Pitt. In the words of one of your favourite writers:

> 'An honest man here lies at rest
> As e'er God with His image blest.
> The friend of man, the friend of truth;
> The friend of age, and guide of youth:
> Few hearts like his, with virtue warm'd,
> Few heads with knowledge so inform'd:
> If there's another world, he lives in bliss;
> If there is none, he made the best of this.'

(*Epitaph on my own Friend William Muir, at Tarbolten,* by Robert Burns)

Epilogue

GM left the control of his estate, worth £11,832, to his lawyer son Charles Brian and to RM, the latter of whom renounced his right to Probate and Execution of the will to his younger brother.

RM's wife Eugenie inherited Holbrook, on which GM owed £4,000. Bronte was bequeathed to the three children of his son Edwin, who had built it. GM junior inherited the 30 acres near Windsor and some duelling pistols. £1,000 was set aside for Jessie's children (Jessie herself had died nine years earlier), £1,500 for sons Edwin and Colin and £1,200 for Harry, who was unmarried. Charles Brian received £200 and sundry other items. GM's only surviving daughter Eva was given £500 in her own right. He also left £200 to his niece Emily Johnson – the daughter presumably of his late wife Julia's brother John – and £50 to his housekeeper, Mrs (or Miss) Snedon. He gave £100 each to the Benevolent Asylums at Windsor and Sydney and the Randwick Asylum for the Destitute.

RM had already received his 40 acres at Wentworth Falls, and he benefited indirectly from the bequest of Holbrook. Charles Brian's £200 seems by comparison with his male siblings rather modest, but as executor and administrator of the will perhaps he gained in other ways. GM junior's 30 acres were probably worth a fair amount. All in all if wills are indicators the Pitts were what we can assume to be a united family.

GM's company Pitt, Son & Badgery Ltd kept going under the same name and under the directorship of RM and Henry Badgery. Henry took over the chairmanship and remained there until 1903. RM became Managing Director. In 1907 the company resumed paying dividends and moved offices to a brand new purpose-built home in O'Connell Street.

The building – which was sadly demolished in 1970 – boasted a 'Palm Court' with palm trees, hanging baskets, marble floors, fine wood panelling and a lift. It was here that RM and his fellow directors entertained clients, business leaders and celebrities. Among the services provided was shopping – 'anything from a nail to a Mercedes' – finding cooks and governesses, arranging theatre tickets, meeting a train with a consignment of day-old chicks or a small child, choosing wedding presents and even a best man, and supplying transport to take clients to and from sales and auction rooms.

RM was, like his father, a big man with a big personality and a loud voice. There was an aviary in the Palm Court full of songbirds he was fond of imitating, and the story (according to the *Australian Women's Weekly*) goes that one day, being in his customary hurry he slipped on some birdseed, swore loudly, picked himself up from the floor, flung open the aviary door and the birds flew away forever. He was known to be constantly laughing or whistling an aria from an opera; but he was also impatient, and if he was kept waiting because someone left the lift door open on another floor he would yell loudly enough to be heard at Circular Quay.

When RM was living at Coorah he commuted into town every day by rail from Wentworth Falls. He was regarded as the Number One fat stock salesman of New South Wales, but unlike his father his ambitions extended way beyond the state boundaries. He travelled the world, lived to 86, in the latter years (amicably) apart from his wife, who outlived him.

The year after GM died the company began trading in wool, and turnover went from 8,000 bales a year in 1897 to 43,000 bales in 1907. Pitt Sons was taken over in 1972 by Scottish Australian Holdings Ltd, and in 1976 it was acquired by Elder Smith Goldsborough Mort Limited, though it continued operating under its original name.

RM's death in 1935 marked the end of the Pitt family's participation in the company. The only one of RM's sons to join the company was Arthur (aka AGM), a lawyer who was on the board but didn't want to take over the company. It seems GM and RM's talent for entrepreneurship faded with that generation.

Bronte, the original Pitt property where GM was born and raised, stayed in the family until 1919, when GM's son Edwin's two surviving offspring sold it, the year after their father's death. In the 1930s the new owners partitioned the two 100-acre properties and Mary's original grant, which she'd named Pitt Farm, ended up divided into six portions. Thomas's grant, Nelson Farm, remained intact under its next owners, William and Mary Betts, apart from 25 acres which they sold off in 1961. Their daughter Margaret lives there now and has restored Edwin Pitt's old homestead to its original glory. Without her friendly and informative cooperation the family story would be that much poorer.

As for Holbrook: a scroll through Trove shows it stayed in the hands of RM and Eugenie until it was eventually sold in 1915. They were living in Wentworth Falls from around 1890 (according to cousin Libby) but spent some of the time at the Kirribilli house after GM's death – their youngest daughter Doris was born at Holbrook in January 1897 and their eldest, Adele, was married from there in 1903. In January 1905 Eugenie advertised for a laundress for Wentworth Falls and a General Servant for North Sydney, which implies they were living in both locations. Then in April of the same year it became a boarding house, advertising rooms to let with access to Boating, Fishing, Sea Baths, billiards and tennis courts. The house had been turned into twenty rooms and was managed by a Mrs Ann Smith. Among the tenants was a 'Mr AJM Pitt' (possibly the above-mentioned AGM, or Arthur), whose room was damaged along with others in a fire in April 1909.

In November 1913 RM eventually put the house up for auction. It was advertised in the press as 'Holbrook Mansion and Grounds', with 22 rooms and beautiful lawns etc, and subdivision into 'Three magnificent allotments', but it didn't achieve its reserve price. So it was advertised again the following year, this time subdivided into seven allotments, and eventually sold in September 1915 for, according to rumour, around £12,000. The house itself remained as a boarding house until 1922, when it was demolished and the land divided up yet again to accommodate several large blocks of flats.

Several family members, regrettably, disappeared from view – the Scott family in particular.

In the 1841 census a William Scott is shown living in a house in Richmond with three other males: one aged between 14 and 21 (possibly his son John), one between 21 and 45 and one over 60, who may have been his father. At that time William himself was 41 and his son John 16. The others males could have been workers on the property. Of his three daughters – Betsey, 14, Augusta, 10, and Frances, 8 – there is no sign.

What does one make of that? There is no indication of exactly where William's property was, but it is possible it was close by Bronte. There is no sign on the same census of any of the Scott children living at Bronte – except, possibly, Betsey.

As we know Betsey married John Timmins in 1848, and the following year John married Elizabeth Shields. Augusta had four children by two different fathers and Frances one child by Arnold Harpin (no record of when they married). Then it all goes quiet until William dies in 1868, in Richmond, aged 68, the year before GM and Julia left the district.

Someone out there may know more about the family, in which case I would be delighted to hear from them.

Henry Badgery meanwhile married twice more after the death of Julia, first to Alice May King in 1896 and then to Sybilla Louisa Hooke in 1900. After he left Pitt Sons he founded a stock and station agency named Badgery Brothers, named for his sons, of which he was managing director until his death in 1917. The firm continued until 1918 when it too was absorbed into Goldsborough Mort.

The company name of Pitt, Son & Badgery exists to this day. There are very few people in the agricultural businesses who are not familiar with the name, if not with its dynamic founder.

I think GM would have enjoyed knowing his name lives on. Whether or not the paltry efforts of his great great granddaughter have come near to doing justice to the memory of such a great man is another matter. She can only say she has done her best.

Afterword

Of course the story is not complete. No family history ever is. I would be delighted to hear from anyone who can fill in any of the gaps in my family saga, or to correct any of my conclusions on everything from the handling of livestock to parliamentary procedure in 19th century Australia, or anything else.

I have created a Pitt family history website at marymatchampitt.wordpress.com, with outline information on the various branches of the first generation of Pitts, including the Faithfulls, Wilshires, Woods, Jenkins and Laycocks. Please feel free to leave (friendly) comments on the site.

I have also started a Pitt family Facebook group at https://www.facebook.com/groups/341776523285974/?ref=bookmarks

Whether or not you are related to the Pitt family I would love to hear from you.

Acknowledgments

A special thank you once again to Michael Burge, for his help and advice with the manuscript and for his beautiful cover designs. A man of many talents and infinite patience.

Thank you to Di and Chris McCarthy for their expertise on all things agricultural, without whom I would not have been able to write this book.

Thanks again to my cousin Libby White, who has accompanied me on most of my expeditions throughout New South Wales, and whose late mother Barbara Lamble was responsible for my setting off down this path in the first place.

Thank you to Penny Nelson for her editing.

Thank you to all the relatives who have contacted me over the years with vital information about various branches of the extended family. In particular Marg Kaan (a descendant of the Mantons), Gail Sutton (from William and Margaret Scott), Michelle Kaplan (Julia Johnson's sister Sarah), Jeff Pitt and Michael Want (GM's brother Robert), Carol Liston (Robert Aull), Carol Roberts (James Wilshire junior), Jeanette Dixon (GM Pitt junior), Clayton Simpson (Aboriginal Pitts) and his cousin Dorothy Tighe-Pitt (ditto).

Thanks to Barry Corr for his vast knowledge of and help with Aboriginal research, and to Richard Green for his Darug translation skills.

Thanks also to Michael Le Couteur for his advice and research on early stock and station agents in New South Wales.

And finally, a big thank you to the Royal Australian Historical Society for funding my trip to Moree in 2015 to research GM and William Scott's early adventures on the land.

Author biography

Patsy Trench is a bilingual Anglo-Aussie, born and bred in England to an Australian mother and Anglo-Irish father. She began her working life as an actress, in the UK and in Australia, where the highlights were working alongside the legendary Chips Rafferty and Skippy the bush kangaroo. She has been a scriptwriter, script editor, playscout and lyricist and co-founder of The Children's Musical Theatre of London.

She is the mother of two adult children and lives in London with a Freedom Pass. When not writing books she organizes theatre tours and teaches theatre part-time at Kingston University to visiting students from overseas.

Also by Patsy Trench:

The Worst Country in the World (2012): about GM's grandmother Mary Pitt. 'The true story of an Australian pioneer family'.

The Awakening of Claudia Faraday (2019): a novel set in 1920s England about a society woman behaving badly.

The Purpose of Prudence de Vere (2019): The remarkable memoir of Claudia's best friend, good-time girl and free spirit.

References and chapter notes

Abbreviations

ADB	Australian Dictionary of Biography
Col Sec	Colonial Secretary
HRA	Historical Records of Australia
HRNSW	Historical Records of New South Wales
JRAHS	Journal of the Royal Australian Historical Society
SMH	*Sydney Morning Herald*
SRNSW	State Records of New South Wales

Prologue
The description of GM's funeral is from *Sydney Stock and Station Journal*, 16 October 1896, p6.

Introduction
The title of my book *The Worst Country in the World* was based on a comment by Major Robert Ross, Lt Governor of New South Wales, ten months after the arrival of the First Fleet in Port Jackson in 1788: 'I do not scruple to pronounce that in the whole world there is not a worse country than what we have yet seen of this.'
 Edward Bell, unsuccessful squatter but later private secretary to Governor La Trobe in Victoria, is from *Station Life in Australia*, by Peter Taylor, pp6&7.

Chapter 1: GM, head of the family
Thomas Pitt's obituary is from *Sydney Gazette*, 3 February 1821.
 George's reaction to his father's death is invented, as is GM working alongside Scott to keep the farm going. Details about 'bloat' – caused by the eating of a native plant called trefoil – are thanks to Di and Chris McCarthy.
 James Scott being sent to an orphanage is from SRNSW, Col Sec Index

1788-1825. Under James Scott it reads: '1818 July 25, Mother dead, father at the Coal River. Recommended for the new orphan school.' (Reel 6047; 4/1740 pp253-4) 1819 Jan 1, 'Admitted to the Male Orphan School; Mr Pitt his parent/guardian.' (Fiche 3307; 4/7208 pp3-4) (Thanks to Gail Sutton, a descendant of William's sister Margaret.)

Chapter 2: Staying on
Thomas's grants are from censuses of the time. He was also given land in the Badgerys Creek area, though there's no record of him having farmed there. There is a Pitt Street in Badgerys Creek and another in Richmond itself, both named after Thomas. Elizabeth's advertisement is from *Sydney Gazette*, 10 February 1821, p2.

Chapter 3: Scandal
The scenes between William and Elizabeth are imaginary. But the children they had together are real.

A 'Selkie' is a Scottish mythical seal with the ability to change into a human on dry land.

Chapter 4: The Hawkesbury
The joint names of the Nepean and Hawkesbury rivers come from two early expeditions that set out from Parramatta and Sydney at the same time, travelling in different directions, and discovered what they thought were two rivers several hundred miles apart. It wasn't until later they realised they were one and the same.

Cowper's quote is from a letter to colonial secretary Campbell. (HRNSW 7, p285)

The early beginnings of Richmond School is from *Early Days of Windsor*, Jas. Steele. Mr Harris's quote is from *Macquarie Country*, D G Bowd, p182.

The description of the school building is from *Hawkesbury 1794 – 1994: the first 200 years*, Jan Barkley & Michelle Nichols.

Information on Mathew Hughes is from *Early Days of Windsor* and *Macquarie Country*, p183. As a non-commissioned corporal in the British army it's unlikely Hughes had received more than an elementary school education and, possibly, one or two years at secondary level. 'Convict and emancipist teachers, New South Wales, 1789-1830', by Geoffrey Burkhardt (online).

Richard Barker was convicted of an unspecified crime at Lincoln Assizes and transported for 7 years on board *Speke*, arriving Sydney 18 May 1821.

The two other government servants in the 1825 muster were a lifer called George Draper (arrived *Asia 1*, 24 July 1822) and James Manley (arrived *Batavia* 5 April 1818, sentence not stated). Manley doesn't appear on any convict lists, or on the convict list for *Batavia*, so it's possible he changed his name.

In the 1828 census Elizabeth's workers were George Draper, 21, govt servant, *Asia 2* 1823, Labourer (Life), Ref 1584 (This contradicts the 1825 census, which states George Draper arrived on *Asia 1* in July 1822. Online records state there was a George Draper arrived *Asia 1* in July 1822, and a Joseph Draper arrived on *Asia 2* in 1823); Charles Norford, 26, govt servant, *Sesostris*, 1826, Labourer (life), N427; Robert Sidebottom, 36, came free, *Anne 2*, 1811, Labourer, S884; Henry Town, 37, FS (free by servitude), *G Stewart*, 1819, 7 years, Labourer, T1067.

Information on William Broggy (aka Brophy) is from Merv Webster, a descendant, who has written a book about the Broggy family called *Not Famous Just Battlers*.

Elizabeth being allocated a founder and stockman is from *Sydney Gazette*, 5 July 1832.

The Kurrajong relative is Michael Want, a descendant of GM's younger brother Robert. Michael (and others) reckons part of the stock may have been kept at the Kurrajong property unsupervised, despite the fact that the fencing in those days was rough and ready.

The tale of the caterpillars is from *Sydney Gazette*, 31 March 1825, p2.

Details of the Hawkesbury floods are from the Hawkesbury Museum.

The scene between William and GM is invented.

The Peter Cunningham quote is from *Squatter's Castle: the Life and Times of Edward David Stewart Ogilvie 1814 – 1896*, by George Farwell.

Chapter 5: The Aboriginal connection

I owe the discovery of the Aboriginal song recorded by GM to Dr Geoff Ford in his thesis *Darkiñung Recognition*, p102.

'The true proprietors of the soil' is from Governor King's letter to William Bligh, 1807, HRA 1, p65.

According to Mark Saddler, a Wiradjuri man living in Wagga Wagga, 'owner' is not a word an Aboriginal person recognises.

Up until 1800 26 white people were claimed to have been killed by natives on the Hawkesbury. Evidence was not available of the number of Aborigines killed. (HRA 1, 2, 2 January 1800, p422)

Governor Macquarie's comments the Appin Massacre are from *The Governor's Diary & Memorandum Book*, 10 April 1816. Also from *When the Sky Fell Down*, by Keith Willey.

Interestingly most of the reports of the Appin massacre are from secondary sources, or from the 'Journal and Report of Captain James Wallis' (who was in charge of the governor's troops) 10–17 April, 1816, Col Sec's Correspondence, 4/1735, 52–4, SRNSW. The only mention of it in newspapers is in the *Sydney Gazette*, 11 May 1816, in which, having described the killing of the Aborigines it says: 'The humanity with which this necessary but unpleasant duty has been conducted throughout, by the Officers appointed to this command, claims our warmest commendations: and although the result has not been altogether so successful as might have been wished, yet there is little doubt but it will ultimately tend to restrain similar outrages, and a recurrence of those barbarities which the natives have of late so frequently committed on the unprotected Settlers and their Families.'

Macquarie's 4 June declaration is from *Sydney Gazette*, 4 May 1816, p1.

James (Toby) Ryan's story is from his *Reminiscences Of Australia*.

Aboriginal people using the crossing at the Yarramundi is from a personal email from Carol Liston.

Chapter 6: At home

A woman's household duties is from Mary Gilmore's *Old Days: Old Ways*.

Information on the Agnes Banks markets is from Dictionary of Sydney (online).

The Crawleys and the bushrangers story is from *Sydney Gazette*, 31 March 1825, p2. The article mentions a 'Robert Hall' but since later that year Aull petitioned for a reward for capturing bushrangers I'm assuming it was him.

Toby Ryan's description of 'Wild' Jack Donohoe is from *History of Penrith: First 50 Years*, Toby Ryan, *Nepean Times*, 22 October 1949, p3. Also from Donahoe's ADB online.

The state of the roads is from *Hawkesbury Courier*, 11 July 1844. (Cited in *Macquarie Country*, D G Bowd.)

Hannah Laycock's will is from *Lives Obscurely Great* by Sheila Tearle.

Chapter 7: Distraction

It was Nelson's brother in law, George Matcham, who was responsible for the migration of his first cousin and our family pioneer Mary Pitt and her children. Mary arrived with letters of recommendation from Nelson's father, and the Nelson name proved invaluable to various members of the family down the years; as was reflected in the names of their various properties such as Nelson's Farm, Bronte and Trafalgar.

GM and Scott's visit to the Governor Darling and the scene following are inventions.

Chapter 8: The convict stain

At the end of the 16th century in Britain there were around 50 offences that carried the death penalty; two centuries later that had risen to more than 200 and included setting fire to coalmines, sending threatening letters, bigamy, consorting with gypsies and stealing a shroud from a grave. *Bound for Botany Bay*, by Alan Brooke & David Brandon.

The comparisons of literacy between convicts and others is from *Convict Workers*, ed Stephen Nicholas, p44.

The description of John Johnson is taken from Home Office Convict Prison Hulk Registers and Letter Books, 1802-1849. HO 9/8. PRO Reel (ML 4881).

The removal of destitute people back to the parish of their birth was part of the 1662 Poor Laws, which decreed the parish in which someone was born was responsible for looking after them should they be in need.

Negotiating the Gaol Books at the National Archives: the court system in England and Wales fell into three categories: magistrates' courts for minor offences, local county courts or quarter sessions, assizes where the most serious criminal trials were heard twice a year by judges appointed by the monarch.

The records contain: 2.1 Crown and Gaol Books for names of the accused, charges, plea, verdict and sentence, 2.2 Indictments: parchment rolls containing charges, plea, verdict and sentence, 2.3 Depositions: pre-trial witness statements (only those for capital cases survive), photographs, maps, appeal papers, 2.4 Other records include pleadings, statements of claim and counterclaim, draft minutes of trials, correspondence, jury lists, financial business etc.

I clicked on Crown & Gaol Books, and then I waited. The code for the Stafford Assizes Gaol Book (where John was tried) is ASSI 2/28. The indictment, which took a while to find as you have to scroll through page by page, is coded ASSI 5/128/16, Stafford Assizes, Lent 1808.

The 'Grand Jury' looked at all the cases beforehand and decided which should be brought to trial. The 'Petty Jury' were separate and were responsible for attending the trials and giving their verdicts. For Mary the Surrey Crown and Gaol Books for Lent 1808 is coded ASSI 31/20. The Indictments are ASSI 94/1616.

Chapter 9: Crime and punishment

Crimes and punishments in 19th century England are from *Crime, Policing and Punishment in England, 1750-1914*, pp109-111 & p119, David Taylor, *Victorian Crime and Punishment* (online), and *Bound for Botany Bay*, pp9 & 11.

The reports on Johns Johnson and Baddeley are from *Staffordshire Advertiser*, 28 November 1807, p4.

The history of the Baddeley family is from *History of the Staffordshire Potteries*, Simeon Shaw.

Life in the Pottery towns of early 19th century is from *The Potteries*, ed ADM Phillips, and *Leek Remembered* by Val Priestman. The 1840 testimony of working conditions is from William Griffiths, Overlooker, cited in *Evidence taken in the Staffordshire potteries*, by Samuel Scriven.

Conditions on board the hulks is from James Hardy Vaux, cited in *The English Prison Hulks* by W Branch Johnson, and *Bound for Botany Bay*, p26. John Johnson's transfer to the convict ship and Baddeley's death is from Home Office: Convict Prison Hulk Registers and Letter Books, 1802-1849, HO 9/8 (under JJ on prison hulk).

Chapter 10: Mary and John

Mary's departure on *Aeolus* is from Index to NSW convict indents 1788-1842.

Fiche 632, p297, film 393, 4/4004.

The unlikelihood of female convicts being able to return home did not go unnoticed. Later that year, 1808, the *Freeman's Journal* published a letter from the Sheriff of London to the Secretary of State for the Colonies Lord Hawkesbury expressing his concern that "the women it may be readily conceived are doomed by such a distant transportation, to pass the remainder of their days in that remote region frequently for first and very slight offences . . . attended by no circumstances indicative of radical or habitual depravity; and others unite to this last recommendation, that of having families of young children, husbands, and other relatives, the conscious separation from whom, for the remainder of life, involves more acute suffering and more complicated misery, than would the punishment of death itself." There was no indication that the authorities did anything to address these concerns.

Castlereagh's remarks on the 'pimping sessions' (my term) are from his letter to governor-to-be Colonel Macquarie written from Downing Street, London, 14 May 1809. (HRA 1, 7, p84)

Mr Plummer's comment, also to Colonel Macquarie, a friend, was part of a lengthy letter written on 4 May 1809 in England, setting out the various ways the colony might 'speedily and completely accomplish its original design of being a school of reform to the convicts in general who are transported there'. (HRNSW 7, p197) A similar description of female convict assignment was expressed by a local resident G F Hammersley in 'A few observations on the situation of female convicts in NSW'. (NSW State Library)

The quote from *Sydney Gazette* is dated 29 January 1809.

The description of the Female Factory is from *Factory Above the Gaol* by Michaela Ann Cameron, 2015 (cited in Dictionary of Sydney online), and *Sydney Gazette*, 7 May 1809, p1.

Governor Hunter's remark is from a letter to Lord Portland, 18 November 1796, HRNSW III, p182 (cited in *Convict Women*, Kay Daniels). Governor King's comment is also from *Convict Women*. Macquarie's quotes are from Macquarie to Lord Castlereagh, 8 March 1810, Sydney (HRA 1, 7, p221); and Macquarie to Lord Liverpool, 17 November 1812 (HRA 1, 7, p614).

Information on the nature of the female convicts is from *'Women transported: Myth and reality'*, Gay Hendriksen, Curator, Parramatta Heritage Centre, National Archives of Australia in Canberra on 14 June 2009 (online).

Margaret Catchpole was transported for life for stealing a horse, and then breaking out of gaol while awaiting transportation. She had led an adventurous life in her home county of Suffolk, hence the books written about her, not all of which bear much resemblance to reality. She travelled to Sydney in the same fleet as the Pitt family and she acted as midwife to many of the Pitt mothers, and nursed Mary Pitt in her old age. Mary Pitt at one point asked Margaret to come and live with her but she refused, preferring her independence. She died from influenza caught on our family property Bronte in 1819. I wrote about Margaret's remarkable story more fully in *The Worst Country in the World*.

The report on the convicts on their arrival is from *Sydney Gazette*, 3 March 1810, p2. What happened to them next is from 'Free Settler or Felon?' (jenwillets.com)

Macquarie's quote is from *Sydney Gazette*, 7 January 1810, p1.

There is no room here to narrate the full story of the Rum Rebellion, so-called. In short, Governor Bligh had made himself so unpopular in the colony, especially with the New South Wales Corps, that members of the Corps led by Major Johnston and at the instigation of the wealthy settler John Macarthur marched on Government House in January 1808 and arrested him, then assumed authority in the colony for nearly two years until the arrival of Governor Macquarie late in 1809.

Macquarie's letter to Castlereagh is dated 8 March 1810. (HRA 1, 7, p221)

The definition of 'mechanic' is from Alexander Macleay, colonial secretary, New South Wales Calendar and General Post Office directory, 1836. (RAHS)

The history of early pottery in Sydney is from *Local Pottery and Dairying at the DMR Site, Brickfields, Sydney, New South Wales*, by Mary Casey (pdf), *Australasian Historical Archeology*, 1999 (online).

John's ticket of leave is from Copies of Letters Sent: Local And Overseas, 1809-1813, Col Sec's Papers, No 10/2 4/4427; Reel 601 p471 (Ancestry). The handwritten note reads: 'Secretary's Office, 22 June 1810. Sir, His Excellency the Governor having given a Ticket of Leave to John Johnston [sic] (a Potter) Convict of ship Anne, Clarke Master, to enable him to employ himself for his own Benefit; you are of course to discontinue the Issuing of Rations to him from the present date. I have the honour to be Jnº Thoˢ Campbell. To Wm Broughton Esq., Act. Comm.'

Chapter 11: The little brown jug
This chapter is invented and the Landstaffs are fictional characters. Mrs Landstaff's indenture is based on a genuine contract drawn up in 1827 between Hannah Jones, a Sydney dressmaker, and her apprentice Eliza Ward, from *Life Lines: Australian Women's Letters and Diaries 1788 to 1840*, eds Patricia Clarke and Dale Spender.

The scenes between Mary and John are likewise imaginary.

Chapter 12: The smile
Mary and John's wedding is from St Phillip's Church register. 1178/1811 V18111178 3A (District CA).

Mary's ticket of leave is from Registers of Certificates of Freedom, 4 Feb 1810 - 26 Aug 1814, SRNSW, Kingswood, NSW. 11/212, 4/4427; Reel 601 p.447. (Ancestry)

The 1814 muster is from *New South Wales General Muster*, ed. Carol J Baxter, p 118.

John's grant of 40 acres at Airds is from Col Sec's records. 'Johnson, John of Sydney. 1816 Jan 16: On list of persons to receive grants of land in 1816 (Fiche 3266; 9/2652 p.28).'

John's Conditional Pardon is from New South Wales Australia Convict Records of Conditional and Absolute Pardons, SRNSW, Kingswood. Reel No 774. Roll No 149. Vol no 4/4430. (Ancestry)

The 1822 muster is from *General Muster and Land and Stock Muster of NSW, 1822*, ed Carol J Baxter. Ref A11356, P259.

Records of various John Johnsons are from Col Sec's papers 1788-1856. Special Bundles, 1794–1825 X Fiche 3290, 4/4570D pp.5, 82; Fiche 3291, 4/4570D pp.89, 96, 98, 104, 121 (Ancestry).

References to John Johnson 'publican and builder' are from Col Sec's papers (Reel 6061; 4/1779 p.173c & Fiche 3293; 5/3821.1 p.4).

Mary having three convicts working for her is from 'List of Convicts Registered in the Employ of Jn Johnson of George Street': Rowland, Thos, Tibbles, Wm. Whithouse; Col Sec's records. Fiche 3138; 4/1842B No.417, pp701-6.

Mary & John's land grants are from NRS 13836 Registers of land grants and leases – John's grant (7-447, Reel 2561, p61); Col Sec's papers, Memorials to the Governor, 1810-1826, No 417, pp701-6 (Ancestry) – Mary; Col Sec's Papers, Special Bundles, 1794-1825, p93 (Ancestry) – Mary.

The 1828 census is from *Census of N.S.W, 1828*, ed Malcom R Sainty & Keith A Johnson, p210. According to the cross reference index two convicts, Rowland and John Reed, are listed as employed by Mary Johnston [sic]; one, John Whitehouse (who also appeared on the previous memorial requesting land), as employed by Mary Johnson; and one possible, Mary Hill (nee Johnson), with no employer listed.

Chapter 13: Robert Aull

This scene is an invention, though the story Robert told about *Francis & Eliza's* capture is true. I have no idea what Julia thought of her future stepfather but it's not too far-fetched to assume that she would have, initially at least, resented the appearance of a surrogate father-figure.

The story of the hijacking of *Francis & Eliza* is from *Sydney Gazette*, 12 August 1815, p2; *Caledonia Mercury*, 27 February 1815; *Freemans Journal*, 22 August 1815, p4; and 'Free Settler or Felon?' jenwilletts.com.

Captain Champlain of *Warrior* refuted these versions of the story in *The Nile Register*, claiming he found *Francis & Eliza* in a state of mutiny with the convicts in control, and it was only by placing some of his men on board that he was able to restore order.

Captain Harrison of *Francis & Eliza* did recommend to Governor Macquarie the convicts be given Conditional Pardons for their exemplary behaviour. Macquarie agreed, but the powers that be back in England insisted they serve at least part of their sentence. (Macquarie to Bathurst, 18 March 1816, HRA 1, 9, p55. Cited in Carol Liston's thesis, Chapter 2)

Aull's crime and punishment is from Return of Frauds and Forgeries in Department of Stamp Office of Ireland, 1812-16, p389: *Belfast Newsletter*, 17 September 1813. (Cited in *Free Settler or Felon?* jenwilletts.com)

The story of the lady convict and the Captain of the *Warrior* is from *The Literary Panorama and National Register*, Charles Taylor, p487 (as above).

Jane Thompson's details are from PCUG (PC Users' Group online) and Col Sec's papers, Copies of Letters Sent Within The Colony, 1814-1827, Reel 6004; 4/3494, p141; Col Sec's Correspondence Series: NRS 937; Reels 6004-6016 (and on Ancestry).

Robert Aull as constable and pound keeper is from *Sydney Gazette* 1 Dec 1821, 5 April 1822 & 14 Aug 1823 supp. (cited in Carol Liston's thesis). His aiding with the capture of a convict is from Col Sec's papers, Reel 6009; 4/3506 p.334 (Ancestry), letter from F Goulburn, Col Sec.

His petitioning for a reward for apprehending bushrangers is from Col Sec's papers, Reel 6064; 4/1787 p.148 (and Ancestry); and for misusing a servant *Sydney Gazette*, 23 Jan 1828 (cited in Carol Liston's thesis).

Jane Aull's death is from SAG Kerrison Jones Index (cited in Carol Liston's thesis). There was a child Isabella listed as born in 1828, but since she disappears from the records thereafter I am assuming Jane died in childbirth and the baby did not survive.

Robert and Mary's marriage is from New South Wales BDM online: (Reg No 773/1829 V1829773 13)

Chapter 14: Upper Richmond

The lagoon was known by several Anglicised monikers until it settled into the name 'Yarramundi', an adaptation of Yaramundy, the Aboriginal Darug clan chief it was named after. He was a medicine man and was known early on to European settlers when he accompanied Governor Phillip's exploration of the Hawkesbury in 1790.

The quote about Mrs Aull is from *The Australian*, 9 July 1830, p4 (Carol Liston's thesis); NSW Publicans' Licenses 1830-1849 (Ancestry). The JPs who granted the licence included William Cox Jnr and Archibald Bell.

Governor Hunter's sighting of a platypus is from Dictionary of Sydney, Agnes Banks.

Many women in early colonial Australia produced children in their 40s. Sarah Broughton, the bishop's wife, had a child when she was 47 (though she died 6 months later).

Aull's threatening notice is from *The Australian*, 26 October 1832, p1 (cited in Carol Liston's thesis). His bankruptcy is also from Carol Liston's thesis. Digory Forrest was, I since discovered, brother of Austin Forrest, first husband of GM's aunt Jemima.

Aull acquiring The Pilgrim Inn is from Carol Liston's thesis, as is his selling off of his assets.

Robert Aull indicted for assaulting a policeman is from *The Australian*, 24 May 1833, p3. For impounding Swine: *Commercial Journal & Advertiser*, 31 October 1838, p4. The housekeeper's complaint: *Commercial Journal and Advertiser*, Saturday 15 June 1839, p3.

Aull's certificate of discharge is from *Maitland Mercury*, 24 June 1846, p2.

Requirements of the 1841 census are from NSW State Records online. The status options were: Born in the colony (BC), came free (CF), other free persons – ie emancipists – ticket of leave, in government employment or private assignment.

Chapter 15: Interpreting our ancestors

Janelle Cust is the writer of the impeccably researched *The Family of Mary Pitt*.

The Pitt family website is www.marymatchampitt.wordpress.com.

Governor Macquarie was famously (and controversially) in favour of the rehabilitation of time-expired convicts, though his views on granting land to single women tell another story: 'I consider it a bad practice (except in some extraordinary and pressing case of necessity) and very injurious to the interests of the colony to give grants to single women.' He believed they were unable to cultivate land. (Macquarie to Bigge, 12 Jan 1821, HRA 1, 7, pp351-2)

Goulburn's letter regarding Mary's land grant is from Col Sec's papers (Fiche 3266; 9/2652 p93) George Faithfull's letter to La Trobe is from Museums Public Library: Letters from Victorian Pioneers, pp15/16 (online).

Joan Scott's death announcement is from *Surry* ship's log, CY 1113, ML.

Chapter 16: Death and marriages

Elizabeth's funeral and wake are inventions. Aunt Lucy's curious glances are based on a story passed down the generations that she refused to have anything to do with her son's wife because she was the daughter of convicts.

GM's sister Eliza, who had spent much of her youth living with her grandmother Hannah Laycock in Sydney, married her cousin Austin Forrest Wilshire (Hester and James Wilshire's son), named after Jemima's first husband Austin Forrest. Jemima's younger son William Warren Jenkins also married his cousin Matilda Pitt Wilshire, the Wilshires' fifth daughter; and Matilda's younger brother Thomas Matcham Pitt Wilshire later married Helen Faithfull, William Faithfull's daughter by his second wife.

Details of GM and Julia's marriage are from Barbara Lamble, though the celebrations that followed are my inventions. Their honeymoon is from *Sydney Gazette*, 24 September 1835, p3.

Chapter 17: William Scott

William Scott's musings are invented, though the story of his background is true. 'Nurse' is the Australian equivalent of what in Britain we'd call a nanny.

Chapter 18: The land of golden soil

The title of the chapter is from Australia's national anthem 'Advance Australia Fair'.

'Bush rangers with a base' is from *Sydney Gazette,* 9 September 1826 (cited in *Station Life,* p2).

The population figures are from *Landed Enterprise and Penal Society,* Brian H Fletcher; the area that comprised the Nineteen Counties from *Sheep, Squatters, and the Evolution of Land Rights In Australia: 1787-1847,* Sumner J. La Croix, University of Hawaii (online).

Conditions imposed on people seeking to take up land is from *Station Life,* p2. The Act was aimed mostly at new migrants. GM's cousin William Pitt Faithfull applied for land under this Act, having proved he had over £2,000 in capital, but to his annoyance he was only granted two square miles, half what he was hoping for. It didn't prevent him from eventually becoming one of NSW's most successful farmers and the founder of Springfield, near Goulburn.

Duties of Land Commissioners is from *Squatting on Crown Land,* J F Campbell, JRAHS Vol 15/2, 1929.

The conversation between GM and Will at the end of the chapter is invented.

Chapter 19: The big journey

The quote in Janelle Cust's book is from Treasury, Letters received 1847, SRNSW 4/2788, Wm Scott 47/4126.

The custom for Aboriginal people to adopt European names is from *The Naming Of Aborigines,* by Edgar Beale, JRAHS Jan/Feb 1980.

The shooting of Tom Pitt is from *Maitland Weekly Mercury,* 6 April 1901, p4. (Thanks to Clayton Simpson Pitt.)

Details of Sir Thomas Mitchell's journey, are from his *Three Expeditions into the Interior of Eastern Australia.*

Chapter 20: The drover

Thanks to Di and Chris McCarthy for details of droving methods today and in the past.

Cows' habits are from various sources including *The Overlanders* and *Station Life.*

Banjo Paterson's *Saltbush Bill* is about sheep of course, but a similar rule applied to cattle. *Saltbush Bill* tells how one particularly experienced (and canny) drover managed to extend his stay on a squatter's land by picking a fight with the jackeroo – who was English, and a new-chum, naturally – making it last all day and allowing the jackaroo to win in the end so he could proudly return to the homestead claiming he'd licked the interloper; meanwhile the drover's sheep had strayed way beyond the legal limit of half a mile from the track and had spent the day merrily chomping on the squatter's grass, scattering so far and so wide it took a week to muster them.

Finding handy trees to climb in case of necessity is from *Some Ups and Downs of an old Richmondite,* by Alfred Smith.

Jack Timmins's father John was transported from Ireland for political reasons. Jack's riding up to Bronte to ask for a job is from *The Tail Goes with the Hide,* Gene Makim. His alleged powers over his dogs is from *Reminiscences of Richmond,* 'Cooramill' (Sam Boughton).

Chapter 21: Three expeditions
Bell's Line of Road is named after Sir Archibald Bell the younger, a surveyor, who discovered a new route through the Blue Mountains.

Details of Mary Laycock's descendants in the Wollumbi Museum are from Wollumbi District Anglican Marriages, 1856-1900; Wollumbi District Church of England Baptisms, 1856-1905, Cessnock District Historical and Family History Society, 1998.

John Blaxland was the elder brother of Gregory Blaxland, one of the three explorers who first negotiated a route through the Blue Mountains in 1813. The others were William Wentworth and William Lawson.

'Sydney's smallpox outbreak of 1789 - an act of biological warfare against Aboriginal tribes', by Chris Warren, is from ABC Radio National *'Ockham's Razor',* 17 April 2014. (Cited in Sovereign Union - First Nations Asserting Sovereignty, online.)

A British company with aristocratic connections, the Australian Agricultural Company were officially granted a million acres of land by the British Government, some of which they took up on the coast near Port Stephens, some of it on the Liverpool Plains in 1833.

Allan Cunningham, botanist and explorer, visited the Gwydir district in 1827 and named the river after his patron.

Chapter 22: The squatter
'Old Kiley' features in Paterson's *On Kiley's Run.* He was a farmer of the old school who worked his butt off and was generous to everyone until the drought got him, the banks foreclosed on him and he died of a broken heart.

George Farwell's description of squatters is from the Introduction to *Squatter's Castle.*

The Anthony Trollope quote is from *Australia & New Zealand,* p76.

Details of the Dights and Howes are from The University of Queensland online (https://espace.library.uq.edu.au/).

The squatters displaced from their properties on the Liverpool Plains is from *The Rising Sun,* by R J Webb, p17.

Following the cattle to find the best grazing land is from *Station Life,* p16. The talents of the best stockmen is also from *Station Life,* p42. The quote about the Sandersons is from *Old Days: Old Ways.*

Chapter 23: Moree

Edward Bulwer-Lytton, after whom Charles Dickens's son was named, was a popular novelist who coined the phrases 'the great unwashed', 'the pen is mightier than the sword' and 'It was a dark and stormy night.' He was also a politician and held the office of Secretary of State for the Colonies for a year. (Wikipedia)

Edward Dickens was not the only failed son of a successful father. Our family patron George Matcham, responsible for his cousin Mary Pitt's emigration back in 1801, also sent his youngest son to the colony. But despite having enough money to buy his own property Charles Horatio Nelson Matcham never thrived, and he too died unhappy, unmarried and forgotten, and was buried in an obscure corner of a graveyard in Yass.

Information on Edward 'Plorn' Dickens is from 'Dickens of a time', Steve Meacham, *SMH*, 24 December 2002. Plorn was a disappointment to his father, who thought 'Australia would suit Edward better as he was fond of animals and being on horseback . . . I hope he may take better to the Bush than to Books.' *Charles Dickens and his Australia* by Coral Lansbury, RAHS Journal Vol 52/2, June 1966, p115.

Chapter 24: The puzzle explained

Malcolm Fraser's quote about the liberal party is from *The Age*, 26 May 2010.

The extent of Thomas Hall's station is from the Govt Gazette of 1848, cited in the JRAHS, Vol 17, p51.

How to build a humpy is from *Station Life*, p24.

George Bull as Scott and Pitt's overseer is from Treasury, Letters received 1847, SRNSW 4/2788, Wm Scott 47/4126 (cited in *The Family of Mary Pitt*).

Chapter 25: Dispossession

The skirmishes between squatters and Aboriginal people is from *Exploration and settlement of the N W Plains*, James Jervis, JRAHS 48, pt 5, p383.

The Myall Creek massacre and the trial are from numerous sources, particularly *Australia, A New History of the Great Southern Land*, by Frank Welsh, p180, and C F Boughton, Chronicles 31.

D G Bowd's quote is from *Macquarie Country*.

The Bobby Pringle quote is from *The Rising Sun*, p21.

The dispute over Bullerue is based on Scott's letters to Governor Gipps 11 August 1845 (Treasury, Letters Received 1847, SRNSW, 4/2788, William Scott, ref 45/581); as is the meeting between Scott and Allman. The character of Francis Allman is taken from his online biography, by A J Gray.

The extra fee George Hall was paying for his three properties included the levy per head of stock imposed on squatters by the 1839 Act, viz 3d per annum 'for every head of horned cattle' and 6d for every horse. (*Squatting on Crown Lands*, p97). Scott and Pitt's licences are from Commissioner Mitchell's returns, 1846.

Chapter 26: The price of capitalism
Wentworth's complaints to governors is from *Squatting on Crown Lands*, p222. Gipps's response is from the ADB online, Samuel Clyde McCulloch.

The March 1847 Act is from *Recollections of an Australian Squatter*, W A Brodribb, Appendix.

The description of Coorar is from the Govt Gazette 1848, No 81, p1175.

GM's journey is from *Stock and Station Jour*nal, 13 December 1932.

The transfer of Coorar is from the Govt Gazette.

John Hoskisson was known as the 'grandfather' of the Hawkesbury, mostly because he was born there and lived there all his life, and at his death in 1874 he was the oldest male born in the colony. The illiterate son of a convict who was killed by Aborigines before he was born, Hoskisson managed to accumulate a huge amount of property in both the Windsor area and further afield. When he died he was the biggest property-owner on the Hawkesbury. (*Macquarie Country*)

GM appointed to the committee of the Hawkesbury Agricultural Society is from Minutes of the Society, quoted in *Those Were the Days*, J C Fitzgerald, p 107; and *Hawkesbury Courier*, 17 July 1845, p2.

Joining the committee of the Hawkesbury Benevolent Society, *Hawkesbury Courier*, 17 April 1845, p2; the C of E Lay Association of NSW, *Hawkesbury Courier*, 7 August 1845, p3; steward at Hawkesbury Races, *Hawkesbury Courier*, 26 March 1846, p4, & 13 August 1846, p3; trustee for Savings Bank of NSW, Govt Gazette 1847, Vol 1, p525, 12 May; GM also joined a citizens' group pressing for a road from Windsor to Bathurst, *Hawkesbury Courier*, 10 Sept 1846, p3; taking out a loan, Govt Gazette 1847, Vol 1, 12 May, p525 (cited in *The Family of Mary Pitt*).

Chapter 27: The women
Information on the Cox family is from ADB online and *Macquarie Country*.

Catherine Helen Spence details are from the Australian Women's History Network (online), and the Constitution (Female Suffrage) Act 1895 (SA).

The Drover's Wife is a short story by Henry Lawson.

The tribulations of Mary Thomas are from *Lifelines*, p158/160.

The Sunday pilgrimage to St Peter's Church is from *Those Were the Days*.

Duties of the women of the house and segregation at formal events is from *Old Days: Old Ways*.

Robert Aull's notice appeared in the *Colonist*, 6 Feb 1839, p3; 9 Feb 1839, p1; 13 Feb p1; and *SMH*, 8 Feb 1839.

The 1841 census is for Ham Common, County of Cumberland. (State records letters 40/4342, 4/2504.2 and 40/4350.) Information on Jane Bibben is courtesy of her great great granddaughter Sue Austin.

The birth of a James Aull is courtesy of Michelle Kaplan, a descendant of Mary and John Johnson through their daughter Sarah.

Robert preserving his wife's interest in the land is from Conveyance, R G Deeds Registration. Deed of Indemnity lease and release, Aull, Jeffrey & Bedeck, 9, 10 Dec; Book 2, 100, 101 (courtesy of Carol Liston).

The expectation of a mother to produce a child every year is from *Those Were the Days*.

Chapter 28: The law and the Aborigines
'Going Circuit at the Antipodes' originally appeared in *Household Words* in 1852. It was reproduced in *The Wingham Chronicle and Manning River Observer*, 5 September 1919, p4.

The identity of the writer is from *Household Words – A list of contributors*, by Anne Lohri.

In the early days of settlement Aboriginal people could not appear in court at all as they could not swear an oath on the Bible. Governor Gipps tried to introduce an 'Aborigines' Evidence Bill' allowing them to testify if their evidence was corroborated, but the British Government vetoed it.

Dickens thought nothing of 'taking a story and playing with it until it was practically rewritten', according to Coral Lansbury in *Charles Dickens and his Australia* (JRAHS).

Fryingpan's alleged crime is from *Maitland Mercury*, 22 March 1843, p1.

The postponement of the trial(s) is from *Hunter River Gazette*, 19 March 1842, p3.

The description of Fryingpan's trial is from *SMH*, 22 March 1843, p2.

The quote about Gipps is from *Colonial Observer*, 3 September 1842, p2.

The *Herald* quote, and Gipps's apparent loss of heart, are from *Waterloo Creek*, Roger Milliss.

Chapter 29: Self government
The extract from Molesworth's notes is cited in *Fatal Shore*, by Robert Hughes, p494. Molesworth presided over a select committee under the Whig government in 1837/8 to look into transportation.

Population figures are from *Australia*, Welsh, p151.

William Bowman was the son of an early settler, John Bowman, whose support of Governor Bligh against the New South Wales Corps during the Rum Rebellion in 1808 resulted in his imprisonment, ostensibly for calling Nicholas Bayly, an old enemy (and incidentally married to Elizabeth Pitt's sister Sarah), 'a rogue' (ADB online, Brian Fletcher). John Bowman's brother William, the younger William's uncle, arrived in New South Wales in 1801 on *Nile*, in the same fleet as Mary Pitt and the same ship as Margaret Catchpole and the Rouse family.

The public meetings in support of the parliamentary candidates was reported in *Colonial Observer*, 18 January 1843. The fracas on election day is from *SMH*, 22 June 1843, p2; and from *Australasian Chronicle*, 22 June 1843, p2.

According to *Macquarie Country* the final vote was 129 for Bowman and

126 for Fitzgerald, and a total of 287 votes in all. (The maths doesn't add up but I can't find any other verification for these numbers.)

Chapter 30: Local matters

Timmins's absence from the birth of his first child is from *The Tail Goes with the Hide*. The choice of a Presbyterian church for his marriage to Betsey Scott is odd: Jack's Irish parents were Catholics and they brought their children up likewise, according to the 1828 census; and in the 1841 census young William is marked as either C of E or Catholic. It's possible Betsey turned to Presbyterianism in recognition of her ancestral Scottish roots.

Timmins's dog breeding exploits, by John Chandler, are from *The Australian Cattle Dog Social Club of North Queensland* (online).

The gift of a watch is courtesy of Susan Mary Rayner/Green.

GM's community activities in Richmond are from *Hawkesbury Courier* on the following dates in 1845: 17 April, 15 May, 17 & 24 July, 7 August, 4 Sept; 12 February, 10 & 17 September 1846. Govt Gazette, Vol 1, 12 May 1847, p525. Govt Gazette 5 December, 1854.

Categories in the ploughing competition: *Those Were the Days*, p107.

GM's property deals are from Bk 28, No 422 & Bk 32, No 724, DL; LA, V&P, 1859/60, 3, P664 (cited in *The Family of Mary Pitt*).

In 1850 GM gave a Ben Mortimer £5 for recovering the body of a Tom Hornery from the Yarramundi Lagoon. The only connection I can find between GM and the drowned man was that Hornery – also known as Thomas Groves among other names – was the husband of Jane Bibben, who'd been recruited from the orphanage to work for the Pitt family in 1840.

The rumour of GM standing for the Legislative Council is from *SMH*, 2 November 1855, p8.

James Robert Wilshire was the second son of James Wilshire, businessman and early settler, who married GM's aunt Hester Pitt. He was mayor of Sydney in 1844 and at the time GM petitioned for his help he represented Sydney in the Legislative Council. GM's protests against the Richmond Bridge Company are from *SMH*, 27 November 1856, p4.

The queues forming to cross the river are from *Reminiscences of Australia*, Ryan, p172. GM's demand for compensation is from *SMH*, 5 June 1856, p3; and the dismissal of his petition from *Empire*, 26 November 1856, p4.

The completion of Richmond Bridge is from *SMH*, 2 August 1859, p8.

The Alfred Smith quote is from *Some Ups and Downs of an old Richmondite*.

The inaugural meeting of the Volunteers is from *Those Were the Days*, p154. According to this account there were 100 signatures taken at that meeting; elsewhere it's said there were 25 or 35.

Boughton's quote is from *Reminiscences of Richmond*, p53. Sam Boughton was born in Richmond in 1841, so according to his date he would have been ten years old when he watched GM and the others being drilled (or more likely 19, in 1860).

'Catchpoleiana' is a word possibly coined by J C Fitzgerald, author of *Those Were the Days*. Margaret's fame, or notoriety, was mostly thanks to a partly-fictional biography of her written by the grandson of her one-time employers, the Cobbold family of Ipswich. She died on the Faithfull property next door to Bronte and is buried in St Peter's churchyard in Richmond.

Opium in teething powders is from *Black Kettle and Full Moon*, Geoffrey Blainey.

Chapter 31: Australia and how to find it
The Australian Colonies: Where They Are and How to Get to Them is from *Australia*, p204.

The explosion in the population is from *Australia*, p248, and 'Australia, historical demographical data of the whole country' (online).

The doubling of salaries of government officials to keep them from the goldfields is from *Australia: Origins to Eureka*, Thomas Keneally; farm labourers deserting their posts is from *Colonial Australia*, Frank Crowley. Ladies forced to open their own front doors is from *Australia*, p204.

'Batmania' is from Melbourne metblogs (online).

Adelaide was named after King William IV's wife.

The establishment of the colonies of Queensland and Western Australia is from WorldAtlas (online). Full self government in WA was granted in 1890.

The 1850 Australian Colonies Government Act is from *Australia*, p187.

By 1861 all the Australian colonies bar Tasmania had adopted universal male suffrage (excluding members of the forces, the police, and in some states the clergy), secret ballots, equal electoral districts and salaries for members of parliament; nearly sixty years before the Mother Country.

The extension of the franchise is from Parliament of New South Wales (online).

Melbourne's burgeoning population is from *Australia*, p248.

The dinner held to honour Darvall and Piddington is from *SMH*, 17 September 1860, p2.

Chapter 32: The romance of the bush
Information on Aboriginal scarring is from Mark Saddler.

The Don Watson quote is from *The Bush*.

'Ah Chee's' quote is from 'The Delights of the Bush', first published in *The Bulletin* and cited in *The Best Australian Bush Stories*, ed Jim Haynes.

Banjo Paterson's 'The Trouble with Merinos' was published in *The Bulletin* in 1895.

Definitions of mateship are from C E W Bean, 'a major influence on the Anzac legend', cited in *Larrikins, Bush Tales & Other Great Australian Stories*, Graham Seal.

Predicting weather is from 'A seasonal guide to weather and wives', *Larrikins, Bush Tales*.

Wholesale buyers forming a cartel at the markets is from *Station Life*.

To add insult to injury for the farmer was the introduction, in 1859, of the rabbit – initially imported by a settler for the fun purpose of shooting them. Over the next fifty years the devastation they wreaked as they ate their way throughout the colony was described by Peter Taylor in *Station Life* as 'of Biblical proportions'.

Chapter 33: The law and the Europeans

In the 'Registers of Accepted Tenders for new runs' (undated), Courah [sic] is listed as 25,600 acres (72^2 is 46,080 acres). Either GM did not quite get the land he applied for or there is a discrepancy in the records. Other entries appear in acres.

GM's land deals:

(i) In March 1849 he briefly held 1200 acres near Putty, next door to Putty Farm, where his sister Mary lived (19 March 1849, 1200 acres County Hunter Parish unnamed near Putty. Entry crossed out, and written against it 'Advertised in the Govt Gazette 29th August 1849 for sale W 121 for sale on the 27 September 1849 at the Police Office Macdonald River'). (Ancestry)

(ii) In 1850 GM and his brother Robert bought 1½ acres in the Highlands, which he sold three years later. (Bk 28, No 422, DL, cited in *The Family of Mary Pitt*, p176)

(iii) The same year he bought 32 acres between the Hawkesbury and 'the lagoon' [Yarramundi presumably] and sold it three months later at a profit of over 25%. (Bk 34, No346, DL, cited in *The Family of Mary Pitt*, p176)

(iv) On 1 January 1852 he acquired, with Thomas Sullivan, 22,400 acres near Wellington called Garagary. (Return Of Crown Lands Held Under License – Wellington 1866, Warren Library. 'Term of present tenure 31 December 1865. annual rent £10. Assessment £20.')

(v) In 1854 Coorar was transferred to GM's neighbour J Husskisson [sic]. (Govt Gazette: 'It is hereby certified, for general information, that the interest of the previous occupants in the Undermentioned Runs of Crown Lands has been transferred, with the sanction of the Government, to the persons hereinafter particularised, in accordance with the Regulations of 1 January 1848.')

(vi) Two years later GM and Sullivan bought a licence for 16,000 acres at Gunningbar in the Wellington District.

(vii) In 1857, GM and Dr C D Whittaker sold Bangheet in the Gwydir District to F W Rusden. 'No muster taken.' (Govt Gazette)

(viii) In 1858 GM and Sullivan rented a 16,000 acre property called Warmerawa in the Wellington District. (Return Of Crown Lands Held Under License – Wellington 1866. 'Assessment £10. Commencement 4 June 1858. Term Annual – not converted.')

(ix) In 1859 GM acquired '1 rood 30 perches' in Richmond and got rid of Lower Grahway, 19,200 acres in the Wellington District, to Joseph Cope.

(Govt Gazette)

Wellington's population is from Return Of Crown Lands Held Under License – Wellington 1866.

Rusden v Pitt and Whittaker was reported in *Maitland Mercury*, 19 March 1861, p2.

Chapter 34: Birth of a salesman

'R.J.W.' may have been Robert Joseph Webster, businessman, parliamentarian and, briefly, farmer.

The announcement of GM selling Sloper Cox's stock is from *SMH*, 6 October 1857, p7. Sloper Cox was the third son of William Cox junior. GM's auctioneer's licence is from NSW Govt Gazette, 22 February 1859, p421.

GM buying land near Fullagher's saleyards is from BK 58, No 920, DL (cited in *The Family of Mary Pitt*).

Tom Harvey bemoaning the loss of his sheep at Walgett is from *SMH*, October 22, 1965, p6.

The role of the auctioneer is thanks to Di and Chris McCarthy. Di's father was a stock and station agent wth Pitt, Son & Badgery in Cootamundra.

Euston to Milton Keynes is around half an hour.

GM selling to his brother in law is from *SMH*, 3 September 1861, p7.

The quote from the Homebush website is from The Sydney Royal Easter Show (online).

Thomas Dawson's property is from *SMH*, 14 July 1860, p10.

Regarding the Laycock family's connection to Homebush: the first mention I can find of 'Mr. Laycock's Farm on the Parramatta Road commonly called Home Bush' is in the *Sydney Gazette*, 24 November 1805, p2. The rumour the property was won and lost over a game of cards is from Wikipedia (online):

Pitt and Sullivan setting up as stock and station agents is from *SMH*, 20 February 1862, p2. The properties they leased at Wellington were Salisbury Plains and Back Gangary (Bligh & Wellington Districts General, Warren Library, 9 October 2009).

Chapter 35: Politics

GM's decision to contest the Windsor election is from *SMH*, Tuesday 22 November 1864, p3. The report of the meeting at the Windsor courthouse is from *SMH*, 24 November 1864, p10.

Windsor with one representative is from *Macquarie Country*.

Political leanings, or lack of, among the parliamentary parties is from *Australia*, p217. A few years previously, in 1855, the then Governor Sir William Denison had complained there were as many parties as there were members. Stuart Donaldson's quote is also from *Australia*, p220.

The unfair balance of the vote against rural workers is from *A Land Half Won*, Geoffrey Blainey, p221.

The certainty GM would be returned is from *Maitland Mercury*, 26 November 1836, p2.

Chapter 36 Railroads and rivalry
The opening of the Richmond railway is from *SMH*, 30 November 1864, p5.

The proliferation of railway gauges is from *Australia*, p272.

The Irish chief engineer, Francis Webb Sheilds, was replaced by a Scot named James Wallace. ('Main Suburban railway line', Wikipedia, online)

Early difficulties with building railways is from 'Sydney Railway Company Corporate Body' (online).

The story of the murder on the Murray is from 'Stateless Old Jack, Beyond All Borders', *SMH*, 14 April 2012.

Chapter 37: Weddings and inundations
According to Jeannette Dixon, a descendant of GM junior through his eldest son John Matcham, Sunnyside was a wedding gift from Elizabeth's parents John and Elizabeth Town (née Onus). John Town's grandfather, also John Town, arrived in the colony as a convict.

The GM Pitt juniors' 'open door' is from *Those Were the Days*.

Information on William Garling is from Trove.

Illegitimacy in the Town family is again according to Jeanette Dixon. Andrew and Elizabeth shared a grandfather, the convict John Town, but different grandmothers. Andrew was legitimately descended from John Town's marriage to Mary Pickett while Elizabeth, who was older, was descended from his mistress Sarah Gordon.

Henry and Julia Badgery's move to Maitland is from *From the Hawkesbury to the Monaro*, Bobbie Hardy.

The description of the Hawkesbury River is from NSW SES (State Emergency Service) online.

Heights of Hawkesbury floods are recorded at Windsor Bridge and displayed at Windsor Museum. Details of the 1864 flood are from 'Hawkesbury heritage & happenings: Hawkesbury River floods' (online).

The fate of the Eather family in the 1867 flood is from 'Inquest on six bodies of six of the Eather family', *SMH*, 1 July 1867, p3. Two further bodies were recovered subsequently, the remaining four were never found.

The beaches covered in debris is from *SMH* 25 June 1867, quoted in the Windsor Museum.

Other information on the flood is from the following: *SMH*, 24 June 1867, p5. *Empire*, 24 June 1867, p4: *Empire*, 28 June 1867, p4: *Sydney Mail*, 29 June 1867, p9: *SMH*, 1 July 1867, p3.

Margaret Betts said there was a bad flood in 1991 (Hawkesbury records have that down as 1990) when the river burst its banks at Yarramundi and flooded the lower part of her property at Bronte, ripping out the fencing and washing away the soil. Thirty years earlier, in 1961, her father lost 20 cattle, trapped behind fences. None of the other 20th century floods have reached more than halfway up her hill.

There is some doubt about whether RM stayed in Richmond or accompanied his parents to Manly in 1869. Since he joined his father's company in 1871 I assumed he did the latter, yet on his marriage certificate in 1874 it gives his place of residence as Richmond.

Chapter 38: Manly Beach

The description of Bronte is from *Some Ups and Downs of an old Richmondite*.

It's not known exactly when the current house at Bronte was built. Margaret Betts is sure it was after the 1867 flood, and a friend with knowledge of such things who visited it recently dated it around 1870.

Sam Boughton's comment on GM is from *Reminiscences of Richmond*. He also quotes a poem that GM apparently delivered at a wedding about a hard-drinking woman and her long-suffering husband.

The ferry service between Manly and the city is from 'Sydney Heritage Fleet: North Shore Steam Ferry Company' (online).

The description of Fairlight is from *SMH*, 20 March 1869, p3.

The Inspector of Nuisances is from *Sand in our Souls*, Leone Huntsman.

Mr Gocher's challenge is from *Manly & Pittwater, its Beauty and Progress*, P W Gledhill, Manly, Warringah and Pittwater Historical Society, 1948. According to local historian John McGrinchy most Sydney suburbs outlawed sea bathing from the late 1870s on, though police were instructed not to prosecute unless they thought public decency was being threatened.

Henry Gilbert Smith's contribution to Manly is from *Manly & Pittwater*. His nickname 'The Father of Manly' is from 'The Manly Heritage Plaques Walk', manly.com (online).

Smith's departure from Manly is from 'Manly founder's home at Fairlight a lost treasure', by John Morcombe, *Manly Daily*, 19 August 2016.

Manly with no hospital etc is from *Reminiscences of Old Manly*, George H Aurousseau, 29 September 1952 (pdf).

GM and Julia's community activities are from *SMH*, 25 January 1872, p2.

GM on the Manly ferry is from *Reminiscences of Old Manly*.

GM's fishing expedition is from *SMH*, 23 March 1874, p4. (Cited in *The Family of Mary Pitt*)

RM's quote is from *SMH*, 1 October 1935, p12.

The behaviour of theatre audiences is from Australian Culture 1789-2000, by Paul Bentley, The Wolanski Foundation Project, October 1999 (online).

Opera came to Australia courtesy of the Lyster Opera Company, who may well have been responsible for RM's later reputed love of opera.

The Anthony Trollope quote is from *Australia and New Zealand, Vol 1*.

The beginnings of the telegraph service is from *Manly & Pittwater*: 'A solitary telegraph wire stretched from Sydney to Manly via the Spit and was opened for service on the Corso 1 July 1876. Among the subscribers was a H

S Badgery, 'Oyama', Manly.' GM and RM both attended the banquet to honour the arrival of the telegraph in February 1876 and no doubt his son in law and future partner Henry Badgery did too.

Manly residents buying water is from *Reminiscences of Old Manly*.

The description of Eugenie Blanchard is from 'The Boudoir had a Grand Piano', *Australian Women's Weekly*, Kay Keavny, 25 March 1970, p13.

The history of Mauritius is from maurinet.com, Museums Victoria and The Mahatma Gandhi Institute (all online).

Chapter 39: The Mauritian connection

To describe Yves Blanchard as a 'sea captain' is an exaggeration, according to aunt Barbara: he owned a small boat which he used to deter pirates.

List of migrants is from Unassisted Migration List for *Exporter*, Ancestry.

There is a sad story attached to Antoine Masse, passed on to me by Marg Kaan. Later in 1836 he is listed as 'Antony Masse' at the 'Normal Institution' – a private day and boarding school set up by a Reverend Henry Carmichael – among scholars awarded prizes for 'for general ability in their different classes, and as an incitement to future, exertions'. (*The Australian*, 16 December 1836.) But eleven years later, in 1847/8, he appears as an inmate of Tarban Creek Lunatic Asylum, and there is an Antoine Masse who died, aged 79, at the Rockwood Asylum in May 1904. His mother Francoise, who died in 1888, had made provision for her son's burial in her will.

Permission to open the tomb is from 'ITEM 24 White Population 1831 No 474 Date April 2 Class 5' (Mauritian Archives, Marg Kaan)

According to aunt Barbara's notes, taken from *Mauritian Genealogie* by Edward Druyker, Julien Ives Blanchard married Angelique Mariette Mauritius in 1813.

Emilie's migration on board *Guide*, with Frederick Manton and Uranie, is from 'History of immigration from Mauritius', Museum Victoria (online). Also Unassisted migration list for Emilie Blanchard, Ancestry.

Uranie and her husband Richard continued to live at Mon Reduit for thirteen years until the Mantons sold it. Some time later they were given a grant near Tumut. From the 'Biography of Richard Manton Jeffrey' (online).

More details of Mon Reduit are from *Of the Star and the Key*, Edward Duyker (thanks to Marg Kaan). The ruins of the old building were still there in 2015 – a Manton descendant, Christopher Shain, photographed them (online).

Emilie was one of the earliest Mauritians to migrate to Australia. There had been an influx of Mauritian 'convicts' in the early days of European settlement, and a bigger influx of chancers during the goldrush of the 1850s. So one can safely claim that the Blanchards were, in this context, pioneers.

The abolition of slavery was not an overnight thing in Mauritius. There had been strong lobbying for it from groups of 'Coloureds' – mostly emancipated slaves – ever since the British took over the island in 1810, which was met by an even stronger lobby of 'affluent Whites' who for obvious reasons were keen to hang onto the status quo. At the time of the Masse migration abolition was still in its four-year probationary period, during which slaves became 'apprentices', with wages (albeit minimal). (From *A Comprehensive History Of Mauritius*, Sydney Selvon.)

JC Blanchard's allotment in Yass is from 'Julien Charles Blanchard Town Purchase 319' (Ancestry); and of Hoombango from 'License to Depasture Land beyond the Limits of Location' (Ancestry).

Chapter 40: The Blanchards & Sparrows
Passengers on *Tropic* are from List of Unassisted Passengers on *Tropic* (Ancestry); and *Sydney Gazette*, 28 May 1839. The origin of their journey and Anna's age are from Barbara Lamble, via her daughter Libby White.

Details of the Mantons is from 'The Mantons of Port Philip', Marg Kaan, Port Philip Pioneeers Group (online).

Marg tells me my aunt Barbara said Anna was 'brought to Australia to marry Julien Blanchard'. I have no details or evidence of this. There is a sixteen-month gap between Anna's arrival and her marriage. So who knows?

It's ironic that in the 1830s only certain professions qualified for assisted migration, which did not include surgeons apparently. When I migrated to Australia as a 'ten pound pom' in the late 1960s nobody cared or asked about my profession. I was an actress, not something the colony had a shortage of I don't think.

Thomas Sparrow's letter is from *Sydney Monitor*, 18 September 1839, p2. His child may have been William, born in 1839 according to NSW BDM (online).

Thomas's death is from *SMH*, 15 October 1842, p3.

The passenger lists of migrants in the *Hobart Colonial Times* mention only 'Mr and Mrs and Miss Sparrow'. Thomas Sparrow senior, named on Anna's marriage certificate as 'late', presumably died before his offspring emigrated.

The wedding announcement is from *Australasian Chronicle*, 12 Sept 1840, p3. The fact that JC and Anna married in both a Catholic and an Anglican church presumably means Anna was a Protestant.

Their residences are from Electoral rolls 1842-43 and 1849-50 respectively (Ancestry). The Ladies' School is from Sands Directories 1865 and 1875.

Anna's musical talent was evidently shared by her sister in law Emilie Manton, and was passed down to Anna's daughter Eugenie and to her daughter Muriel, my grandmother. Muriel, known as Mimi, was invited to travel to Europe to study piano, but her father forbade it because at thirteen she was considered too young, and 'No daughter of mine needs to earn a living'. So another potentially brilliant career bit the dust.

JC and Anna's children are from NSW BDM (online).

RM meeting Eugenie and its aftermath are inventions. RM's description of Eugenie is taken from a photo of her at a young age, part of the Pitt family collection. Eugenie's 'coolness' is also invented, though she did show signs of snobbishness in her later life. RM calling her mother Anna an 'angel' and father 'a French prig' are according to aunt Barbara, again via Libby White.

Eugenie's age on the marriage certificate has to be a mistake, as she was actually only 17.

RM and Eugenie living at Manly is from Bk 159, No 750, DL (cited in *The Family of Mary Pitt*).

The description of Hill-Side Cottage is from *SMH*, 4 May 1878, p16; and of Leona *SMH*, 13 September 1878, p10, and 16 January 1879, p8.

RM's term as alderman and topics discussed at council meetings are thanks to John MacRitchie, local historian at Manly Library and author of *A History of Manly Council* (2016).

Chapter 41: Kirribilli

The description of Holbrook is from *SMH*, 24 February 1875, p8, and from 'At home in North Sydney', Holbrook House Estate (online).

GM and Julia advertising for staff is from *SMH*, 15 September 1876, p8: The price they paid for Holbrook is from *The Family of Mary Pitt*.

Admiralty House, previously known as Wotonga House, was once let to James Robert Wilshire, GM's cousin.

The trimming of the ferry is from *Early Neutral Bay*, L F Mann, JRAHS Vol XVIII, pt4, Sydney 1932, p207. Ferrymen routinely carried counterweights to balance the boat (*Municipality of North Sydney*, G V F Mann).

The state of the North Shore streets is from *Freeman's Journal*, 16 May 1885 (cited in *The Opposite Shore, North Sydney and its People*, Eric Russell).

GM attending a banquet at the Masonic Hall is from *SMH* 19 Feb 1876, p5.

Meeting to discuss the water situation is from *SMH*, 31 March 1876, p4.

The sale of Coorar and Carar is from *Maitland Mercury*, 16 Jan 1877, p5.

In 1874 GM was executor to John Hoskisson's will, so I am assuming this JH was his son.

The squabbling between councils is from *Freeman's Journal*, 10 March, 18 August, 24 August 1878, 15 February 1879.

Chapter 42: The North Shore Lazarus

The North Shore 'Lazarus' is from the *Freeman's Journal*, 16 July 1881, p9.

'A Correspondent's' letter is from *Evening News*, 11 March 1882, p5.

Mr Glacken's comments are from *Evening News*, 26 January 1883, p2.

Petitions from the mayors to members of the government are from *Daily Telegraph*, 27 October 1883, p6: 'Nomad's' rants are from 'North Shore Notes' by Nomad. *Freeman's Journal*, 16 May 1885, p9.

Lord Carrington's first appearance on the North Shore was written up by several newspapers, including, in great detail and with some humour, *The Globe*, 24 May 1886, p3.

GM's donation for drainage is from *Evening News*, 26 March 1885, p5. The spring at Mount Street is from *Municipality of North Sydney*.

The mains pipe laid across the harbour is from *Illustrated Sydney News*, 9 May 1885, p11. The opening is from *SMH*, 4 July 1885, p11.

'Burglary and blasting' hitting the residents of Kirribilli and GM's offer of his coach and horses is from *Freeman's Journal*, 10 October 1891, p19.

The *Freeman's Journal's* reaction to the amalgamation of the councils is dated 9 May 1890.

GM's poetry-free speech to the Minister of Works is from *Evening News*, 8 June 1883, p2.

Chapter 43: Captain Cook, then and now

The report of the Captain Cook celebrations is from *SMH*, 26 February 1879, pp7&8. Why the celebrations took place in February 1879 I've no idea: Cook landed at Botany Bay on 29 April 1770.

The especially-written verse of *Rule Britannia* went:
> With lion heart that nought could tame,
> Our Hero sailed for shore unknown ;
> Crowned with the laurel wreath of Fame
> He won these lands we call our own.
> Hail, Australia, hail to thee!
> Fairest Daughter of the Sea!

The friend who reminded me of the 1970 commemoration was Michael Burge. The description of that event is from 'Commemoration and contestation at Kurnell' by Dr Stephen Gapps, Australian National Maritime Museum blog, 11 May 2015 (online).

Stan Grant's comments: 'It is a 'damaging myth' that Captain Cook discovered Australia' is from ABC News online.

Chapter 44: Julia

This scene is from my imagination.

Chapter 45: Pitt, Son & Badgery

Information on Henry Badgery is from *From the Hawkesbury to the Monaro*, and ADB online, by G P Walsh.

According to Bobbie Hardy, Henry and his family moved to Sydney late in 1877. Sands Directories has him living in Roslyn Terrace, Darlinghurst, Sydney in 1879, although Hardy maintains that 'By early 1879 the expense of living in this pleasant urban environment weighed on Henry's mind and he vacated Roslyn Terrace and sent 'Jue' and the children off to Bronte, his father-in-law's farm in Richmond.'

Badgery joining GM's company is from *SMH*, 10 February 1879, p2.

GM's statement to parliament is from NSW Legislative Assembly, Votes & Proceedings, 1877/78. Roll No 53, p849-852 (National Library).

Details of the new saleyards are from *Sydney Daily Telegraph*, 1 November

1882, p3. The opening is from *Daily Telegraph*, 2 November 1882, p3.

Badgery's complaints about the state of the saleyards is from 'At Homebush. With Pen and Pencil', *Sunday Times*, 14 April 1895, p3.

GM junior's survey of the Blue Mountains is from *The Story of Wentworth Falls*, M D McLaurin, Blue Mountains Historical Society. (Cited in *Coorah, The Life of Pitt House*, by Joan Edwards and Michael Burge.)

GM's eligibility for a grant of land as a volunteer is from The Volunteer Force Regulation Act 1867, Part VII, clause 45.

Reports on the progress of Coorah are from *Katoomba Times*, 13 July 1889, p3, & Sept 1889, p2. GM's 'launching' of it is from 'Coorah - Garden of a million blooms', by 'E Ficifolia', *SMH*, 22 February 1934, p6.

According to *The Life of Pitt House* from 1905 a Mr and Mrs Gorringe were working at Coorah as housekeeper and gardener. So RM and Eugenie may have initially used the house as a weekender, along with Eugenie's (unmarried) sister Mae, until they moved there completely in around 1915. RM as a patron of Grand Opera is also from *The Life of Pitt House*.

The description of Pitt Son & Badgery's building in George Street is from *Illustrated Sydney News*, 23 December 1882, p17. P, S & B's becoming a limited company is from *50 Years of Wool and Stock: The Remarkable Record of Pitt, Son & Badgery Ltd*.

The creators of the Homebush saleyards initially wanted to use the name Flemington but were dissuaded, to avoid confusion with the Melbourne saleyards of the same name. It seems the name caught on eventually anyway.

Chapter 46: The world without a sun
'The world without a sun' is from a speech delivered by GM in honour of MPs 'Mr Darvall' and 'Mr Piddington', *SMH*, 17 September 1860, p2.

Edwin's wife Julia Johnson was possibly John Johnson junior's daughter, so Julia and GM's niece.

GM's Latin translates as 'A man only gets what he deserves'.

JC Blanchard died on 8 July 1883, aged 75, of 'Hepatic disorder aggravated by a cold', according to his death certificate. He was buried at Petersham. Anna died on 3rd March 1885 of uterine cancer, from which she had been suffering for eight months. She was buried at Waverley Cemetery.

The coroner called to determine the cause of death of Mary Laycock is from *Maitland Mercury*, 25 July 1878, p5.

Chapter 47: Battling on
GM's activities following Julia's death are from *Evening News*, 6 August 1888, p8, *Daily Telegraph*, 26 June 1888, *SMH*, 3 Jan 1888 and *SMH*, 5 July 1888.

His letters to the press complaining about parliamentarians are from *SMH*, 5 May 1888, p8: and *Evening News*, 28 July 1888, p3.

Concerning the ferry company: *SMH*, 10 May 1888, p4. The response from 'Salus Populi' is from *SMH*, 11 May 1888, p10.

Riots in Newcastle: *Newcastle Morning Herald*, 20 October 1888, p2.

GM's views on strikes are from *Evening News*, 11 October 1888, p6, and *Evening News*, 16 October 1888, p5.

Chapter 48: Conclusion

Girls refusing to dance with blacklegs is from *The Australian Legend*, Russel Ward. (Cited in *Mateship and Moneymaking: Australian Shearing*, Rory O'Malley)

Julia Badgery's funeral is from *Windsor and Richmond Gazette*, 4 August 1894, p10.

19th century treatments for Bright's Disease are from Wikipedia.

Tributes paid to GM on his death are from *Australian Star*, 12 October 1896, p5; *SMH*, 13 October, p4; *Daily Telegraph*, 13 October 1896, p5; *Daily Telegraph*, 13 October 1896, p5; *Evening News*, 12 October 1896, p6. The description of his coffin is from *Australian Star*, 13 Oct, 13 October 1896, p5.

The description of his funeral is from *Sydney Stock and Station Journal*, 16 October 1896, p6.

'Young and free' Australians is from Australia's National Anthem.

Epilogue

GM gave Eugenie and RM the option of paying the £4000 owed on Holbrook right away or paying 4% interest over ten years (*The Family of Mary Pitt*).

GM's will is from 'Registers of Copies of Wills 1800-1901, SAG Will 4/12756', cited in *The Family of Mary Pitt*.

The description of RM is from *Australian Women's Weekly*, Kay Keavny, 25 March 1970, p12.

Pitt, Son & Badgery's turnover is from *The Remarkable Story of Pitt, Son & Badgery Ltd*. Its acquisition is 1972 is from ANU Archives (online).

Details of Pitt and Nelson's Farms are from *The Family of Mary Pitt*.

Doris's birth and Adele's wedding at Holbrook are from *SMH*, 3 Feb 1897, p1, and *Stock and Station Journal*, 15 May 1903, p3.

Eugenie's ads are from *SMH*, 23 Jan 1905, p2.

Holbrook's becoming a boarding house is from *SMH*, 26 April 1905, p4.

AJ Pitt lodging there is from *The Star*, 2 April 1909, p1. I assume he was a family member.

Holbrook advertised for sale is from *Sunday Times*, 9 November 1913, p4. The fact that each of the rooms was considered big enough to act as an early 20th century 'bedsitter' is an indication of their generous size.

Further ads and the eventual sale of the house is from *Daily Telegraph*, 4 Sept 1915, p12. It was advertised for auction again in 1816. The demolition of the boarding house is from 'At home in North Sydney' (online).

What knowledge I have of the Scott children came from Chris Daley, who is a descendant of one of them. Unfortunately she has dropped off the radar.

Henry Badgery's marriages are from ADB online and NSW BDMs.

Bibliography

PUBLISHED BOOKS

Barcan, Alan, *A Short History of Education in New South Wales*, Martindale Press, Sydney, 1965

Barkley, Jan & Nichols, Michelle, *Hawkesbury 1794-1994: the first 200 years*, Windsor, Hawkesbury City Council, 1994

Barkley-Jack, Jan, *Hawkesbury Settlement Revealed*, Rosenberg Publishing Pty Ltd, 2009

Blainey, Geoffrey, *A Land Half Won*, Macmillan, Melbourne, 1982

Blainey, Geoffrey, *Black Kettle and Full Moon*, Penguin, Australia, 2003

Boughton, Sam (aka 'Cooramill'), *Reminiscences of Richmond*, collated by Cathy McHardy, Kurrajong, 2010 (Originally published in the *Hawkesbury Herald*, 20 March 1903 to 26 August 1904)

Bowd, D G, *Macquarie Country*, Library of Australian History, 1979

Branch Johnson, W, The English *Prison Hulks*, Phillimore, London & Chichester, 1970

Brodribb, William Adams, *Recollections of an Australian Squatter*, John Woods, 1883

Brodsky, Isadore, *North Sydney 1788-1962*, Municipal Council of North Sydney, 1963

Brook, Jack, *Shut Out From the World*, Deerubbin Press, 1999 (originally Berowra Press, 1891)

Brook, J, Kohen, J L, *The Parramatta Native Institution and the Black Town*, NSW University Press, NSW, 1991

Brooke, Alan & David Brandon, *Bound for Botany Bay*, National Archives, London, 2005

Champion, Shelagh & George, *Manly, Warringah and Pittwater*, 1998-1998, NSW, 1990

Clarke, Patricia & Spender, Dale (eds), *Lifelines: Australian women's letters and diaries 1788-1840*, Allen & Unwin, Sydney, 1992

Crowley, Frank (ed), *Colonial Australia, Vol 1*, Thomas Nelson, Melbourne, 1980

Cumpston, J H L, *Thomas Mitchell – Surveyor General and Explorer*, T & W Boone, London, 1938

Cust, Janelle, *The Family of Mary Pitt*, Gordon, 2009

Cunningham, Peter, *Two Years in New South Wales*, Henry Colburn, London, 1927

Daniels, Kay, *Convict Women*, Allen & Unwin, Sydney 1998

Dark, Eleanor, *The Timeless Land*, Macmillan, Australia, 1941

Duyker, Edward, *Of the Star and the Key*, Australian Mauritian Research Group, NSW, 1988

Edwards, Joan & Burge, Michael, *Coorah: The life of Pitt House*, Blue Mountains Grammar School, NSW, 1989

Evans L & Nicholls P (eds), *Convicts and Colonial Society*, Macmillan, 1984

Farwell, George, *Squatter's Castle: the Story of a Pastoral Dynasty*, Landsdowne Press, Melbourne, 1973

Fitzpatrick, John Charles Lucas, *Those were the Days*, NSW Bookstall Co Ltd., Sydney, 1923

Fletcher, Brian H, *Landed Enterprise and Penal Society*, Sydney University Press, 1976

Foster, William C, *Sir Thomas Livingstone Mitchell and his World, 1792-1855: surveyor general of New South Wales, 1828-1855*, Sydney Institution of Surveyors, 1985

Freeland, J M, *Architecture in Australia*, National Library of Australia, 1967

Gilmore, Mary, *Old Days: Old Ways*, Angus & Robertson, Sydney, 1934

Gledhill, Percy Walter, *Manly and Pittwater: its beauty and progress*, Manly, Warringah and Pittwater Historical Society, 1948

Guilfoyle, John, *Bloody Agents*, Boolarong Press, Queensland, 2009

Hardy, Bobbie, *From the Hawkesbury to the Monaro*, Kangaroo Press, NSW, 1989

Haynes, Jim, *The Best Australian Bush Stories*, Allen & Unwin, Australia, 2013

Hughes, Robert, *The Fatal Shore*, Pan Books, London, 1987

Huntsman, Leone, *Sand in Our Souls: The Beach in Australian History*, Melbourne University Press, 2001

Ingleton, Geoffrey, *True Patriots All*, Angus & Robertson, Australia, 1965

Inglis, KS, *Australian Colonists*, Melbourne University Press, 1974.

Keneally, Thomas, *Australia: Origins to Eureka*, Allen & Unwin, Australia, 2011

Lohrli, Anne, *Household Words: A Weekly Journal, 1850-1859*, University of Toronto Press, 1973

McDonald, D. I, *They Came to a Valley; Wellington 1817-1967*, Wellington Historical Society, 1968

McKenzie, Kirsten, *Scandal in the Colonies: Sydney and Cape Town 1820-1850*, Melbourne University Press, Carlton, 2005

McLaurin, M D, *The Story of Wentworth Falls*, Blue Mountains Historical Society, 1947

Mahaffey, Kath, *The Watercourse Country*, Moree & District Historical Society, 1983

Makim, Gene, *The Tail Goes with the Hide*

Mann, G V F, *Municipality of North Sydney: History and Progress from 1788 - 1938*, Municipal Council of North Sydney, 1938

Marshall, John, *Twenty Years Experience in Australia*, Smith, Elder & Co., London, 1837

Millis, Roger, *Waterloo Creek*, McPhee Gribble, Victoria, 1992

Mitchell, Major T L, *Three Expeditions into the Interior of Eastern Australia*, T & W Boone, London, 1838

Nicholas, Stephen (ed), *Convict Workers*, Cambridge University Press, 1988

O'Malley, Rory, *Mateship and Moneymaking. Shearing: the clash of union solidarity*, XLibris, 2003

Oxley, Deborah, *Convict Maids*, Cambridge University Press, 1996

Paterson, Banjo, *The Man from the Snowy River and Other Verses (Saltbush Bill)*, Angus & Robertson, Australia, 1895

Paterson, Banjo, *The Trouble with Merinos*, The Bulletin, 1895

Phillips, ADM & Sutton, Alan, eds, *The Potteries: Continuity and Change in a Staffordshire Conurbation*, Allan Strutton, Stroud, 1993

Priestman, Val, *Leek Remembered*

Roberts, Stephen H, *The Squatting Age in Australia 1835-1847*, Melbourne University Press, 1935 (reprinted 1975)

Robson, Lloyd, *Convict Settlers in Australia*, Melbourne University Press, 1995

Ross, Valerie, *Hawkesbury Story*, Library of Australian History, Sydney, 1989

Russell, Eric, *The Opposite Shore, North Sydney and its People*, North Shore Historical Society, 1990

Ryan, James T. ('Toby') *Reminiscences of Australia*, George Robertson, Sydney, 1894 (Facsimile edn 1982)

Seal, Graham, *Larrikins, Bush Tales and other Great Australian Stories*, Allen & Unwin, Australia, 2014

Selvon, Sydney, *A Comprehensive History of Mauritius*, MDS, Mauritius, 2005

Shaw, Simeon, *History of the Staffordshire Potteries*, Scott, Greenwood & Co, Hanley, 1829

Smith, Alfred, *Some Ups and Downs of an old Richmondite*, Nepean History Society, 1991

Steele, James, *The Early Days of Windsor*, Tyrrell's, Sydney, 1910

Swancott, Charles, *Manly 1788-1968*, D S Ford, Sydney, 1968

Taylor, David, *Crime, Policing and Punishment in England, 1750-1914*, Macmillan Press Ltd., London, 1998

Taylor, Peter, *Station Life in Australia: pioneers and pastoralists*, Allen & Unwin, Sydney, 1988

Tearle, Sheila, 'Hannah Laycock of King's Grove Farm', from *Lives Obscurely*

Great, Society of Women Writers, Sydney, 1980

Trench, Patsy, *The Worst Country in the World*, Prefab Publications, London, 2012

Trollope, Anthony, *Australia & New Zealand, Vol 1*, Chapman & Hall, London, 1876

Ville, Simon, *The Rural Entrepreneurs: A history of the stock and station agent industry in Australia & NZ*, Cambridge University Press, 2000

Ward, Russel, *The Australian Legend*, Oxford University Press, 1978 (orig edition 1958)

Watson, Don, *The Bush*, Penguin, Australia, 2014

Webb, R, *The Rising Sun – A History of Moree & District*, The Moree & District Historical Society Inc., 1962

Webby, Elizabeth, ed, *Colonial Voices*, University of Queensland, 1989

Webster, R H, *The Ancient Art of Auction*, Real Estate Institute of Australia Ltd, 1988

Webster, R, H & Bray, Colin J, *A Century Of Service*, Stock & Station Agents Assoc of NSW, 1990

Welsh, Frank, *Australia: A new history of the Great Southern Land*, Allen Lane, London 2004

Willey, Keith, *When the Sky Fell Down*, Collins, Sydney 1979

Wright, Judith, *The Generations of Men*, Oxford University Press, Melbourne 1959

JOURNAL OF THE ROYAL AUSTRALIAN HISTORICAL SOCIETY

Beale, Edgar, 1980, *The Naming of Aborigines*, Newsletter No.186: 3-4, Jan/Feb 1980

Campbell, JF, *Squatting on Crown Lands in NSW*, Vol 15 pt 2, 1929

Jervis, James, *Exploration and settlement of the N W Plains*, Vol 48 pt 5, p383

Lansbury, Coral, *Charles Dickens and his Australia* Vol 52 pt 2, June 1966, p115

Lawson, W., *A history of industrial pottery production in New South Wales*, Vol 57 (1):17-39, 1971

Mann, L F, *Early Neutral Bay*, JRAHS, Vol 18 pt4, Sydney 1932, p207

NEWSPAPERS & JOURNALS (AUSTRALIA)

The Age, Australasian Chronicle, The Australian, Australasian Anthropological Journal (1897), Australian Star, Australian Women's Weekly, The Bulletin, Caledonia Mercury, Colonial Observer, Colonist, Commercial Journal & Advertiser, Empire, Evening News, Freeman's Journal, Hawkesbury Courier, Hobart Colonial Times, Hunter River Gazette, Illustrated Sydney News, Katoomba Times, Maitland Mercury, Manly Daily, Newcastle Morning Herald, The Star, Sunday Times, Sydney Daily Telegraph, Sydney Gazette, Sydney Monitor, Sydney Stock and Station Journal, Sydney Morning Herald, Windsor and Richmond Gazette, Wingham Chronicle and Manning River Observer

NEWSPAPERS & JOURNALS (UK)
Belfast Newsletter
Staffordshire Advertiser

NATIONAL ARCHIVES (UK)
Assize courts, Crown & Gaol Books: http://nationalarchives.gov.uk/help-with-your-research/research-guides/criminal-trials-english-assize-courts-1559-1971-key-to-records/

MITCHELL LIBRARY
Boughton, C F, Historical articles on the early history of Moree, from *The North-West Champion*, Sept 1949 to Oct 1954 (ML Q981.6/B 1-273)
Edwardson, Wm, (Chief officer) *Journal of a Voyage in the Ship Surrey Captain Thomas Raine with Convicts from Cork to Port Jackson, New South Wales, 1816*. (Mss A 2044, Reel CY 1113)
Hammersley, G H, A Few Observations on the Situation of the Female Convicts in New South Wales, 1807 - 1894 (ML papers A 657)
HRA & HRNSW
NSW Legislative Assembly, Votes & Proceedings, 1877/78. Roll No 53, p849-852

LOCAL LIBRARIES (Australia)
Return of Crown Lands Held Under License – Wellington 1866 (Warren Library).
Minutes Book Borough of East St Leonards 1879-1885 (Stanton Library).

STATE RECORDS OF NSW
Government Gazettes: Supplement to the Government Gazette, Claims to Leases of Crown Lands, Gwydir District, 9 September 1848, No 81, p1175
SZ1014 Fiche 3307, (attendance at school)
Treasury, Letters received 1847, 4/2788, Wm Scott 47/4126 (Scott's land grant)
Letters received 1826-49 Misc persons M-Y, 4/2406.4, Reel 2213, 38/3985. (ditto)
Treasury, certificates for depasturing licenses 1839-40 Reel 5068, 4/92, No 2 (taking up land 1848)

ONLINE RESOURCES
ABC News: 'It is a "damaging myth that Captain Cook discovered Australia", Stan Grant, 23 August 2017: http://www.abc.net.au/news/2017-08-23/stan-grant:-damaging-myth-captain-cook-discovered-australia/8833536
Aeolus: http://www.jenwilletts.com/convict_ship_aeolus_1809.htm

Australian births, deaths & marriages: http://www.bdm.nsw.gov.au

Australian National Maritime Museum blog. 'Commemoration and contestation at Kurnell' by Dr Stephen Gapps, 11 May 2015: https://anmm.blog/2015/05/11/commemoration-and-contestation-at-kurnell/

Colonial Secretary's papers: http://colsec.records.nsw.gov.au

Convict and emancipist teachers: http://dehanz.net.au/entries/convict-emancipist-teachers/

Convict records: http://www.convictrecords.com.au/convicts

Criminal trials in the English assize courts: http://nationalarchives.gov.uk/help-with-your-research/research-guides/criminal-trials-english-assize-courts-1559-1971-key-to-records/

Dictionary of Sydney, Agnes Banks: http://dictionaryofsydney.org/entry/agnes_banks, Lorraine Stacker, 2008

The Factory above the gaol, Michaela Cameron, 20016: https://femalefactoryonline.org/about/history/the-factory-above-the-gaol/

Governor's Diary & Memorandum Book, Macquarie, 10 April 1816. http://www.mq.edu.au/macquarie-archive/lema/1816/1816april.html

Hawkesbury floods: http://hawkesburyheritage.blogspot.co.uk/2013/06/hawkesbury-river-floods.html

History of Aboriginal Sydney: https://ses.library.usyd.edu.au/bitstream/2123/8253/2/Sukovic%20Read%20Information%20Online%202011.pdf

History of Immigration from Mauritius: http://immigration.museum.vic.gov.au/origins/history.aspx?pid=40

Homebush website: http://www.eastershow.com.au/explore-plan/food-drink-shop/the-stables/

Irish Convicts to New South Wales, Peter Mayberry: http://members.pcug.org.au/~ppmay/cgi-bin/irish/irish.cgi

Kingston, Beverley, Basket, Bag and Trolley: a History of Shopping in Australia: http://www.environment.nsw.gov.au/resources/heritagebranch/heritage/alotinstorech2.pdf

Land grants index: www.records.nsw.gov.au/guides

Letters from Victorian pioneers: http://www.ebooksread.com/authors-eng/museums-public-library/letters-from-victorian-pioneers-being-a-series-of-papers-on-the-early-occupatio-ala/page-15-letters-from-victorian-pioneers-being-a-series-of-papers-on-the-early-occupation-ala.shtml

Mahamta Gandhi Institute: www.mgirti.org

The Mantons of Port Phillip, Marg Kaan: http://www.portphillippioneersgroup.org.au/pppg5ii.htm

Main Surburban Railway line: https://en.wikipedia.org/wiki/ Main_Suburban_railway_line#History)

Mauritius Attractions: https://mauritiusattractions.com/mauritius-history-i-79.html

Mauritius Island Online: www.maurinet.com
Melbourne Metblogs: http://melbourne.metblogs.com/2007/06/13/batmania
Museums Victoria: www.museumvictoria.com.au
NSW Records: https://www.records.nsw.gov.au
Parliament of New South Wales: https://www.parliament.nsw.gov.au /about/Pages/1856-to-1889-Responsible-Government-and-Colonial-.aspx
Parramatta Female Factories: https://parramattafemalefactories.wordpress.com/historical-context-for-female-factories/
Return of Frauds and Forgeries in Department of Stamp Office of Ireland, 1812-16, *Belfast Newsletter*, 17 September 1813: http://eppi.dippam.ac.uk/documents/9037/eppi_pages/203525
Richards, Leanne, A short history of the Australian theatre to 1910: http://www.hat-archive.com/shorthistory.htm
Sands Directories: http://cdn.cityofsydney.nsw.gov.au/learn/history/archives/sands/1870-1879/1879-part3.pdf
Scriven's Report on Child Labour in the pottery industry: http://www.thepotteries.org/history/scriven4.htm
NSW SES: https://www.ses.nsw.gov.au/news/all-news/2017/reflecting-on-the-record-1867-hawkesbury-nepean-flood/
Shain, Christopher website: http://shain.com.au/?p=173
Simply Austra*lia*: http://simplyaustralia.net/index.html
Surveys & maps: maps & imagery, parish maps, www.lands.nsw.gov.au, www.home.pacific.net.au/2tandd, www.coraweb.com.au
Sydney Heritage Fleet: North Shore Steam Ferry Company: www.shf.org.au/archives-research/photographic-collections/william-bill-allen-collection/north-shore-steam-ferry-company/
John (Jack) Timmins, John Chandler: http://www.wolfweb.com.au/acd/johntimmins.html
Victorian Crime & Punishment: http://vcp.e2bn.org_
Warren, Chris, 'Sydney's Outbreak of Smallpox 1789', ABC Radio National 'Ockham's Razor', 17 April 2014: http://nationalunitygovernment.org/content/was-sydneys-smallpox-outbreak-1789-act-biological-warfare-against-aboriginal-tribes
Western Australia: https://www.worldatlas.com/webimage/countrys/oceania/australia/westernaustralia/watimeln.htm
Willetts, Jen: *Free Settler or Felon?* https://www.jenwilletts.com/

ONLINE BIOGRAPHIES (ADB)
Allman, Francis, by A J Gray: http://adb.anu.edu.au/biography/allman-francis-1699
Badgery, Henry, by G P Walsh, http://adb.anu.edu.au/biography/badgery-henry-septimus-47

Bowman, John, by B T Fletcher: http://adb.anu.edu.au/biography/bowman-john-1813
Cox, William, by Edna Hickson: http://adb.anu.edu.au/biography/cox-william-1934
Donohoe, Jack, by Russel Ward: http://adb.anu.edu.au/biography/donohoe-john-jack-1985
Gipps, Sir George, by Samuel Clyde McCulloch: http://adb.anu.edu.au/biography/gipps-sir-george-2098
Jeffreys, Richard Manton: https://www.wikitree.com/wiki/Jeffery-710
Macquarie, Lachlan, by N D McLachlan:
http://adb.anu.edu.au/biography/macquarie-lachlan-2419
Pitt, GM, by G P Walsh: http://adb.anu.edu.au/biography/pitt-george-matcham-4403GM Pitt
Wilshire, James Robert by G P Walsh:
http://adb.anu.edu.au/biography/wilshire-james-robert-4865

PRIVATELY PUBLISHED
50 Years of Wool and Stock: The Remarkable Record of Pitt, Son & Badgery Ltd., Sydney, 1938

CENSUSES and MUSTERS
New South Wales general muster 1814, ed. Carol J Baxter, ABGR in association with The Society of Australian Genealogists, Sydney, 1988
General Muster and Land and Stock Muster of NSW, 1822, ed Carol J Baxter, ABGR, North Sydney, 1988
Census of N.S.W, 1828, ed Malcom R Sainty and Keith A Johnson, Library of Australian History, Sydney, 1980
New South Wales Census of the Year 1841 (Ancestry

OTHER
Aurousseau, George H, *Reminiscences of Old Manly*, 29 September 1952
McGeoch, J.A.H, 'The Role and Art of the Auctioneer', *Wood Hall News*, No. 22, December 1971
MacRitchie, John, *A History of Manly Council*, 2016
Wollumbi District Church of England Baptisms, 1856-1905, both Cessnock District Historical and Family History Society, 1998 (Wollumbi Museum)

Index

Abbott, Tony 161
Aboriginal people 6, 41-46, 49, 114-116, 128, 134, 135, 144-49, 151, 156, 165-168, 183, 185-189, 199, 202, 205, 229, 234, 261, 263, 264, 288, 289, 296, 309, 310
Adelaide 41, 178, 198, 226, 288
Aeolus 79-81
'Ah Chee' 203
Allman, Francis 168-171
Anne 74, 83, 84
Appin Massacre 44
Assize Courts 60, 62, 69
auctioneering 3, 4, 210-213, 228, 229, 268, 270, 272, 274
Aull family
    Elizabeth 110
    James 181, 182
    Jane 105
        See Thompson, Jane
    Mary 53, 56, 106-111, 119, 123, 178, 180-182, 232, 267
        See Moore, Mary and Johnson, Mary
    Mary junior 110
    Robert 49, 53, 56, 101-111, 120, 122, 180-182, 296
    William 110
Australasian Anthropological Journal 41

Australia (film) 137
Australian 107, 108
Australian Agricultural Company 148, 152, 162
Australian National Library 112
Baddeley, John 62, 65, 71, 72, 75
Badgery family
    Henry Septimus 229, 268-270, 272, 285, 291, 293, 323
    James 229, 276
    Julia 229, 269, 276, 285, 293, *See* Pitt, Julia junior
    Badgery Brothers 294
Badgerys Creek 44, 229
Baldwin, Otto and Harvest 152, 162
Bangheet 207-209
Banks, Joseph 263
Bathurst 50, 100, 109, 141, 193, 197, 231
Bayley, Marshall 251
Betts, Margaret 48, 232, 292
Betts, William and Mary 292
Bibben, Jane 181
Big River 133-136, 150, 158, 160, 162, 172
Blacket, Edmund 236
Blanchard family
    Anna 247, 248
    See Sparrow, Anna

Charles 242
Francoise Royer 241
See Masse, Francoise
Julien Charles 239-243, 245-247, 321, 322
Julien Yves 241, 320
Marie Emilie (JC's sister) 242-245, See Manton, Emilie
Marie Emilie Eugenie 239, 240, 247-249 See Pitt, Eugenie
Blaxland brothers 144, 176
Bligh, William, governor 35, 80, 92
Blue Mountains 34, 46, 128, 231, 273
Blue Mountains Grammar School 273
Botany Bay 59, 75, 117, 263
Boughton Papers 158
Boughton, Charles 159
Boughton, Sam 195, 196
Bound for Botany Bay 70
Bourke, Sir Richard, governor 122, 129, 130, 145, 260
Bowd, DG 166
Bowman, George 141, 152, 165
Bowman, John 313
Bowman, William 191, 313
Boyd, Benjamin 176
Brickfields 85, 266, 305
Brisbane, Sir Thomas, governor 113, 190
Britannia 35
British government 42, 128, 189, 190, 199
British Library 70, 241
Bronte 52, 54, 120, 122, 124-126, 140, 142, 176, 179, 228, 232, 233, 269, 277, 290, 292
Brunker & Wolfe 229, 269
Bull, George 133, 163, 183, 185, 186
Bullerue 166, 168, 172, 176, 183, 185

Bulletin 203
Burns, Robbie ... 2, 36, 214, 286, 289
bushrangers 6, 49, 105
Byron, Lord 214
Canberra 160, 227
Captivity 73-75
Carrington, Lord, governor 258
Castlereagh, Lord 80, 84, 105
Catchpole, Margaret ... 82, 152, 196
censuses 42, 43, 48, 51, 99, 100, 105, 110, 115, 133, 181, 182, 293
Chisholm, Caroline 178
Circular Quay 237, 252, 254, 265, 291
Clarence River 135
Clarke, George 135
Colley, Elizabeth 70
Colonial Observer 187, 313
Colonist 180
Constitution Act 1843 190
Convict assignment 80, 85
convicts 6, 11, 13, 29, 33-35, 38-40, 48, 49, 53, 55, 59-61, 70, 74, 79-85, 89-92, 98-106, 111, 113, 115, 116, 120, 121, 125, 126, 135, 136, 141, 142, 165, 183, 189, 190, 196, 204, 232, 266, 267, 282, 300
Cook, Captain 260-264, 323
Coorah (Blue Mountains) 273, 274, 291, 324
Coorar (Gwydir) 133, 158, 159, 172, 174, 207, 253
Cowper, Reverend William 34, 97
Cowper, Sir Charles 217-219, 223, 224
Cox, Sloper 211, 212, 229
Cox, William 34, 109, 177
Craig, Richard 135
Crawley, Mr and Mrs 49
Crimes and punishments 62, 68, 329
Crown Lands 109, 128, 129, 133, 173, 197

335

Crown Lands Act 1861 (free selection) 218
Cunningham family 70
   Elizabeth 65-67
   Jane 66, 70
   Thomas 63, 66, 67, 70
Cunningham, Allan 150, 288
Cunningham, Peter 40
Cust, Janelle 112, 133
Daily Telegraph 287, 325
Dangar, Henry 165
Darkiñung people 46
Darug 41-43, 46, 114, 115, 166, 296
Darvall, John Bayley 199, 200
Dawson, Thomas 215
Deas Thomson, Sir Edward 188, 223
Deerubbin 32
Dickens family
   Arthur d'Orsay Tennyson 157
   Charles 157, 183-185, 239
   Edward Bullwer Lytton 157
   Henry 157
Dight, Hannah 152
Donohoe, 'Wild' Jack 49, 50
Drover's Wife 137, 178
droving 6, 35, 132, 136-139, 141, 177, 192, 193, 203, 206
Drysdale, Russell 137
Duke of Wellington 183, 184, 186, 187
East St Leonards 254, 256
Eather family 230
economic depression 109, 164, 166, 191, 275, 284
education 33-35, 44, 73, 126, 159, 179, 220, 221, 236, 239, 261, 274
Egerton, Captain 195
Elders Smith Goldsborough Mort 292, 294
elections 190, 191, 194, 222-224, 257, 281
Endeavour 263
Evening News 259, 281-283, 287, 281-283, 322, 324, 325
Fairlight 234, 236, 238, 251
Faithfull family
   George ... 34, 36, 115, 121, 126, 188
   Susanna 10, 120, 196
   William 10, 33, 120, 121, 193
   William Pitt 122, 188
family history 4, 6, 51, 59, 63, 68, 100, 111-113, 116, 136, 157, 158, 181, 185, 228, 240, 254, 283, 295
Family of Mary Pitt 308, 322, 325
Farwell, George 151
Federation 227, 285
Female Factory 81, 89, 105, 304
First Fleet 70, 80, 264
Fitzgerald, Robert ... 141, 152, 174, 176, 191, 194
Fitzroy, Sir Charles, governor 172, 174, 197
Flinders, Matthew 240
floods 32, 80, 98, 144, 152, 194, 195, 203, 205, 223, 229-232, 318
Ford, Dr Geoff 46
forgery 56, 59, 60, 62, 64, 65, 67, 71, 104, 108
Francis & Eliza 101, 102, 104
Franklin, Miles 178, 242
Fraser, Malcolm 160, 161
free selection 217-219
Freedom March 1965 156
Freeman's Journal ... 253, 256, 257, 259
Fryingpan 183, 185-187
Fullagher's saleyards 212
Fullwood, Albert Henry 228
Fulton, Reverend Henry 35
Garah 159
Garling family
   Frederick 228
   Jessie .... 229, 276, *See* Pitt, Jessie
   William 228, 276, 318
Gilmore, Mary 47, 49, 154, 178, 266

Gipps, Sir George, governor... 166, 170, 171, 173, 174, 187, 188, 191, 312
GM Pitt & Son 238, 253
Going Circuit at the Antipodes ... 183
goldrush 197-200, 204, 224, 227, 289
Goulburn, Frederick.................. 113
Government Pottery 85
Governor Darling 53, 107, 110, 111, 120, 122, 178, 182
Grant, Stan 263, 264, 323
Green, Richard 41, 296
Grenville, Kate 41
Gwydir district ... 1, 132-134, 140, 150, 152, 158, 162, 164, 165, 167, 170, 183, 192, 193, 208, 253, 273, 286
Hall brothers.......165, 169, 176, 192
    George............................ 167, 172
    Thomas. 162, 167-172, 192, 193
Hardy, Bobbie 269, 318
Harpur, Joseph............................. 35
Harris, Mr 34
Hawke, Bob 161
Hawkesbury 1, 22, 32, 33, 41, 43, 47, 50, 51, 80, 122, 126, 128, 133, 140, 142, 152, 166, 193-195, 200, 223, 229, 231, 232, 266, 286, 318
Hawkesbury Agricultural Association 176, 193, 229, 268
Hawkesbury library.................. 160
Herald 188
Hobartville.................. 195, 229, 276
Hogsflesh, Mr............................... 35
Holbrook 251, 252, 258, 273, 276, 286, 290, 292, 293
Homebush 215, 229, 270-272, 275, 317
Hoskisson, John .174, 176, 212, 253
Hoskisson, John junior 253
Household Words 183, 184
Hughes, Mathew 34, 35

Hunter Valley 152
Hunter, John, governor 81, 82, 108
Hyde Park............................ 260, 264
Illustrated Sydney News 274, 330
Inall, Edward 51, 126
Jackman, Hugh.......................... 137
Jeffrey, Richard Manton............242
Jenkins, Jemima 120, 121, 196
Johnson family
    Charlotte.................................98
    Elizabeth..............................61, 72
    John 59-66, 68, 69, 71-75, 83-85, 93-100, 302, 303, 305, 306
    John junior 98, 103, 181, 182, 290
    Julia 54, 56, 67, 101-104, 106-108, 111, 119-123, 265, 277, 278, 296, *See* Pitt, Julia
    Mary 59, 60, 82, 98-101, 106, 113, 182, 232, 306 *See* Moore, Mary and Aull, Mary
    Mary Ann 98, 101-103
    Sarah 98, 181, 296
Kaan, Marg 241, 242, 296, 320, 321
Kamilaroi 115, 134, 135, 149, 153, 164-166
Katoomba Times...........................273
Kerr, Sir John, governor-general 161
Kindur...............................135, 150
King George III............................44
King, Anna 178
King, Philip Gidley, governor ..81, 82
Kirribilli 251, 254, 256-259, 265, 273, 287
Kurrajong 33, 52, 108, 109, 113, 122, 141, 143, 175, 192, 231, 276
Lamble, Barbara 60, 112, 273, 296, 308, 321
Land Commissioners.................130
Landstaff, Edna 89-93, 95, 98
Landstaff, Harold...................91, 92

Lawson, Henry............137, 178, 203
Laycock family 122
   Hannah 10, 28, 49, 51, 121, 126,
   Samuel.............10, 14, 15, 17, 28
   Thomas WEB..........51, 121, 122
   Thomas, quartermaster 51, 215
   William............................51, 120
Legislative Assembly ... 194, 195, 199, 220, 222, 269
Legislative Council 157, 187, 188, 190, 194, 198-200, 223
Liverpool Plains 109, 133, 136, 141, 147, 148, 152, 158, 162, 164-166, 168
Liverpool Ranges.......146, 148, 152
London............. 2-4, 61, 64, 82, 116
Luhrmann, Baz............................137
Macarthur, Elizabeth................177
Macarthur, John 177
Macquarie, Lachlan, governor .43, 44, 81, 82, 84, 85, 93, 113, 114, 128, 129, 188, 190, 264
Mahaffey, Kath............................ 159
Maitland 229, 269, 281
Maitland Assize Court............. 183
Maitland Mercury.................186, 221
Makim, Gene 192, 193
Male Orphan School.................. 115
Manly 232-234, 236, 237, 239, 251, 253, 258, 276, 277, 285, 319
Manton family....................242, 321
Manton, Emilie 320, 321
Manton, Frederick 242, 320
Marsden, Reverend Samuel.......83
Martin, James.......................217, 220
Masse family
   Alexis Antoine 241, 242
   Anthony (Antoine)......241, 320
   Eugenie..................................241
   Eulalie...................................241
   Francoise 241, *See* Blanchard, Francoise Royer
Mauritius 239, 240-243, 320
McCarthy, Chris & Di 3, 212, 296, 299, 309, 317
McKnight, Roger 203
McNamara, Michael 157, 158
Melba, Dame Nellie 273
Melbourne 122, 190, 198, 199, 225, 227, 288
Michie, Archibald...... 183, 184, 185
migration 5, 91, 129, 189, 190, 197, 198, 240, 242, 243
Milwood, James............................99
Mitchell, Roderick............. 171, 172
Mitchell, Sir Thomas Livingstone 130, 136, 139-150, 159, 171, 288,
Molesworth, Sir William...........189
Mon Reduit................. 242, 243, 320
Monaro...269
Moore, Mary 59, 60, 62, 63, 65-67, 69-71, 75, 79-83, 85, 89-98, 303, 305 *See* Johnson, Mary and Aull, Mary
Moree 133-136, 156-159, 174, 177, 193, 297
Moree Champion...........................134
Moree Historical Society.. 157, 159
Moree library 156, 157, 158
Murray river................................226
Murray, Les 203
Myall Creek massacre 165, 188
National Archives 61, 62
Nelson, Admiral....... 9, 52, 111, 287
Nepean river 32, 108, 194
new chums 5, 6, 164
New South Wales Corps 35, 80, 84, 93, 177, 215
Nineteen Counties 129, 130, 163, 164, 288
Norfolk Island..............................39
North Richmond 228, 276
North Shore 234, 252, 254, 256-59, 277, 280
North Shore Ferry Company ...280
North Sydney 253, 254, 258, 259, 277, 292, 322
Nowland, William.....................152

Onus, John 152
orphanages 11, 178, 181
Overlanders (film) 137
Oyama 285
Pardon, Absolute 99
Pardon, Conditional 98, 105
parliament   6, 200, 202, 239, 269, 271, 280
Parnell, Thomas 152
Parramatta 44, 81, 105, 128, 224, 272
Paterson, Banjo 137, 138, 151, 202, 203
   Clancy of the Overflow .. 137, 203
   Man from Snowy River 203
   Saltbush Bill 137, 138
   Waltzing Matilda 204
Paterson, Colonel William 80
Paterson, Susan 178
penal colony 4, 6, 59, 125
Penrith 49
Perth 198, 226, 288
Phillip, Arthur, governor ... 81, 234
Piddington, WR 199, 200
Pitt and Nelson's Farms ...   11, 18, 21, 46, 181, 292
Pitt family
   18, 21, 22, 33, 48, 51, 59, 112, 116, 124, 125, 127, 134, 192, 215, 231, 234, 238, 251, 268, 276-279, 290, 292, 295
   Arthur (AGM) 249, 292, 293
   Charles Bryan 196, 232, 277, 290
   Colin 196, 232, 277, 290
   Edwin 196, 232, 233, 276, 277, 290, 292
   Eliza 10, 14, 51, 121, 126
   Elizabeth 9-11, 14, 15, 18-31, 33, 35, 48-52, 113, 115, 116, 119-121, 124, 126, 141, 196, 215, 230
   Eugenie 247-249, 273, 276, 290, 292, 321, 322 *See*
Blanchard, M E Eugenie
   Eva Laura 182, 196, 232, 265, 276, 277, 290
   George Matcham 1-3, 6, 9-16, 18, 19, 21, 24, 31, 34, 36-42, 46, 48, 50, 52, 53-56, 59, 111, 114-116, 119-122, 124-126, 131-136, 139-142, 144-146, 148, 149, 152, 153, 156, 158, 159, 162, 163, 165, 167, 170-172, 174-176, 179-181, 190-196, 199-201, 205-209, 211, 212, 214-217, 219, 221-224, 227-230, 232-234, 236-238, 251-259, 262, 264-273, 276, 277, 279-294, 296, 297
   George Matcham junior 131, 180, 181, 196, 228, 273, 276, 277, 290
   Harry Austin   196, 232, 277, 290
   Jessie.........   181, 196, 277, 290 *See* Garling, Jessie
   Julia ..... 123, 124, 131, 180-182, 196, 228, 232-234, 237, 251, 265-267, 276-90, 293 *See* Johnson, Julia
   Julia junior.... 196, 229, 268, 269
   Mary ... 1, 5, 6, 18, 43, 120, 122, 128, 230, 238, 287, 292
   Mary Matcham 14, 15, 18, 121, 122, *See* Laycock, Mary Matcham
   Muriel (Mimi) 249, 321
   Robert (Mary's husband)   33
   Robert Matcham (RM) 41, 42, 196, 232, 236, 238, 239, 253, 270, 273, 276, 277, 290-293
   Robert (GM's brother) 10, 52, 121, 122, 276, 296
   Sarah (Robert's wife) 276
   Thomas 9-11, 13, 14, 17, 18, 23, 25, 27, 28, 33, 34, 35, 46, 47-49, 51, 52, 113, 115, 116,

120, 126, 176, 230, 292, 300
Thomas junior 131
William Henry 10, 51
Pitts, Aboriginal 134, 135
Arthur 134
Tom 134, 135
Clayton Simpson 134, 296
Tighe-Pitt, Dorothy 134, 296
Pitt, Son & Badgery   1, 211, 268, 270, 274, 275, 280, 284-286, 288, 291-294, 323-325
Pitt Town 231
Plunkett, John Hubert, attorney general 165, 187
population 6, 42, 43, 72, 73, 129, 158, 190, 197, 199, 202, 218, 220, 227, 238-240, 264, 288
Port Jackson 84, 241
Port Jackson Steamship Company 237
Port Phillip 122, 198, 332
Potteries (England) 71-73
potteries (Sydney) 85
prison hulks 73-75
prisons 60, 73, 125, 186, 267
Pursip, Agnes 18, 22-24, 30, 31, 50
Putty Farm 51
Queen Elizabeth II 263
Queen Victoria 174, 195, 200, 262, 264
Queensland 198, 225, 286, 315
Rafferty, Chips 137
railways 223-226, 239, 252, 253, 257, 272, 285, 318
Reibey, Mary 178
Richmond 1, 2, 9, 17, 32, 34-36, 42, 47, 49, 52, 105, 107, 110, 111, 126, 133, 170, 171, 176, 179, 180, 182, 191, 193-195, 211, 222-224, 228-232, 251, 268, 269, 277, 279, 285-287, 293
Richmond Bridge 194
Richmond Bridge Company 194
Richmond Road Trust 193

Richmond School 34, 35
Rising Sun....159, 166, 175, 310, 311
Roberts, Tom 228
Robertson, John 218
Robinson, Sir Hercules, governor 261
Rowland, Thomas 99, 100
Royal Australian Historical Society 3, 136, 157, 297
Rusden, Francis 208, 209
Ryan, James ('Toby')   .. 45, 49, 50,
Saddler, Mark 115
saleyards 3, 205, 206, 211, 212, 215, 234, 270-272, 275, 287
Scott family 51, 112, 115, 192, 293
Augusta 31, 293
Elizabeth (Betsey) 31, 126, 192, 193, 293
Frances 31, 293
James junior 11, 115, 126, 299, 300
James senior 115, 116, 125
Joan 115, 116, 125
John 31, 121, 126, 293
Margaret 11, 14, 19, 51, 115, 126, 296
William 10-15, 18-21, 23-25, 27, 29, 31, 35-40, 50-56, 115, 116, 119, 121, 122, 124-127, 130-134, 136, 140, 141, 144, 148, 149, 152, 153, 158-160, 162, 163, 165-172, 176, 179, 183, 185, 192, 193, 293, 296, 297
Scott, Sir Walter 200
Secret River 41
Self government 189
settlers 5, 22, 34, 43, 44, 46, 83, 84, 89, 91, 111, 115, 131, 166, 190, 198, 205
Shoalhaven River 128
slavery 39, 91, 220, 240, 242, 243, 282
smallpox 146, 310, 333
Smith, Alfred 195, 233, 310

Smith, Babette 59
Smith, Henry Gilbert 234-236, 319
Smith, Mrs Ann.......................... 292
Some Ups and Downs of an old Richmondite 310
South Australia 178, 198, 225, 226
Sparrow, Anna .. 244-248, 322, 324
   See Blanchard, Anna
Sparrow, Thomas 244, 247, 321
Spence, Catherine Helen 178
Squatter's Castle 151
squatters 6, 115, 129, 130, 139, 148, 149, 151-155, 162, 165, 166, 168, 173, 177, 178, 188, 219
St James's Church 106, 265
St Matthew's Church 122, 224, 237
St Peter's Church 1, 119, 179, 228, 232, 269, 285, 286
Stafford Advertiser 71
Stafford Assizes 62
Stanton Library 254
State Records of New South Wales 159, 160
Station Life 299, 316
Stirling, Sir James, governor of Western Australia 198
stock and station agents 1, 3, 206, 213-215, 229, 237, 268, 269, 272, 274, 277, 286, 296
Stock and Station Journal 133, 175, 286, 287, 325
stockmen 154, 165, 173, 177
Stoke on Trent 72
Streeton, Arthur 228
Styles, Reverend Mr 122
suffrage 178, 190, 198-200, 217, 219, 280, 282, 289
Sullivan, Thomas ... 207, 215, 216, 237
Sunnyside 228, 276
Surrey Assizes 62
Surry 115, 116
Sutton, Gail 115, 296, 300
swagmen 177, 204

Sydney 9, 10, 14, 15, 18-20, 25, 32, 49-51, 56, 60, 61, 71, 75, 79, 81-85, 90, 92, 97, 99, 105-108, 113, 117, 120-122, 126, 128, 130, 135, 136, 140-143, 149, 156, 160, 165, 175, 185, 189, 190, 194, 197, 199, 202, 204, 215, 223-225, 227, 230, 234, 239, 242, 253, 254, 257, 258, 260-262, 266, 268, 272-274, 277, 287, 288, 290, 292, 305, 310
Sydney Gazette 81, 84, 92, 113, 123, 129
Sydney Monitor 246, 321
Sydney Morning Herald 180, 185, 188, 211, 217, 224, 237
Tamworth 136, 147, 148
Tasmania 84, 198, 286, 288
theft 56, 59, 60, 62, 63, 65-70, 73, 92, 165
Thomas, Mary 178, 198
Thompson, Jane 105
   See Aull, Jane
Those were the Days 233, 182, 312-315, 318
Threlkeld, Reverend 187, 188
Tibbitts, William 99
tickets of leave 85, 98
Timmins, Jack 132, 140, 141, 162, 192, 193, 293, 314
Timmins, William 192
Tolpuddle Martyrs 59
Town, Andrew 229
Town, Elizabeth 228, 229
Trafalgar 109, 126, 140, 276
transportation 29, 34, 35, 56, 59-63, 65-67, 70-72, 74, 79, 104, 105, 115, 125, 184-186, 189, 286, 287, 289
Trench, Tony 3, 137, 204, 225
Trollope, Anthony 239
Trove 111, 112, 256, 292, 318
Upper Richmond 107, 108, 181, 182, 266, 267

Uranie 242, 320
Van Diemen's Land   39, 84, 184, 186, 198, 288
Vestey, Lord 273
Victoria 197-199, 225, 226
Volunteers 195, 201, 220, 273
Wagga Wagga 3, 115, 212, 225, 226
Walker, William 200, 217, 219, 220-222
Ward, Russel 203
Warrior 102
Watercourse Country 159
Watson, Don 203
Webb, R J 159, 166
Weebollabolla 167
Wellington 1, 176, 194, 216, 317
Welsh, Frank 190
Wentworth Falls..   273, 290-292,
Wentworth, D'Arcy 215
Wentworth, William 173, 176, 189-191
Western Australia   198, 225, 286, 315
White, Libby 136, 140, 145, 146, 148, 156, 160, 241, 296

Whitlam, Gough 161
Whittaker, Dr Charles .   207-209, 228
Wiradjuri 115
Wilshire family
   Austin Forrest 126
   Hester 10, 15, 120, 121, 196
   James 10, 108, 120
   James Robert 194, 195, 296
Windsor 35, 49, 53, 105, 122, 176, 178, 190, 191, 193-195, 199, 211, 216, 217, 219, 222-224, 230, 231, 290, 318
Wingen burning mountain 145, 146
Wiseman's Ferry 49, 142
Wollumbi 144
Wood, Lucy 10, 120, 121, 196
Yarramundi 46, 53, 107, 108, 140, 194
Yass 242, 243
Yilaalu 158, 159
Young, Sir John, governor 223, 224

www.ingramcontent.com/pod-product-compliance
Lightning Source LLC
Chambersburg PA
CBHW030430010526
44118CB00011B/568